MW01533838

THE IMPORTANT DIFFERENCE

THE DIFFERENCE BETWEEN BONDAGE AND FREEDOM

ENE I. ETTE, Ph.D., FCP, FCCP, FAAPS

FOREWORD MRS. ESTHER A. ETTE, B.PHARM., M.S.

Scripture quotations in this book were taken from the publications below and we therefore wish to credit them:

American Standard Version (Public Domain) [ASV]

"Scripture quotations taken from the Amplified® Bible, Copyright © 1954, 1958, 1962, 1964, 1965, 1987 by The Lockman Foundation. Used by permission." (www.Lockman.org) [AMP]

Darby Translation (Public Domain) [DARBY]

Scripture quotations taken from Greek Interlinear New Testament © 2010 Scripture4all Foundation - www.scripture4all.org [GKINT NT]

Scripture quotations marked HCSB are taken from the Holman Christian Standard Bible®, Copyright © 1999, 2000, 2002, 2003, 2009 by Holman Bible Publishers. Used by permission. Holman Christian Standard Bible®, Holman CSB®, and HCSB® are federally registered trademarks of Holman Bible Publishers.

King James Version (Public Domain) [KJV]

"Scripture taken from The Message. Copyright © 1993, 1994, 1995, 1996, 2000, 2001, 2002. Used by permission of NavPress Publishing Group." [MESSAGE]

THE MOUNCE REVERSE-INTERLINEAR NEW TESTAMENT Copyright © 2011 by Robert H Mounce and William D Mounce. Used by permission. All rights reserved worldwide. [MOUNCE]

NET Bible® copyright© 1996-2006 Biblical Studies Press, LLC. http://netbible.com All rights reserved.

"Scripture quotations taken from the New American Standard Bible®, Copyright © 1960, 1962, 1963, 1968, 1971, 197right2, 1973,1975, 1977, 1995 by The Lockman Foundation. Used by permission." (www.Lockman.org) [NASB]

The names: THE NET BIBLE®, NEW ENGLISH TRANSLATION COPYRIGHT © 1996 BY BIBLICAL STUDIES PRESS, LLC. NET Bible® IS A REGISTERED TRADEMARK THE NET BIBLE® LOGO, SERVICE TRADEMARK COPYRIGHT © 1997 BY BIBLICAL STUDIES PRESS, LLC. ALL RIGHTS RESERVED.

"Scripture taken from the New King James Version®. Copyright © 1982 by Thomas Nelson, Inc. Used by permission. All rights reserved." [NKJV]

THE HOLY BIBLE, NEW INTERNATIONAL VERSION®, NIV® Copyright © 1973, 1978, 1984, 2011 by Biblica, Inc.® Used by permission. All rights reserved worldwide.

Scripture quotations marked (NLT) are taken from the Holy Bible, New Living Translation, copyright © 1996, 2004, 2007 by Tyndale House Foundation. Used by permission of Tyndale House Publishers, Inc., Carol Stream, Illinois 60188. All rights reserved.

The Living Bible copyright © 1971 by Tyndale House Foundation. Used by permission of Tyndale House Publishers Inc., Carol Stream, Illinois 60188. All rights reserved. The Living Bible, TLB, and the The Living Bible logo are registered trademarks of Tyndale House Publishers.

The New Testament : A New Translation. James Moffatt (Public Domain) [MOFFATT]

The New Testament in Modern English, J. B. Phillips. 1962 edition, HaperCollins. [PHILLIPS]

Weymouth New Testament Bible (Public Domain) [WEY]

Young Literal Translation (Public Domain) [YLT]

Scriptures are reproduced as obtained from the different versions of the Bible, and in some cases, I have added emphasis with italics. Some Scripture passages are cited without reference to any version of the Bible, indicating non-preference for a Bible version.

No part of this book may be reproduced or transmitted in any form or by any means, graphic, electronic, or mechanical, including photocopying, recording, taping or by any information storage or retrieval system, without the permission of the author.

Cover design by: Mfonabasi E. Ette

LOVE: THE IMPORTANT DIFFERENCE

ISBN: 978-0-9903114-4-7

Copyright © 2016 by Ene I. Ette, Ph.D., FCP, FCCP, FAAPS

All rights reserved

Published in the U.S.A. by

Alaythace Publishing

Natick

© Ene I. Ette, Ph.D., FCP, FCCP, FAAPS

DEDICATION

This book is dedicated to The Holy Spirit Who has taught me love of the God-kind.

TABLE OF CONTENTS

FOREWORD

Love: The Important Difference is a very wise, thought provoking and revealing book. It will take you on a soul searching journey that will reveal your diligence with the measure of *Agape* love that God poured into your heart at your new birth experience.

As I wrote this, I could not but call to remembrance how God brought my beloved husband into my life. Ours was not a love at first sight. In the natural, our tastes seem so incompatible. Our coming together was a demonstration of *Agape* love defined by the actions it prompts. What was very clear was that each of us loved God and wanted God's will and nothing else in seeking a life partner. Our individual "yes Lord" in obedience and out of our love for God, made *Agape* (God's love) the foundation and bed rock of our marriage. Space will not permit me to describe how rewarding it has been to see God working through the Holy Spirit to build the romance and other blessings of our union on this firm rock of *Agape*.

Agape will be your shield and defense as you choose to walk in this God-kind of love. You will watch God fight your battles for you as you hold your peace. God's protective shield actually covers His children walking in *Agape* love. You will also experience as Apostle Paul rightly stated, "love never fails." *Agape* love never fails a child of God who chooses to walk in the God-kind of love. You will not fail if you do. It is the theme of this book, and it governs human relations, giving, and victorious Christian living. I commend this book to you. Read and reread it; put what you read to work, and you will find yourself working in victory.

1. INTRODUCTION

Since by your obedience to the truth you have purified yourselves for a sincere love of the believers, [see that you] love one another from the heart [always unselfishly seeking the best for one another], for you have been born again [that is, reborn from above—spiritually transformed, renewed, and set apart for His purpose] not of seed which is perishable but [from that which is] imperishable and immortal, that is, through the living and everlasting word of God. [1 Peter 1: 22-23, AMP]

The Scripture passage above was written by Peter, the apostle that our Lord taught loving Him from the heart. Thus, Peter speaks in the above passage of two kinds of love – the sincere (unfeigned brotherly) love (*phileo* in Greek) for believers, and love from the heart (*agapao* in Greek). *Agapao* is used approximately seven times as much as *phileo* in the New Testatment.

Phileo is friendship love, and it is unimpassioned. It is love that is a response to the delight (pleasure) one takes in another. It is based on what two friends have in common. Fondness, liking, and affection are words that best describe *phileo* (friendship love). *Phileo* love between Christians is one Christian heart responding to another because of what or Who we have in common. This love is non-ethical. Salvation is what all Christians have in common, and Jesus Christ Who lives in us is the One we have in common.

The Apostle Peter exhorts us to combine friendship love for one another with *Agape* love which is the God-kind of love poured into our hearts through the Holy Spirit that indwells every truly born again child of God. [Romans 5: 5] *Agapao* is the verb of the noun form *Agape*. *Agape* love is a love of devotion that is aroused by a sense of worth in an object that causes a person to prize it. The love (*Agape*) of God for humanity expressed in John 3: 16 springs from His heart in response to the high value He places on each one of us. That is why the Father sent Jesus to die for us. "For God so [**greatly**] **loved and dearly prized the world**, that He [even] gave His [One and] only begotten Son, so that whoever believes and trusts in Him [as Savior] shall not perish, but have eternal life." [John 3: 16, AMP; emphasis mine] Love is His nature, and He is *Agape* (Love).

Peter was able to write to the brethren and to us today because the Lord, after His resurrection, educated Peter on loving (*agapao*) Him more than his fishing profession. Peter had deserted the Lord and went fishing after he had denied the Lord thrice before His crucifixion. In the Lord's interaction with Peter, the Lord spoke of *Agape* love, but Peter spoke of friendship love (*phileo*). [My use of the Greek word *Agape* with love is to reinforce the fact that the focus of this book is on love of the God-kind, and it is emphasized throughout the book.] The Lord asked Peter twice whether he had *Agape* love for him, but Peter who did not have an understanding of *Agape* love responded that he had friendship love for the Lord. We pick up the interaction in John 21:

> [15] So when they had finished breakfast, Jesus said to Simon Peter, "Simon, son of John, do you love (i.e. *agapao*) Me more than these [others do—with total commitment and devotion]?" He said to Him, "Yes, Lord; You know that I love (i.e., *phileo*) You [with a deep, personal affection, as for a close friend]." Jesus said to him, "Feed My lambs."
>
> [16] Again He said to him a second time, "Simon, son of John, do you love (i.e. *agapao*) Me [with total commitment and devotion]?" He said to Him, "Yes, Lord; You know that I love (i.e., *phileo*) You [with a deep, personal affection, as for a close friend]." Jesus said to him, "Shepherd My sheep."
>
> [17] He said to him the third time, "Simon, son of John, do you love Me [with a deep, personal affection for Me, as for a close friend]?" Peter was grieved that He asked him the third time, "Do you [really] love (i.e. *phileo*) Me [with a deep, personal affection, as for a close friend]?" And he said to Him, "Lord, You know everything; You know that I love (i.e.

phileo) You [with a deep, personal affection, as for a close friend]." Jesus said to him, "Feed My sheep. [John 21: 15-18, AMP; emphasis mine]

When you read John 21 in context you will find that the Lord was indicating to Peter that if he had a love of devotion (*agape*) for Him, he would not have deserted Him during the darkest moment of His life when He suffered for our sins. Thus, He went on to tell Peter how he would die because of his love of devotion for him.

> [18] I assure you and most solemnly say to you, when you were younger you dressed yourself and walked wherever you wished; but when you grow old, you will stretch out your hands and arms, and someone else will dress you, and carry you where you do not wish to go."
> [19] Now He said this to indicate the kind of death by which Peter would glorify God. And after saying this, He said to him, "Follow Me [walk the same path of life that I have walked]!" [John 21: 18-19, AMP]

This love of devotion is what the Lord demands from us because He has poured His love into our hearts through His Spirit in us. This love of devotion (*Agape* love) is what the Holy Spirit instructed Peter to admonish us to have for one another. This love of devotion will enable you stand with your spouse through thick and thin in your marriage. It will enable you to reach out a helping hand to those in need; give for the spreading of the Gospel to a lost and dying world; and stand your ground against the assault of the enemy and win. It is *Agape* love that will put you over in every circumstance that is of the devil's making. Yes, *Agape* love is the focus of this book because it is the love that brings liberty. It governs human relations, the stewardship of what God has blessed us with, and victorious Christian living on this earth. The book is organized around these themes.

Scripture passages are quoted from different translations and paraphrases of the Bible to aid clarity and bring home the points to you as the Holy Spirit revealed them to me. Where I have paraphrased Scripture passages, I have used italics to indicate such. I have also italicized some statements I have made for emphasis. I have included testimonies to build your faith and demonstrate that the Love and Word of God will work for you, if you will work them. Some points are repeated on purpose for faith building. Choose victory over defeat, freedom over bondage, and success over failure by working in *Agape* love. Enjoy *Love: The Important Difference,* and the Lord bless you as you read/study it. Share the truth you learn from this book with others and be doubly blessed in the Name of Jesus.

PART 1: LOVE OF THE GOD-KIND

(*AGAPE* LOVE)

2. LOVE OF THE GOD-KIND

He who does not love has not become acquainted with God [does not and never did know Him], for God is love. [1 John 4: 8, AMP]

God is love. [1 John 4: 8] "Love" is translated from the Greek word *agape*. *Agape* is the God kind of love. The love of God (*Agape* love) is selfless and sacrificial, unlike human love that is selfish. It is unrestrained, unrestricted, unconditional love that is other-focused.

We are the object of God's love. Therefore, *Agape* love is best understood from the deeds it prompts. It is not an impulse from feeling, rather it is a love of devotion. For the benefit of the one loved, *Agape* love will deny self. *Agape* love is a love that seeks the welfare of all. [Romans 15: 2] Love seeks the occasion and opportunity to do good to all. *Agape* love is "mindful to be a blessing, especially to those of the household of faith [those who belong to God's family with you, the believers]." [Galatians 6: 10, AMP] The love of God is best observed and comprehended in the gift of Jesus, His Son, that He sent to die for the remission of our sins. The Scripture passages below explain it all:

> ⁹ To us, the greatest demonstration of God's love for us has been his sending his only Son into the world to give us life through him. [1 John 4: 9, PHILLIPS]

Agape love is best understood from the deeds it prompts. It is not an impulse from feeling, rather it is a love of devotion.

[10] This is real love - not that we loved God, but that he loved us and sent his Son as a sacrifice to take away our sins. [1 John 4: 10, NLT]

[16] For God so greatly loved and dearly prized the world that He [even] gave up His only begotten (unique) Son, so that whoever believes in (trusts in, clings to, relies on) Him shall not perish (come to destruction, be lost) but have eternal (everlasting) life. [John 3: 16, AMP]

God's love for us is dependent on God and not on us. "But God shows and clearly proves His [own] love for us by the fact that while we were still sinners, Christ (the Messiah, the Anointed One) died for us." [Romans 5: 8, AMP]

Agape love is not a feeling but a person, the person of God, because God is *Agape* love. Just as you can observe or experience the effect of the wind when it blows, similarly you can experience or observe the effect of God's *agape* love. We understand the feelings of God, *Agape* Love, by looking at Jesus during His earth walk because Jesus is the express image of the Father. [Hebrews 1: 3] He showed compassion, exercised patience, groaned, and wept. He demonstrated His passion and zeal for the Father by carrying out the will of the Father. Jesus' actions only mirrored the Father's. [John 5:30; 8: 26, 28; 14: 10] As Jesus is, so are we in this world. [1 John 4:17, AMP]

The good news is that every born again child of God has *Agape* love in him. It is not something we have to struggle for because God deposited it in us on the day we received Jesus as our Lord and Savior. "God's love has been poured out in our hearts through the Holy Spirit Who has been given to us." [Romans 5: 5, AMP] By this, God made His *Agape* love available in us. We have the ability to love as God does because we have His *Agape* love. We have to rely on Him to be able to love as He does because as He is so are we in this world. [1 John 4: 17, AMP]

God cannot ask us to do what He has not equipped us to do. Therefore, our love must be God-focused and in exercising it, we must do it to please God. When we please God in our daily walk as it relates to our relationship with Him and our fellow man, we fulfill His command (His Word):

> [15] If you [really] love Me, you will keep (obey) My commands.
>
> [21] The person who has My commands and keeps them is the one who [really] loves Me; and whoever [really] loves Me will be loved by My Father, and I [too] will love him and will show (reveal, manifest) Myself to him. [I will let Myself be clearly seen by him and make Myself real to him.]
>
> [23]Jesus answered, If a person [really] loves Me, he will keep My word [obey My teaching]; and My Father will love him, and We will come to him and make Our home (abode, special dwelling place) with him. [John 14: 15, 21, 23, AMP]

> [34] I give you a new commandment: that you should love one another. Just as I have loved you, so you too should love one another.
>
> [35] By this shall all [men] know that you are My disciples, if you love one another [if you keep on showing love among yourselves]. [John 13: 34-35, AMP]

Notice that Jesus explained that the person who has His commands (His Word) and keeps them is the one who really loves Him. You cannot say you love Jesus or God the Father and do not obey His Word. If you say you love God and yet disobey His Word, you are only fooling yourself. Either the love of God is not in you, or you just choose to disobey God.

We can only love God the Father if we accept the sacrifice of His Son and make Him the Lord of our lives. Once we do, He equips us with *agape* love to love our fellow man and ourselves. Man without God is selfish, and every child of God has to grow in this *Agape* love. *Agape* love (Christ's love) is not driven by feeling. *Agape* love is not only directed towards those we have affection for, but seeks the good of all. The Holy Spirit through Paul admonishes us thus, "Let each one of us make it a practice to please (make happy) his neighbor for his good *and* for his true welfare, to edify him [to strengthen him and build him up spiritually]." [Romans 15: 2, AMP] To be able to grow in the God kind of love we must know its characteristics.

The Characteristics of the God Kind of Love

Since God is *Agape*, to understand the characteristics of *agape* love we need to look at some of the qualities of God. God is truth, and He is a God of integrity. He is altogether good, patient, and His mercy and loving kindness endures forever. He is

> **Love makes being a blessing life's purpose.**

righteous and all His works are perfect and His ways are just. To gain more insight into the mercy and loving kindness of God, let us examine 1 Corinthians 13: 4–8 where the Holy Spirit through the Apostle Paul describes to us the characteristics of *Agape* love.

> [4] Love endures long and is patient and kind; love never is envious nor boils over with jealousy, is not boastful or vainglorious, does not display itself haughtily.
>
> [5] It is not conceited (arrogant and inflated with pride); it is not rude (unmannerly) and does not act unbecomingly. Love (God's love in us) does not insist on its own rights or its own way, for it is not self-seeking; it is not touchy or fretful or resentful; it takes no account of the evil done to it [it pays no attention to a suffered wrong].
>
> [6] It does not rejoice at injustice and unrighteousness, but rejoices when right and truth prevail.
>
> [7] Love bears up under anything and everything that comes, is ever ready to believe the best of every person, its hopes are fadeless under all circumstances, and it endures everything [without weakening].
>
> [8a] Love never fails [never fades out or becomes obsolete or comes to an end]. 1 Corinthians 13:4-8, AMP]

In the first three verses of 1 Corinthians 13 Paul explained that our Christian works (operating in the gifts of the Spirit, as the Lord wills, that enables us to prophecy, do charitable work, yield to martyrdom, etc.) without love are a waste.

> [1-3] If in the languages of men I speak and the languages of angels but do not have love [**Greek word here used of God's love produced in the**

heart of the yielded saint by the Holy Spirit, a love that impels one to deny himself for the sake of the loved one], I have already become and at present am sounding brass or a clanging cymbal. And if I have the gift of uttering divine revelations and know all the mysteries and all the knowledge, and if I have all the faith so that I am able to keep on removing mountain after mountain, but am not possessing love, I am nothing. And if I use all my possessions to feed the poor, and if I deliver up my body [as a martyr] in order that I may glory, but do not have love, I am being profited in not even one thing. [1 Corinthians 13: 1-3, WUEST]

It is, therefore, important for us to take time to understand the different characteristics of the *agape* love delineated in 1 Corinthians 13:4-8. The description of these characteristics below stems from my study of 1 Corinthians 13:4-8 from different translations and paraphrases of the Bible and the meanings of the key words as translated from Greek in the Strong's Concordance (2010) and Thayer's Lexicon (1995). Since *Agape* love is inseparable from God, I have taken the liberty to use same in the discourse below. In doing so, I have used *Agape* love or Love repeatedly to reinforce the fact that *Agape* love is animate and not inanimate. *Agape* love makes us servants. Love makes being a blessing life's purpose.

Long Suffering, Patience, and Kindness
The God kind of love is longsuffering and kind. *Agape* love does this by exercising self-restraint in the face of provocation. Love is merciful and patient. Love has long patience and never gives up, as long as patience is required. Love is benevolent and does not succumb under trial or surrender to circumstance. *Agape* love makes us willing servants. Love makes being a blessing life's purpose or assignment.

Contentment (No Envy or Jealousy)
Agape love is not jealous or envious. Love does not burn with or boil over with jealousy. It does not desire what others have. Jealousy/envy gives birth to confusion, rebellion, and every type of evil imaginable.

[14] But if you have bitter jealousy (envy) and contention (rivalry, selfish ambition) in your hearts, do not pride yourselves on it and thus be in defiance of and false to the Truth.

[16] For wherever there is jealousy (envy) and contention (rivalry and selfish ambition), there will also be confusion (unrest, disharmony, rebellion) and all sorts of evil and vile practices. [James 3: 14, 16, AMP]

Jealousy/envy can cause sickness. "A heart at peace gives life to the body, but envy rots the bones." [Proverbs 14: 30, NIV] Getting rid of jealousy will bring healing to a jealous person.

Humility (No Aggrandizement, Vain Gloriousness, Being Puffed Up, or Unseemly)

The God kind of love is not boastful, proud, arrogant, or vainglorious. Love does not sound his praises. When you operate in *agape* love, you do not make a vain display of your worth or achievements. *Agape* love does not brag, nor is it conceited. Love does not have a high conception of self or attainments. *Agape* love does not feel superior to others. Love is well behaved, and, therefore, does not behave rudely, or act unbecomingly. Humility displayed by *Agape* love is summarized thus:

[3] Don't be selfish; don't try to impress others. Be humble, thinking of others as better than yourselves. [Philippians 2: 3, NLT]

[3] Do nothing from factional motives [through contentiousness, strife, selfishness, or for unworthy ends] or prompted by conceit and empty arrogance. Instead, in the true spirit of humility (lowliness of mind) let each regard the others as better than and superior to himself [thinking more highly of one another than you do of yourselves]. [Philippians 2: 3, AMP]

Love edifies, and does not act arrogantly. [1 Corinthians 8: 1]

Self-Sacrifice and Self-Control (Not Self-Seeking or Easily Provoked)

Agape love does not plot to gain advantage in a situation. Love does "not insist on its own rights or its own way, for it is not self-seeking; it is not touchy or fretful or resentful." [1 Corinthians 13: 5, AMP] Love is not easily angered. *Agape* love is not sharp-tongued, therefore Love chooses his words carefully so as not to provoke a violent response from others. Love has no inventory of wrongs from others and "pays no attention to a suffered wrong." [1 Corinthians 13: 5, AMP]

"Love does no wrong to one's neighbor [it never hurts anybody]. Therefore love meets all the requirements and is the fulfilling of the Law." [Romans 13: 10, AMP] You cannot say, I am going to repay evil for evil. If somebody wronged you, do not think in your heart that it is your turn to repay when you have an opportunity to be a blessing to the person. To enjoy your Christian life you must be ready to do good to those who wronged you. As a Christian, you may be wronged by your Christian brother or sister. Instead of looking for how to pay back your brother, seek ways to be a blessing.

Several years ago, a child of God wronged me. The Lord was teaching me to walk in love at that time. I hearkened to God and forgave the one who wronged me. A few years later, the Lord asked me to be a blessing by standing in the gap for a miracle for this person, and I did. We got the miracle and I had a thrill that I had hearkened to God when He asked me to forgive and be a blessing. I was humbled by God's love. You do not know what tomorrow holds, therefore do your best for others, and desire good for them.

No Evil Thought
Agape love takes no thought and keeps no account of evil done to him. Instead of entering it into his account book, he voluntarily lets go of it. *Agape* love quickly forgives when wronged.

Justice
Agape love rejoices with the Truth. God is *Agape* love, and He is just. That is why *agape* love does not rejoice about evil done to someone else. *Agape* love does not gloat about injustice and unrighteousness, the

wickedness of others, or when they get into trouble. Love does not take pleasure in other people's sins. Rather, it "rejoices when right and truth prevail." [1 Corinthians 13: 6, AMP]

Perseverance, Belief, and Hope

The God kind of love covers a multitude of sins; puts a roof over people and protects them from exposure. It is not our place to expose people's sins. "Above all things have intense and unfailing love for one another, for love covers a multitude of sins [forgives and disregards the offenses of others]." [1 Peter 4: 8, AMP] Please understand the context here. What is not intended here is seeing someone commit a murder and you keep quiet without reporting it to the police. As a child of God and a good citizen, you report such to law enforcement agents for the protection of society.

Agape love believes the best in every situation, and the best of others. Love's hopes are fadeless under all circumstances because love expects and anticipates with pleasure the very best in every situation. *Agape* love has the strength of character to persevere in every situation, with no intention to surrender, give up, or quit. Love does not quit, give up, or surrender because love knows that at the end love wins by standing on the Word of God.

> [19] Many evils confront the [consistently] righteous, but the Lord delivers him out of them all. [Psalm 34: 19, AMP]

> [11] For I know the thoughts and plans that I have for you, says the Lord, thoughts and plans for welfare and peace and not for evil, to give you hope in your final outcome. [Jeremiah 29: 11, AMP]

> [33] I have told you these things, so that in Me you may have [perfect] peace and confidence. In the world you have tribulation and trials and distress and frustration; but be of good cheer [take courage; be confident, certain, undaunted]! For I have overcome the world. [I have deprived it of power to harm you and have conquered it for you.] [John 16: 33, AMP]

Jesus Who is Love has deprived Satan of power to harm us who are the Lord's, and has conquered him for us. Thus, we who are in Christ have conquered Satan and deprived him of power to harm us because we walk in *Agape* love.

Failure Proof

Agape love never fails. Love never loses, or gets out of course. *Agape* love cannot be ineffective because love cannot be separated from God, and God cannot be separated from His Word. God's Word is active, operative, energizing, and effective:

> 12 For the Word that God speaks is alive and full of power [making it active, operative, energizing, and effective]; it is sharper than any two-edged sword, penetrating to the dividing line of the breath of life (soul) and [the immortal] spirit, and of joints and marrow [of the deepest parts of our nature], exposing and sifting and analyzing and judging the very thoughts and purposes of the heart.
> 13 And not a creature exists that is concealed from His sight, but all things are open and exposed, naked and defenseless to the eyes of Him with Whom we have to do. [Hebrews 4: 12-13, AMP]
>
> 37 For with God nothing is ever impossible and no word from God shall be without power or impossible of fulfillment. [Luke 1: 37, AMP]

God never fails because He is love. God word never fails because He is not a liar. You cannot fail, if you walk in love. To enable the Word to work in you, you must be forgiving because our Father is forgiving. Walking in *Agape* love is proof positive that you are a born again child of God.

Agape Love – Evidence of the New Birth

You cannot just wake up and have *Agape* love if you are not a child of God. To have *Agape* love, you must be born again. If you are not, and you want to be, which you should because it is the best thing that can happen to you, please go to the end of this book and pray the prayer of salvation for Jesus to come into your life. When you do, you will experience peace, God's peace, and God will pour His *Agape* love into your heart through His Spirit. "...For God's love has been poured out in our hearts through the Holy Spirit Who has been given to us." [Romans 5:5b, AMP] Get into the Word of God, and put the love of God in your heart to work.

Putting *Agape* love to work in your life by loving your fellow Christian is a distinctive characteristic that you are a child of God and no longer a child of the devil. "We know that we have passed over out of death into Life by the fact that we love the brethren (our fellow Christians). He who does not love abides (remains, is held and kept continually) in [spiritual] death." [1 John 3:14, AMP]

Let the love of God be the constraining force in your life. When you are filled with and controlled by God's Word, you will do what God's Word says. Thus you will not yield to the dictates of the old carnal nature (the flesh), but to the dictates of the Spirit of God in you. You come under a new law, the law of *Agape* love.

Agape Love – The Law of the New Covenant

Jesus gave us a new commandment, the commandment of love, and He said obeying this new commandment marked us out as His own (disciples).

> [34] I give you a new commandment: that you should love one another. Just as I have loved you, so you too should love one another.
> [35] By this shall all [men] know that you are My disciples, if you love one another [if you keep on showing love among yourselves]. [John 13: 34-35, AMP]

Loving others as ourselves is a demonstration to the world that we are the followers of Christ.

> [8] If indeed you [really] fulfill the royal Law in accordance with the Scripture, You shall love your neighbor as [you love] yourself, you do well.

⁹ But if you show servile regard (prejudice, favoritism) for people, you commit sin and are rebuked and convicted by the Law as violators and offenders. [James 2: 8-9, AMP]

Loving one another enables us to fulfill the law. When you do, you live in the light of the law of love.

⁸ Keep out of debt and owe no man anything, except to love one another; for he who loves his neighbor [who practices loving others] has fulfilled the Law [relating to one's fellowmen, meeting all its requirements].
⁹ The commandments, You shall not commit adultery, You shall not kill, You shall not steal, You shall not covet (have an evil desire), and any other commandment, are summed up in the single command, You shall love your neighbor as [you do] yourself.
¹⁰ Love does no wrong to one's neighbor [it never hurts anybody]. Therefore love meets all the requirements and is the fulfilling of the Law. [Romans 13: 8-10, AMP]

The 10 commandments are already written in our hearts, enabling us to set boundaries for our lives.

¹⁹ And I will give them one heart [a new heart] and I will put a new spirit within them; and I will take the stony [unnaturally hardened] heart out of their flesh, and will give them a heart of flesh [sensitive and responsive to the touch of their God], {Ezekiel 11: 19, AMP]

³³ But this is the covenant which I will make with the house of Israel: After those days, says the Lord, I will put My law within them, and on their hearts will I write it; and I will be their God, and they will be My people.
³⁴ And they will no more teach each man his neighbor and each man his brother, saying, Know the Lord, for they will all know Me [recognize, understand, and be acquainted with Me], from the least of them to the greatest, says the Lord. For I will forgive their iniquity, and I will [seriously] remember their sin no more. [Jeremiah 31: 33-34, AMP]

¹⁰ For this is the covenant that I will make with the house of Israel after those days, says the Lord: I will imprint My laws upon their minds, even upon their innermost thoughts and understanding, and engrave

them upon their hearts; and I will be their God, and they shall be My people. [Hebrews 8: 10, AMP]

These prophecies have been fulfilled in every believer in our Lord Jesus Christ today. Do not brow beat yourself about the 10 commandments. They are already written in your heart and they set boundaries for your life. When you decide to go out of those boundaries, you are on your own. When we walk in *Agape* love, we fulfill the law. To help you walk in *Agape*, always ask yourself this question, What I am about to say or do to others, will I like them to say or do the same to me? Do unto others as you would want them to do to you. When you love God, you will love yourself and others. As you do, you will also learn to glorify God with your body which is God's temple.

Glorify God in Your Body

When you love God you will love His temple, your body, and will not abuse it. Since *Agape* love is known by the action it prompts, having *Agape* love towards God is demonstrated by our obedience to Him (His Word). He says we are to glorify Him with our spirits and are bodies which are His as we read in 1 Corinthians 6:

> 17 But the person who is united to the Lord becomes one spirit with Him.
> 18 Shun immorality and all sexual looseness [flee from impurity in thought, word, or deed]. Any other sin which a man commits is one outside the body, but he who commits sexual immorality sins against his own body.
> 19 Do you not know that your body is the temple (the very sanctuary) of the Holy Spirit Who lives within you, Whom you have received [as a Gift] from God? You are not your own, [1 Corinthians 6: 17-19, AMP]
>
> 20 For ye were bought with a price; glorify, then, God in your body and in your spirit, which are God's. [1 Corinthians 6: 20, YLT]

We need to do what our Father tells us, if we are His children. How are we to do what our Father has asked us to do? He did not just ask us to glorify Him with our bodies, He also told us how to do it. We find this in 1 Corinthians 9: 27 and Romans 12: 1-2.

> [27] Instead, I discipline my body and bring it under strict control, so that after preaching to others, I myself will not be disqualified. [1 Corinthians 9: 27, HCSB]

> [1] I appeal to you therefore, brethren, and beg of you in view of [all] the mercies of God, to make a decisive dedication of your bodies [presenting all your members and faculties] as a living sacrifice, holy (devoted, consecrated) and well pleasing to God, which is your reasonable (rational, intelligent) service and spiritual worship.
> [2] Do not be conformed to this world (this age), [fashioned after and adapted to its external, superficial customs], but be transformed (changed) by the [entire] renewal of your mind [by its new ideals and its new attitude], so that you may prove [for yourselves] what is the good and acceptable and perfect will of God, even the thing which is good and acceptable and perfect [in His sight for you]. [1 Romans 12: 1-2, AMP]

We are to discipline our bodies and bring them under the control of our spirits that are yielded to the Spirit of God. To have our spirits yielded to the Spirit of God, our minds (thinking) need to be changed by feeding our spirits with the Word of God. It is the Word that you meditate upon and speak that will change the image you have inside you (your thinking), believing, and acting (your behavior). The Word is fed into your spirit by speaking, and you change your thinking by changing your speaking. For more on this, see my book, *The Power to Transform*.

Unhealthy Eating
Glorifying God in our bodies includes not eating unhealthy food. If you have high cholesterol, you need to reduce your consumption of carbohydrates and fatty food. If you have diabetes, you have to reduce your carbohydrate and fine sugar consumption to a level commensurate with good health. Heed your doctor and dietician's advice on this. Cooperate with God by eating healthily so that you can be healed and

stay healthy. Repent of your poor eating habit. Line up with God, and eat right. Ask the Spirit of God to help you discipline yourself to eat well. Decide to do the right thing for your body, and follow through. If you know what is right to do and do not it, it is a sin [James 4:17, AMP] Disobedience is sin.

Overwork

Putting strain on your body by working too hard does not help you stay healthy. There is a limit to what your body can take, beyond which it will give. Take care of your body because it is God's temple. It is good to work hard, but do not go overboard with it. You can work yourself so hard that you do not know how to relax. What started as strain can lead to stress with its attendant diseases because of being driven by the desire to achieve. Strive to maintain a healthy balance, and Holy Spirit will help you achieve it. Remember that you are to glorify God with your body which is the Lord's.

Addiction and Sexual Immorality

If you surrender your body to sexual immorality, alcohol and drug abuse, smoking, and other forms of addiction are you honoring the Lord with your body? Is that loving God? It is common knowledge that smoking causes lung cancer. Is smoking, therefore, glorifying God with your body, or giving it to the devil to destroy?

Sexual immorality is of the devil. Sexual immorality is sin against your body.

> [13b] The body is not for sexual immorality but for the Lord, and the Lord for the body.
> [14] God raised up the Lord and will also raise us up by His power.
> [15] Don't you know that your bodies are a part of Christ's body? So should I take a part of Christ's body and make it part of a prostitute? Absolutely not!
> [16] Don't you know that anyone joined to a prostitute is one body with her? For Scripture says, The two will become one flesh.

17 But anyone joined to the Lord is one spirit with Him.

18 Run from sexual immorality! "Every sin a person can commit is outside the body." On the contrary, the person who is sexually immoral sins against his own body.

19 Don't you know that your body is a sanctuary of the Holy Spirit who is in you, whom you have from God? You are not your own,

20 for you were bought at a price. Therefore glorify God in your body [1 Corinthians 6: 13b-20, HCSB]

If God created you a man and you say that you are a woman or vice versa, and act unbecomingly; you are wrong. That is what God's word says in the Book of Romans chapter one. Do not be futile in your thinking. Do not exchange your body's natural function for what is unnatural. Do not believe that lie from the devil. God is against every form of ungodliness. Hear what the Holy Spirit says,

22 Claiming to be wise, they became fools [professing to be smart, they made simpletons of themselves].

24 Therefore God gave them up in the lusts of their [own] hearts to sexual impurity, to the dishonoring of their bodies among themselves [abandoning them to the degrading power of sin],

25 Because they exchanged the truth of God for a lie and worshiped and served the creature rather than the Creator, Who is blessed forever! Amen (so be it).

26 For this reason God gave them over and abandoned them to vile affections and degrading passions. For their women exchanged their natural function for an unnatural and abnormal one,

27 And the men also turned from natural relations with women and were set ablaze (burning out, consumed) with lust for one another— men committing shameful acts with men and suffering in their own bodies and personalities the inevitable consequences and penalty of their wrong-doing and going astray, which [their] fitting retribution. [Romans 1: 22-27, AMP]

Do not say you were created that way because when you say that you are trying to make God to be a liar, and He cannot lie. [Titus 1: 2, AMP] The Word says that you are fearfully and wonderfully made. Why do you not believe who God says you are and who He made you to be? Why listen to the devil whose language is lies because there is no truth in him. You cannot say you are a child of God and give yourself to homosexuality, and say that it is how you were born. God is whole. His ways are just, and His works are perfect. [Deuteronomy 32: 4, NIV] There is no confusion in Him, and His works are not works of confusion. He is our Creator Who created you as a man or a woman. He did not create you to be confused about your sexuality.

The devil is a liar. Quit listening to him, and decide to be free now by surrendering to God. The truth is that you have wrong friends that the devil has used to lure you into homosexuality. It is time to be free. Acknowledge and confess Jesus as your Lord and Savior, and be free. To refuse to be free from the shackles of Satan carries with it grave consequences as the Holy Spirit reveals to us in Romans 1:

> [28] And so, since they did not see fit to acknowledge God or approve of Him or consider Him worth the knowing, God gave them over to a base and condemned mind to do things not proper or decent but loathsome,
> [29] Until they were filled (permeated and saturated) with every kind of unrighteousness, iniquity, grasping and covetous greed, and malice. [They were] full of envy and jealousy, murder, strife, deceit and treachery, ill will and cruel ways. [They were] secret backbiters and gossipers,
> [30] Slanderers, hateful to and hating God, full of insolence, arrogance, [and] boasting; inventors of new forms of evil, disobedient and undutiful to parents.
> [31] [They were] without understanding, conscienceless and faithless, heartless and loveless [and] merciless.
> [32] Though they are fully aware of God's righteous decree that those who do such things deserve to die, they not only do them themselves but approve and applaud others who practice them. [Romans 1: 28-32, AMP]

God did not create you to go to hell. Hell was meant for the devil and his demons. The truth is, you were walking in ignorance and were deceived. Now you know the truth, and the consequence of not acting on the truth you know is severe. Sin pays wages. "For the wages which sin pays is death, but the [bountiful] free gift of God is eternal life through (in union with) Jesus Christ our Lord." [Romans 6: 23, AMP] You are reading this because God wants you free. Your conscience tells you that you are wrong, but you have been ignoring it. Stop ignoring that warning from God in the Name of Jesus. Repent and ask God for forgiveness. Claim your deliverance now in the name of Jesus. Jesus has already paid for your deliverance as it is written in Colossians chapter one.

> [12] Giving thanks to the Father, Who has qualified and made us fit to share the portion which is the inheritance of the saints (God's holy people) in the Light.
> [13] [The Father] has delivered and drawn us to Himself out of the control and the dominion of darkness and has transferred us into the kingdom of the Son of His love,
> [14] In Whom we have our redemption through His blood, [which means] the forgiveness of our sins. [Colossians 1: 12-14, AMP]

Accept it, declare same, and walk free in the Name of Jesus. This is true for any kind of bondage (pornography, fornication, adultery, homosexuality, drug addiction, smoking, etc.) you may be dealing with. You may call it a problem or an issue, but God calls it sin. Call it what God calls, and that is the beginning of your deliverance. Jesus has already paid for your deliverance and liberty. It is up to you to accept it and confess your deliverance with your mouth. When you trust (agree with and accept) the Lord and receive what He offers you, He gives you power to be delivered. Accept His Word, act on it , and be free. Say this from your heart and believe it:

> *Jesus you are the Lord of my life. I acknowledge and confess with my lips that You are Lord and in my heart I believe (adhere to, trust in, and rely on the truth) that God raised You from the dead, and I am saved (redeemed, delivered, set free, healed, made whole, and restored). Thank You Father God for delivering me from the dominion and control of darkness and translating me into the Kingdom of the Son of Your love, in Whom I have my redemption through His blood, [which means] the remission of my sins.*

Lord Jesus I accept what You did for me, therefore I am free. I am free from all (name them) that has kept me bound. Hallelujah! Thank You Lord! I am free. I yield to Your Spirit Father God, and I thank You that by Your grace I daily present my body to You as my reasonable act of worship. Thank You Father for my deliverance and freedom in the Name of Jesus. Amen.

If you need more help, get a Bible believing believer who is anointed with the Holy Spirit to minister to you and set you free from the control of the devil who is the enemy of your soul.

Given the characteristics of *Agape* love and the law of love (i.e., love God, and love your neighbor as yourself) that we are to live by, we understand that walking in *Agape* love is to allow God's nature to reign in our lives. This means keeping no account when wronged. It means walking in forgiveness.

3. FORGIVENESS

Be gentle and forbearing with one another and, if one has a difference (a grievance or complaint) against another, readily pardoning each other; even as the Lord has [freely] forgiven you, so must you also [forgive]. [Colossians 3:13, AMP]

Without God's forgiveness, it would not have been possible for us to come to God. He loved us so much that he paid for our sins, and invited us to come and experience His love for us. In addition, he adopted us into His family and raised us up to sit with Christ at his right hand. He did this because of His intense love for us.

> ⁴ But God—so rich is He in His mercy! Because of and in order to satisfy the great and wonderful and intense love with which He loved us,
> ⁵ Even when we were dead (slain) by [our own] shortcomings and trespasses, He made us alive together in fellowship and in union with Christ; [He gave us the very life of Christ Himself, the same new life with which He quickened Him, for] it is by grace (His favor and mercy which you did not deserve) that you are saved (delivered from judgment and made partakers of Christ's salvation).
> ⁶ And He raised us up together with Him and made us sit down together [giving us joint seating with Him] in the heavenly sphere [by virtue of our being] in Christ Jesus (the Messiah, the Anointed One). [Ephesians 2: 4-6, AMP]

Our Father, in turn, wants to extend His love through us to others. Forgiveness is a key component of extending God's love in us to others, even those we do not think deserve our love. The Holy Spirit admonishes us to "be gentle *and* forbearing with one another and, if one has a difference (a grievance or complaint) against another, readily pardoning each other; even as the Lord has [freely] forgiven you, so must you also [forgive]." [Colossians 3: 13, AMP]

Forgiveness originated from God, and we His children who have His Spirit in us can forgive as God has forgiven us. As discussed previously, He has poured out His love into our hearts through His Spirit in us. Thus, it is not our love but the love of God in us. Forgiving others is for our own benefit. We are the primary beneficiaries of our act of forgiveness, and the secondary beneficiaries are those who wrong us.

On an occasion when I was studying this subject of forgiveness, the Word of the Lord came to me:

> *To forgive is My nature. As My child, you have My nature. My nature is to forgive promptly. That is why I say that love keeps no account of a suffered wrong. You must forgive immediately you are wronged. Do not wait for the other party's apology. You may never receive it, but you must forgive immediately to keep your channel of communication with Me open. When you pray for the one who has wronged you, you allow Me to work in that person's life.*

God would not ask us to do what He has not modeled for us. He has given us the ability and capacity to forgive, and He modeled it for us. Let us learn from our Father's model of forgiveness.

Learn from God

The Holy Spirit introduces us to the forgiving heart of the Father in the Gospel of John chapter three:

> [16] For God so greatly loved and dearly prized the world that He [even] gave up His only begotten (unique) Son, so that whoever believes in (trusts in, clings to, relies on) Him shall not perish (come to destruction, be lost) but have eternal (everlasting) life. [John 3:16, AMP]

God sent Jesus to die for us. While we were yet sinners, Christ died for us. [Romans 5: 8 AMP] In fact, Jesus is "the Lamb Who has been slain [in the mind of God] since the time when the foundations of the universe were laid, and Who is looked upon [by God] as the slain Lamb at the present." [Revelation 13: 8, WUEST] We have redemption through the blood of Christ according to the riches of His grace. [Ephesians 1: 5-8, AMP] When we confess our sins, God readily and quickly forgives our sins, and He does it without reservation. [1 John 1: 9, AMP] He does it because He is love. He cannot do otherwise, but to express Himself by demonstrating His love. The discourse in Matthew 18: 23-27 is a good illustration of how God freely, quickly, and readily forgives us our trespasses:

> ²³ Therefore the kingdom of heaven is like a human king who wished to settle accounts with his attendants.
> ²⁴ When he began the accounting, one was brought to him who owed him 10,000 talents [probably about $10,000,000],
> ²⁵ And because he could not pay, his master ordered him to be sold, with his wife and his children and everything that he possessed, and payment to be made.
> ²⁶ So the attendant fell on his knees, begging him, Have patience with me and I will pay you everything.
> ²⁷ And his master's heart was moved with compassion, and he released him and forgave him [cancelling] the debt. [Matthew 18: 23-27, AMP]

God is love, and all who live in love live in God, and God lives in them.

The story is instructive on how much God loves us and freely forgives, just for our asking.

In addition, God does not keep account of our sins. "I, even I, am He Who blots out and cancels your transgressions, for My own sake, and I will not remember your sins." [Isaiah 43: 25, AMP] God does not remember our sins because of what He did for us through Jesus at Calvary. He is slow to anger and abundant in mercy and loving-kindness. He removes our sins as far as the East is from the West, and He does not deal with us according to our sins. King David described God's love thus,

⁸ The Lord is merciful and gracious, slow to anger and plenteous in mercy and loving-kindness.

⁹ He will not always chide or be contending, neither will He keep His anger forever or hold a grudge.

¹⁰ He has not dealt with us after our sins nor rewarded us according to our iniquities.

¹¹ For as the heavens are high above the earth, so great are His mercy and loving-kindness toward those who reverently and worshipfully fear Him.

¹² As far as the east is from the west, so far has He removed our transgressions from us. [Psalm 103: 8-12, AMP]

Apostle Paul reiterated this, when he wrote that *Agape* love keeps no record of wrongs. [1 Corinthians 13: 5, AMP] In addition, God believes the very best of us because He knows who we truly are and He gives us every opportunity to come into who He created us to be. [1 Corinthians 13: 7, AMP] Therefore, we must learn from God our Father and Jesus our Lord how to walk in love.

Our Part

God made us like Himself and gave us His Spirit to love like Him. In doing this, He poured His love into us through His Spirit in us. [Romans 5: 5, AMP] He did this because He is love. [1 John 4: 8, AMP] Every born again child of God has the love of God in him. We can love even as we are loved by God. We have the capability to love just like God. God would not ask us to do what He has not equipped us to do. The love of God is brought into full expression in us when we love one another. It demonstrates that we live in Christ because as Jesus is, so are we in this world. We have to heed the instruction of the Holy Spirit through the Apostle John:

¹² No one has ever seen God. But if we love each other, God lives in us, and his love is brought to full expression in us.

¹³ And God has given us his Spirit as proof that we live in him and he in us.

14 Furthermore, we have seen with our own eyes and now testify that the Father sent his Son to be the Savior of the world.

15 All who confess that Jesus is the Son of God have God living in them, and they live in God.

16 We know how much God loves us, and we have put our trust in his love. God is love, and all who live in love live in God, and God lives in them.

17 And as we live in God, our love grows more perfect. So we will not be afraid on the day of judgment, but we can face him with confidence because we live like Jesus here in this world. [1 John 4: 12-17, NLT]

As God readily and freely forgives, we must forgive readily and freely. As God does not hold grudge or keep a record of our wrongs, so can we. Here are some passages that drive home this point.

8 The Lord is merciful and gracious, slow to anger and plenteous in mercy and loving-kindness.

9 He will not always chide or be contending, neither will He keep His anger forever or hold a grudge.

10 He has not dealt with us after our sins nor rewarded us according to our iniquities.

11 For as the heavens are high above the earth, so great are His mercy and loving-kindness toward those who reverently and worshipfully fear Him.

12 As far as the east is from the west, so far has He removed our transgressions from us. [Psalm 103: 8-12, AMP]

5 It is not conceited (arrogant and inflated with pride); it is not rude (unmannerly) and does not act unbecomingly. Love (God's love in us) does not insist on its own rights or its own way, for it is not self-seeking; it is not touchy or fretful or resentful; it takes no account of the evil done to it [it pays no attention to a suffered wrong]. [1 Corinthians 13: 5, AMP]

As God does not remember our sins, so can we learn from God and refuse to remember the offenses of those who have wronged us. Do not rehearse the hurt. It will only fuel the anger from the offense. For lack of wood fire goes out. "For lack of wood the fire goes out, and where there is no whisperer, quarreling ceases." [Proverbs 26: 6, NIV]

God gave us a big responsibility as His children, his representatives. Jesus gave us, His disciples, the power to forgive sins.

> [21] Again Jesus said, "Peace be with you! As the Father has sent me, I am sending you."
> [22] And with that he breathed on them and said, "Receive the Holy Spirit.
> [23] If you forgive anyone's sins, their sins are forgiven; if you do not forgive them, they are not forgiven." [John 20: 21-23, NIV]

The Lord gave us a big responsibility to forgive or retain sins. We cannot be arrogant and refuse to forgive others because there may be times we need others to forgive us. Equally, we may sin and when we do, we need God's forgiveness. If we refuse to forgive others, we should not expect God to forgive us. The Lord taught us to ask the Father to "forgive us our sins, as we have forgiven those who sin against us." [Matthew 6: 12, NLT] We must learn to forgive and let go. Forgiveness is a gift you give primarily to yourself, and secondarily to others. Unforgiveness is a stumbling block to anyone who harbors it.

A Stumbling Block

A stumbling block is an obstacle that prevents one from making progress. In the context of the Christian life, it is an impediment to spiritual progress that eventually affects other areas of life. Entertaining offense creates a stumbling block in our lives.

Offense
Here is what our Lord Jesus had to say about offense.

> [1] Then said he unto the disciples, It is impossible but that offences will come: but woe unto him, through whom they come! [Luke 17: 1, KJV]

[1] And [Jesus] said to His disciples, Temptations (snares, traps set to entice to sin) are sure to come, but woe to him by or through whom they come! [Luke 17: 1, AMP]

An offense is a temptation, a snare, a trap set to entice to sin, and Satan is the puppet master orchestrating it. He does this through the instrumentality of a human being. His intent is for us to get offended and refuse to forgive and entertain resentment. Jesus taught us not to swallow the bait of unforgiveness from Satan by refusing to forgive those who wrong us. By forgiving an offense, He means we should "give up resentment and consider the offense as recalled and annulled." [Luke 17: 4, AMP]

How do you know that you have not forgiven your offender and given up resentment? If you get angry when you see your offender or your offender's name is mentioned, it means you have retained resentment. You retained resentment because you did not forgive your offender.

Retaining resentment is a subtle thing. You can say, but I forgave when I prayed. I once thought so too until the Lord explained to me as I have written above. You may not probably know until you encounter the person or the person's name is mentioned. A direct or indirect encounter with your offender without anger is a clear proof that you have forgiven your offender and let go of the offense. If you do not forgive, you are letting the root of resentment (bitterness) to grow in you. When bitterness grows in you, you will defile others by spreading it. We must forsake unforgiveness and resentment because they are toxic. If you do not, they will defile you and those who associate with you because you will poison their minds against those who have wronged you. The Holy Spirit admonishes us in the book of Hebrews that we should:

[14] Strive to live in peace with everybody and pursue that consecration and holiness without which no one will [ever] see the Lord.
[15] Exercise foresight and be on the watch to look [after one another], to see that no one falls back from and fails to secure God's grace (His unmerited favor and spiritual blessing), in order that no root of resentment (rancor, bitterness, or hatred) shoots forth and causes

trouble and bitter torment, and the many become contaminated and defiled by it. [Hebrews 12: 14-16, AMP]

Resentment leads to hatred, and hatred can give birth to murder. To hate is to walk in darkness and a person who hates is not walking in the Light:

> [9] Whoever says he is in the Light and [yet] hates his brother [Christian, born-again child of God his Father] is in darkness even until now.
> [10] Whoever loves his brother [believer] abides (lives) in the Light, and in It or in him there is no occasion for stumbling or cause for error or sin.
> [11] But he who hates (detests, despises) his brother [in Christ] is in darkness and walking (living) in the dark; he is straying and does not perceive or know where he is going, because the darkness has blinded his eyes. [1 John 2: 9-11, AMP]

We are to forgive always.

We must choose to walk in the Light as Jesus Who we are one with is Light. That means we must make the quality decision to forgive readily and freely, no matter the circumstance. We must forgive all those who wrong us, Christian or non-Christian. Once you have made that decision, you will find that it is easy to forgive and let go. You may struggle at first, but once you remind yourself of your decision to forgive God will help you to forgive.

Remember, you are operating with and in *Agape* love and not natural human love. You may have to speak to yourself that you have forgiven your offender, and that you love the individual with the love of God. You probably need to do this each time the devil reminds you of the offense and the need of not letting go of it. This is what I have put to work in my life with tremendous benefit. It is important for us to heed the Holy Spirit and love others and not listen to the devil, or our flesh that needs to be crucified. The key is imitating Christ our Lord:

[13] Be gentle and forbearing with one another and, if one has a difference (a grievance or complaint) against another, readily pardoning each other; even as the Lord has [freely] forgiven you, so must you also [forgive]. [Colossians 3:13, AMP]

[32] And become useful and helpful and kind to one another, tenderhearted (compassionate, understanding, loving-hearted), forgiving one another [readily and freely], as God in Christ forgave you. [Ephesians 4: 32, AMP]

Forgiveness is our life style and obligation as children and servants of the most High God. Jesus reminded us to,

[3] Pay attention and always be on your guard [looking out for one another]. If your brother sins (misses the mark), solemnly tell him so and reprove him, and if he repents (feels sorry for having sinned), forgive him.

[4] And even if he sins against you seven times in a day, and turns to you seven times and says, I repent [I am sorry], you must forgive him (give up resentment and consider the offense as recalled and annulled).

[5] The apostles said to the Lord, Increase our faith (that trust and confidence that spring from our belief in God).

[6] And the Lord answered, If you had faith (trust and confidence in God) even [so small] like a grain of mustard seed, you could say to this mulberry tree, Be pulled up by the roots, and be planted in the sea, and it would obey you.

[7] Will any man of you who has a servant plowing or tending sheep say to him when he has come in from the field, Come at once and take your place at the table?

[8] Will he not instead tell him, Get my supper ready and gird yourself and serve me while I eat and drink; then afterward you yourself shall eat and drink?

[9] Is he grateful and does he praise the servant because he did what he was ordered to do?

[10] Even so on your part, when you have done everything that was assigned and commanded you, say, We are unworthy servants [possessing no merit, for we have not gone beyond our obligation]; we have [merely] done what was our duty to do. [Luke 17: 3-10, AMP]

Although it is stated in the above passage in the Book of Luke that we should forgive our brother seven times, if we take it literally, we find in Matthew 18 that we are to forgive 490 times indicating that we should forgive as often as we are wronged.

> 21 Then Peter came up to Him and said, Lord, how many times may my brother sin against me and I forgive him and let it go? [As many as] up to seven times?
> 22 Jesus answered him, I tell you, not up to seven times, but seventy times seven! [Matthew 18: 21-22, AMP]

When we refuse to forgive we literally turn ourselves over to the devil and his demons to torment us.

It is worth noting that seven is number of completeness, indicating that the Lord in Luke 17: 4 was saying to His disciples then and saying to us, His disciples today, to forgive always. In essence, there should be no room for unforgiveness in us. In Luke 17: 3-10 we find the disciples asking for more faith to be able to forgive those who always wronged them. The reply of our Lord is very instructive. He said that we do not need any more faith than we already have to forgive our offenders. He declared, if you had faith as the grain of a mustard seed "you would say to this mulberry tree, 'Be uprooted, and planted in the sea,' and it would obey you." [Luke 17: 6, MOFFATT] By this statement our Lord and Master declared that unforgiveness was a stumbling block on the path of progress in life like the sycamine (mulberry) tree that was probably on their path which He used for the object lesson on forgiveness.

Our Lord made it clear to us that as children of the most High God forgiveness is our obligation to dispense to others. When we forgive others, we are only doing what He expects of us. Unforgiveness is a stumbling block that keeps you from enjoying the very best in life. Unforgiveness carries with it severe consequences.

Consequences of Unforgiveness

There are many consequences of unforgiveness. They include the torture of Satan, unanswered prayer, loss of protection, and rebellion and death. I discuss each one of them below.

Torture from Satan

When we refuse to forgive we literally turn ourselves over to the devil and his demons to torment us. We see this described vividly in the parable of the unmerciful servant. The master forgave the unmerciful servant a debt of about $10,000,000 (Matthew 18: 24, AMP), but the servant would not forgive his fellow servant a debt of about $20.

> 28 But that same attendant, as he went out, found one of his fellow attendants who owed him a hundred denarii [about twenty dollars]; and he caught him by the throat and said, Pay what you owe!
> 29 So his fellow attendant fell down and begged him earnestly, Give me time, and I will pay you all!
> 30 But he was unwilling, and he went out and had him put in prison till he should pay the debt.
> 31 When his fellow attendants saw what had happened, they were greatly distressed, and they went and told everything that had taken place to their master.
> 32 Then his master called him and said to him, You contemptible and wicked attendant! I forgave and cancelled all that [great] debt of yours because you begged me to.
> 33 And should you not have had pity and mercy on your fellow attendant, as I had pity and mercy on you?
> 34 And in wrath his master turned him over to the torturers (the jailers), till he should pay all that he owed.
> 35 So also My heavenly Father will deal with every one of you if you do not freely forgive your brother from your heart his offenses. [Matthew 18: 28-35, AMP]

The torturers (jailers) in Matthew 18: 34 are Satan and his gangs. Do not turnover yourself to the tormentors (i.e., put yourself in jail) by refusing to forgive. Unforgiveness opens the door for Satan to attack you with sickness, disease, and all kinds of problems.

One day in church a young lady asked me to pray for her to be healed of arthritis and deteriorating vision. Her doctor told her that her vertebral column was damaged from arthritis that could result in paralysis. As I was about to pray for her, the Lord asked me to ask her to forgive her father. I explained to her that I could not pray until she did. Of course, I had to give her some testimonies of others who obtained their miracles from God after they forgave those who wronged them and let go of the offenses. She quickly saw the point, forgave her father, and received her healing and the correction of her eyesight. She is still whole today.

> Next time you exercise authority with no results, check up on yourself to determine if you are walking in love.

Unforgiveness is a door opener. It opens the door for the enemy to enter into your life and affairs. When you know that the devil is looking for ways to come against you at the least opportunity, why would you want to cooperate with him? Jesus said,

> [30] .... the prince (evil genius, ruler) of the world is coming. And he has no claim on Me. [He has nothing in common with Me; there is nothing in Me that belongs to him, and he has no power over Me.]
> [31] But [Satan is coming and] I do as the Father has commanded Me, so that the world may know (be convinced) that I love the Father and that I do only what the Father has instructed Me to do. [I act in full agreement with His orders.] [John 14: 30-31, AMP]

When you, through unforgiveness, open the door to the enemy, Jesus cannot defend you. He cannot, because unforgiveness is not of God, but of the devil. The Lord cannot demand from the devil what is the devil's. Unforgiveness makes the devil to have a claim on you. Jesus said, "The prince (evil genius, ruler) of the world is coming. And he has no claim on Me. [He has nothing in common with Me; there is nothing in Me that belongs to him, and he has no power over Me." [John 14: 30, AMP] Satan had no claim on Jesus and Jesus had nothing of Satan's because Jesus was walking in *Agape* love always. Next time you exercise authority with no results, check up on yourself to determine if you are walking in *Agape* love.

> Unforgiveness leaves a breach in your spiritual defense wall, making you an open target for spiritual marauders.

Unanswered Prayer

Unforgiveness is a major reason for unanswered prayers. Jesus when He taught on prayer said,

> [24] For this reason I am telling you, whatever you ask for in prayer, believe (trust and be confident) that it is granted to you, and you will [get it].
>
> [25] And whenever you stand praying, if you have anything against anyone, forgive him and let it drop (leave it, let it go), in order that your Father Who is in heaven may also forgive you your [own] failings and shortcomings and let them drop.
>
> [26] But if you do not forgive, neither will your Father in heaven forgive your failings and shortcomings. [Mark 11: 24–26, AMP]

Since we have heard from the Master's lips that we must forgive and walk in love to have our prayers answered, we should. How can you commune with a loving God if you choose to harbor unforgiveness? If you do, there is no basis for fellowship with Him. He has said, "Do two walk together unless they have agreed to do so?" [Amos 3: 3, NIV] How can God agree with you if you harbor resentment? How can God whose nature is love agree with you if you decide to yield to the enemy and walk in unforgiveness and resentment? If God does not agree with you, it means you are not lining up with His Word. If you do not line up with His

Word in Mark 11: 24–26, you cannot get your prayers answered. Choose to obey the Lord and forgive. Say: *Lord I obey You, and I forgive those who have wronged me. I thank You for forgiving my failings and shortcomings.*

Loss of Protection

Harboring unforgiveness and resentment makes you an open target for the enemy. Having unforgiveness is like having a breach in a defense wall. Unforgiveness leaves a breach in your spiritual defense wall, making you an open target for spiritual marauders. Do not forget that unforgiveness is of the devil and he will come for what is his. You should not give the devil claim over your life by holding unto what is his. [John 14: 30, AMP] The Apostle Paul warned us not to give the devil room in our lives by not letting the sun go down on our anger.

> 26 When angry, do not sin; do not ever let your wrath (your exasperation, your fury or indignation) last until the sun goes down.
> 27 Leave no [such] room or foothold for the devil [give no opportunity to him]. [Ephesians 4: 26-27, AMP]

To give the devil opportunity, is to give him power and occasion to take action against you. Paul was telling us to be quick to forgive, thereby foreclosing on the enemy and leaving him no room to move against us. The Apostle Peter warned us to be vigilant, temperate, and sober of mind so that the enemy would not take advantage of us:

> 8 Be well balanced (temperate, sober of mind), be vigilant and cautious at all times; for that enemy of yours, the devil, roams around like a lion roaring [in fierce hunger], seeking someone to seize upon and devour.
> 9 Withstand him; be firm in faith [against his onset—rooted, established, strong, immovable, and determined], knowing that the same (identical) sufferings are appointed to your brotherhood (the whole body of Christians) throughout the world. [1 Peter 5: 8-9, AMP]

If you walk in love and are not in fear (anxiety, and worry), then you are at peace and there is no breach in your spiritual defense wall for the enemy to attack you. You will not expose yourself to his thoughts of evil and rebellion.

Rebellion and Death

Unforgiveness can lead to rebellion. Examples abound in life and a good example is Absalom in the Bible. Absalom did not forgive Amnon who committed the heinous crime of raping his sister. Let us pick up the story from 2 Samuel 13:

> [1] Now David's son Absalom had a beautiful sister named Tamar. And Amnon, her half brother, fell desperately in love with her.
>
> [2] Amnon became so obsessed with Tamar that he became ill. She was a virgin, and Amnon thought he could never have her.
>
> [6] So Amnon lay down and pretended to be sick. And when the king came to see him, Amnon asked him, "Please let my sister Tamar come and cook my favorite dish as I watch. Then I can eat it from her own hands."
>
> [7] So David agreed and sent Tamar to Amnon's house to prepare some food for him.
>
> [8] When Tamar arrived at Amnon's house, she went to the place where he was lying down so he could watch her mix some dough. Then she baked his favorite dish for him.
>
> [9] But when she set the serving tray before him, he refused to eat. "Everyone get out of here," Amnon told his servants. So they all left.
>
> [10] Then he said to Tamar, "Now bring the food into my bedroom and feed it to me here." So Tamar took his favorite dish to him.
>
> [11] But as she was feeding him, he grabbed her and demanded, "Come to bed with me, my darling sister."
>
> [12] "No, my brother!" she cried. "Don't be foolish! Don't do this to me! Such wicked things aren't done in Israel.
>
> [13] Where could I go in my shame? And you would be called one of the greatest fools in Israel. Please, just speak to the king about it, and he will let you marry me."
>
> [14] But Amnon wouldn't listen to her, and since he was stronger than she was, he raped her.
>
> [15] Then suddenly Amnon's love turned to hate, and he hated her even more than he had loved her. "Get out of here!" he snarled at her.

16 "No, no!" Tamar cried. "Sending me away now is worse than what you've already done to me." But Amnon wouldn't listen to her.

17 He shouted for his servant and demanded, "Throw this woman out, and lock the door behind her!"

18 So the servant put her out and locked the door behind her. She was wearing a long, beautiful robe, as was the custom in those days for the king's virgin daughters.

19 But now Tamar tore her robe and put ashes on her head. And then, with her face in her hands, she went away crying.

20 Her brother Absalom saw her and asked, "Is it true that Amnon has been with you? Well, my sister, keep quiet for now, since he's your brother. Don't you worry about it." So Tamar lived as a desolate woman in her brother Absalom's house.

21 When King David heard what had happened, he was very angry.

22 And though Absalom never spoke to Amnon about this, he hated Amnon deeply because of what he had done to his sister. [2 Samuel 13: 1-22, NLT]

King David was angry, but did nothing. He did not discipline or punish Amnon appropriately. Absalom, I believe, was not only resentful at Amnon, but he was equally offended at his father's inaction. He decided to take matters into his own hands and plotted the murder of his wicked half-brother Amnon. The planning and execution of the plot is described below:

23 Two years later, when Absalom's sheep were being sheared at Baal-hazor near Ephraim, Absalom invited all the king's sons to come to a feast.

24 He went to the king and said, "My sheep-shearers are now at work. Would the king and his servants please come to celebrate the occasion with me?"

25 The king replied, "No, my son. If we all came, we would be too much of a burden on you." Absalom pressed him, but the king would not come, though he gave Absalom his blessing.

26 "Well, then," Absalom said, "if you can't come, how about sending my brother Amnon with us?"

²⁸ Absalom told his men, "Wait until Amnon gets drunk; then at my signal, kill him! Don't be afraid. I'm the one who has given the command. Take courage and do it!"

²⁹ So at Absalom's signal they murdered Amnon. Then the other sons of the king jumped on their mules and fled. [2 Samuel 13: 23-29, NLT]

After the killing of Amnon, Absalom fled Jerusalem. He later came back and Joab, David's general, reconciled Absalom with his father. Absalom later plotted a rebellion against his father, David, because of the resentment he harbored against him. The resentment, of course, was a consequence of him not forgiving his father for the way he handled (or more appropriately did not handle) the case of Amnon raping his sister, Tamar. Unforgiveness led to resentment and bitterness, and the root of bitterness resulted in hatred to the extent that Absalom plotted the destruction of his father. Let us pick the account of Absalom's rebellion in 2 Samuel 15:

¹ After this, Absalom bought a chariot and horses, and he hired fifty bodyguards to run ahead of him.

² He got up early every morning and went out to the gate of the city. When people brought a case to the king for judgment, Absalom would ask where in Israel they were from, and they would tell him their tribe.

³ Then Absalom would say, "You've really got a strong case here! It's too bad the king doesn't have anyone to hear it.

⁴ I wish I were the judge. Then everyone could bring their cases to me for judgment, and I would give them justice!"

⁵ When people tried to bow before him, Absalom wouldn't let them. Instead, he took them by the hand and kissed them.

⁶ Absalom did this with everyone who came to the king for judgment, and so he stole the hearts of all the people of Israel.

⁷ After four years, Absalom said to the king, "Let me go to Hebron to offer a sacrifice to the Lord and fulfill a vow I made to him.

⁸ For while your servant was at Geshur in Aram, I promised to sacrifice to the Lord in Hebron if he would bring me back to Jerusalem."

⁹ "All right," the king told him. "Go and fulfill your vow." So Absalom went to Hebron.

¹⁰ But while he was there, he sent secret messengers to all the tribes of Israel to stir up a rebellion against the king. "As soon as you hear the ram's horn," his message read, "you are to say, 'Absalom has been crowned king in Hebron.'"
¹¹ He took 200 men from Jerusalem with him as guests, but they knew nothing of his intentions.
¹² While Absalom was offering the sacrifices, he sent for Ahithophel, one of David's counselors who lived in Giloh. Soon many others also joined Absalom, and the conspiracy gained momentum.
¹³ A messenger soon arrived in Jerusalem to tell David, "All Israel has joined Absalom in a conspiracy against you!"

> Children who bear grudges against their parents end up rebelling, and some even destroy themselves as Absalom did.

¹⁴ "Then we must flee at once, or it will be too late!" David urged his men. "Hurry! If we get out of the city before Absalom arrives, both we and the city of Jerusalem will be spared from disaster." [2 Samuel 15: 1-14, NLT]

When David realized what his rebellious son had done, he set out to regain his kingdom. David gave his generals orders to regain control of his kingdom and spare his son Absalom as we read below:

¹ David now mustered the men who were with him and appointed generals and captains to lead them.
² He sent the troops out in three groups, placing one group under Joab, one under Joab's brother Abishai son of Zeruiah, and one under Ittai, the man from Gath. The king told his troops, "I am going out with you."
⁵ And the king gave this command to Joab, Abishai, and Ittai: "For my sake, deal gently with young Absalom." And all the troops heard the king give this order to his commanders.
⁹ During the battle, Absalom happened to come upon some of David's men. He tried to escape on his mule, but as he rode beneath the thick

branches of a great tree, his hair got caught in the tree. His mule kept going and left him dangling in the air.

[10] One of David's men saw what had happened and told Joab, "I saw Absalom dangling from a great tree."

[11] "What?" Joab demanded. "You saw him there and didn't kill him? I would have rewarded you with ten pieces of silver and a hero's belt!"

[14] "Enough of this nonsense," Joab said. Then he took three daggers and plunged them into Absalom's heart as he dangled, still alive, in the great tree.

[15] Ten of Joab's young armor bearers then surrounded Absalom and killed him. [2 Samuel 18: 1-5, 9-11, 14-15, NLT]

General Joab had enough of Absalom's rebellion and would not let him live. Looking at it from the theme of our discussion, we can discern that Absalom entertaining offense by refusing to forgive and let go set himself up for death without knowing. God is a righteous judge and vengeance is His, not ours. As wrong as the offense was and may be, God wants us to forgive. Children who bear grudges against their parents end up rebelling, and some even destroy themselves as Absalom did. This is a lesson for all of us. We are to honor our parents and not hate them. It does not mean you condone what your parent(s) did that was wrong. No, you choose to forgive and enjoy God's best for your life. Hallelujah!

Absalom would not have died if he had forgiven his brother who had committed an abominable offense. He needed to turn the matter over to God. He did not forgive his father because he felt that the father did not avenge the sexual abuse of his sister. Unforgiveness led to resentment, and resentment led to rebellion. Rebellion led to death. The consequences are too severe for us to refuse to forgive. We have to imitate our loving heavenly Father Who is always ready to forgive us our sins quickly and freely. The benefits of forgiving others and choosing to walk in *Agape* love are tremendous.

Benefits of Forgiveness

Answered Prayer

Jesus has taught us that choosing to forgive and walking in love is the key to open heaven. For our prayers to be answered we must forgive others and let go of resentment.

> [24] For this reason I am telling you, whatever you ask for in prayer, believe (trust and be confident) that it is granted to you, and you will [get it].
>
> [25] And whenever you stand praying, if you have anything against anyone, forgive him and let it drop (leave it, let it go), in order that your Father Who is in heaven may also forgive you your [own] failings and shortcomings and let them drop.
>
> [26] But if you do not forgive, neither will your Father in heaven forgive your failings and shortcomings. [Mark 11: 24-26, AMP]

I want my prayers answered. Do you want yours answered? Because I want my prayers answered, I have decided to forgive and move on with God when somebody wrongs me out of what I call ignorance.

Jesus said that those who plotted His crucifixion did it in ignorance and He forgave them right on the cross. He prayed for them, "... Father, forgive them, for they know not what they do." [Luke 23: 34, AMP] If we examine the statement of the Pharisees and the members of the Sanhedrin, we would say that they knew what they did:

> [24] So when Pilate saw that he was getting nowhere, but rather that a riot was about to break out, he took water and washed his hands in the presence of the crowd, saying, I am not guilty of nor responsible for this righteous Man's blood; see to it yourselves.
>
> [25] **And all the people answered, Let His blood be on us and on our children!**
>
> [26] So he set free for them Barabbas; and he [had] Jesus whipped, and delivered Him up to be crucified. [Matthew 27: 24-26, AMP; emphasis mine]

From their speech and actions we would conclude that the Jews knew what they were doing, but Jesus said that they did it in ignorance. We have to believe our Lord and Master. It is important to note that both Jews and gentiles crucified the Lord of glory. Pilate was a gentile, a

Roman governor over the Jewish people at the time of the crucifixion of Jesus.

Like the Lord, we need to consider our offenders ignorant, because if they truly knew what they were doing they would not have done it. They were deceived by Satan. When Satan deceives and blinds people, they do his bidding.

We must walk in love for God to accept our offerings (gifts) to Him. The Lord instructs us to get right with those we have grievance against us before offering our gifts at the alter:

> [23] So if when you are offering your gift at the altar you there remember that your brother has any [grievance] against you,
> [24] Leave your gift at the altar and go. First make peace with your brother, and then come back and present your gift.
> [25] Come to terms quickly with your accuser while you are on the way traveling with him, lest your accuser hand you over to the judge, and the judge to the guard, and you be put in prison. [Matthew 5: 23-25, AMP]

I choose to obey God and forgive those who wrong me. I do not know about you, but I want God to bless me when I give. It is biblical to expect God to bless us when we give. [Luke 6: 38, AMP] Unforgiveness, by default, puts you in Satan's jail. When you harbor unforgiveness, you are defenseless. When you forgive, *Agape* Love becomes your defense.

Defense

Love is a defense. *Agape* love is our defense against the wiles and attacks of the enemy. When you walk in love, the devil cannot touch you. He could not touch Jesus when He was on earth, and he cannot touch us when we operate in *Agape* love. Jesus is our example of the love of God in action. The Apostle Peter described the love of God in demonstration in Jesus' life when he wrote:

21 For even to this were you called [it is inseparable from your vocation]. For Christ also suffered for you, leaving you [His personal] example, so that you should follow in His footsteps.

22 He was guilty of no sin, neither was deceit (guile) ever found on His lips.

23 When He was reviled and insulted, He did not revile or offer insult in return; [when] He was abused and suffered, He made no threats [of vengeance]; but he trusted [Himself and everything] to Him Who judges fairly. [1 Peter 2: 21-23, AMP]

When Satan deceives and blinds people, they do his bidding.

Unforgiveness, by default, puts you in Satan's jail.

The Lord never returned insult for insult. He trusted everything to God the Father Who judges righteously. The same should be true of us. The Holy Spirit, through Apostle Peter, admonishes us thus,

9 Never return evil for evil or insult for insult (scolding, tongue-lashing, berating), but on the contrary blessing [praying for their welfare, happiness, and protection, and truly pitying and loving them]. For know that to this you have been called, that you may yourselves inherit a blessing [from God—that you may obtain a blessing as heirs, bringing welfare and happiness and protection].

10 For let him who wants to enjoy life and see good days [good—whether apparent or not] keep his tongue free from evil and his lips from guile (treachery, deceit).

11 Let him turn away from wickedness and shun it, and let him do right. Let him search for peace (harmony; undisturbedness from fears, agitating passions, and moral conflicts) and seek it eagerly. [Do not merely desire peaceful relations with God, with your fellowmen, and with yourself, but pursue, go after them!]

12 For the eyes of the Lord are upon the righteous (those who are upright and in right standing with God), and His ears are attentive to

their prayer. But the face of the Lord is against those who practice evil [to oppose them, to frustrate, and defeat them].

[13] Now who is there to hurt you if you are zealous followers of that which is good? [1 Peter 3: 9-13, AMP]

Peter was essentially telling us to follow the Master's example of not retaliating against those who do evil to us, "but on the contrary blessing [praying for their welfare, happiness, and protection, and truly pitying and loving them]." [1 Peter 3: 9b, AMP] The Holy Spirit wants us to understand that praying for those who have wronged us is a ministry God has given us. He explained to me that if I knew the spiritual condition (the depravity of the souls) of those who have offended me, I would pray for them.

When we walk in love towards those who hate us, God sees to it that we are protected.

God did not stop at saying we should pray for them, He explained in the above passage that there is a reward (a blessing) for us when we pray for those who have offended us. The Lord has undertaken to protect us, and at the same time frustrate and defeat those who practice evil. God says that there is no one who will hurt us if we are zealous followers of that which is good; if we follow after *Agape* love.

Testimony

I have put this Word to work in my life and I know it works just like every other Word from God. Several years ago, I faced a situation at work which got me very upset. I was falsely accused for what I did not do. I went to God in prayer asking for a solution, and the Lord asked me to forgive those who had offended me. He further instructed me to pray for them and gave me 1 Peter 3: 9–13. That was when He explained to me that if I could see the depravity of their souls, I would pity them and pray for them. I heeded the Lord's instruction, forgave them and prayed for them on a regular basis. God manifested His glory in the situation and I was exonerated. In addition, I was promoted. God's Word works and to God be the glory. Because I followed after good, the enemy could not have his way against me.

Joseph's Example

When we walk in love towards those who hate us, God sees to it that we are protected. In the case of Joseph recorded in Genesis chapters 37, we see how God protected Joseph even though his brothers hated him to the point of seeking to kill him.

> [4] But when his brothers saw that their father loved [Joseph] more than all of his brothers, they hated him and could not say, Peace [in friendly greeting] to him or speak peaceably to him.
> [5] Now Joseph had a dream and he told it to his brothers, and they hated him still more.
> [6] And he said to them, Listen now and hear, I pray you, this dream that I have dreamed:
> [7] We [brothers] were binding sheaves in the field, and behold, my sheaf arose and stood upright, and behold, your sheaves stood round about my sheaf and bowed down!
> [8] His brothers said to him, Shall you indeed reign over us? Or are you going to have us as your subjects and dominate us? And they hated him all the more for his dreams and for what he said.
> [9] But Joseph dreamed yet another dream and told it to his brothers [also]. He said, See the moon bowed down and did reverence to me!
> [11] Joseph's brothers envied him and were jealous of him, but his father observed the saying and pondered over it. [Genesis 37: 3-9, 11, AMP]

Jacob, Joseph's father, sent Joseph to go and see whether everything was alright with his brothers (half-brothers) who were shepherding the family's flock in Shechem which was quite some distance from home. When he got to Shechem he was told they had moved further away to Dothan, another town. Joseph finally caught up with his brothers in Dothan, and as soon as they saw him they felt they had the opportunity they had been seeking to kill him. The story continues in Genesis 37 from verse 18 onwards.

> [18] And when they saw him far off, even before he came near to them, they conspired to kill him.
>
> [19] And they said one to another, See, here comes this dreamer and master of dreams.
>
> [20] So come on now, let us kill him and throw his body into some pit; then we will say [to our father], Some wild and ferocious animal has devoured him; and we shall see what will become of his dreams!
>
> [21] Now Reuben heard it and he delivered him out of their hands by saying, Let us not kill him.
>
> [22] And Reuben said to them, Shed no blood, but cast him into this pit or well that is out here in the wilderness and lay no hand on him. He was trying to get Joseph out of their hands in order to rescue him and deliver him again to his father.
>
> [23] When Joseph had come to his brothers, they stripped him of his [distinctive] long garment which he was wearing;
>
> [24] Then they took him and cast him into the [well-like] pit which was empty; there was no water in it.
>
> [25] Then they sat down to eat their lunch. When they looked up, behold, they saw a caravan of Ishmaelites [mixed Arabians] coming from Gilead, with their camels bearing gum [of the styrax tree], balm (balsam), and myrrh or ladanum, going on their way to carry them down to Egypt.
>
> [26] And Judah said to his brothers, What do we gain if we slay our brother and conceal his blood?
>
> [27] Come, let us sell him to the Ishmaelites [and Midianites, these mixed Arabians who are approaching], and let not our hand be upon him, for he is our brother and our flesh. And his brothers consented.
>
> [28] Then as the Midianite [and Ishmaelite] merchants were passing by, the brothers pulled Joseph up and lifted him out of the well. And they sold him for twenty pieces of silver to the Ishmaelites, who took Joseph [captive] into Egypt. [Genesis 37: 18-28, AMP]

Envy and jealousy lead to hatred, and hatred sustained leads to murder. We see this illustrated in Joseph's story above. However, God did not allow the enemy to destroy His own. Thus, He prevailed on Reuben to prevent his brothers from killing Joseph by putting him in the well. God did not stop there; He allowed them to sell Joseph as a slave to the Ishmaelites for Joseph's protection. If Reuben had returned Joseph to their father, the brothers would have sought another occasion to kill him and probably could have succeeded. Why, you may ask? Joseph did not appreciate the fact that his brothers hated him. He probably thought they loved him. If he knew that they hated him he would not have told them his second dream.

> Unforgiveness can lead to poor memory and foggy thinking.

Joseph did not know that "a man's enemies are the members of his own household." [Micah 7: 6b, NIV]. He did not know what we ought to know because the Lord taught that we should "not give that which is holy (the sacred thing) to the dogs, and do not throw your pearls before hogs, lest they trample upon them with their feet and turn and tear you in pieces." [Matthew 7: 6, AMP] He was casting his pearls to hogs and giving what was sacred (his God-given vision) to the dogs who wanted to turn around and tear him in pieces. Joseph in his loving heart shared his vision ignorantly with his brothers who hated him. That would have been his undoing, but God seeing his heart of love stepped in to protect him.

God allowed him to be sold into slavery to protect him and the vision he was carrying. Thereafter, He enabled Joseph to fulfill his vision; that is, elevation to the premiership of Egypt. The purpose of that was to preserve Israel from destruction by famine in Canaan. Joseph revealed this in his encounter with his brothers when they moved to Egypt with their father, Jacob, during the famine. He said, "As for you, you thought evil against me, but God meant it for good, to bring about that many people should be kept alive, as they are this day." [Genesis 50: 20, AMP]

Good Health

Letting the love of God control you is a recipe for good health. Just as unforgiveness opens the door for the devil to attack, forgiveness closes that door. This is what Jesus explained to us in John 14:

> [30] I will not talk with you much more, for the prince (evil genius, ruler) of the world is coming. And he has no claim on Me. [He has nothing in common with Me; there is nothing in Me that belongs to him, and he has no power over Me.] [John 14: 30, AMP]

I shared a testimony of a young woman who had arthritis that would have crippled her, but for the Lord's intervention. She had to forgive her father as the Lord instructed her through me before I could pray for her. When she obeyed the Lord and I prayed for her, she was instantly healed and has remained so till this day. Love allows the healing power of God to flow through us and in us.

When we walk in love, we are at peace. "Wrath is cruel and anger is an overwhelming flood." [Proverbs 27: 4a, AMP] Anger from unforgiveness and resentment increase your sympathetic drive and floods your body with excess discharge of adrenaline and noradrenaline (chemical substances released in the body for fight or freight) which constrict your arteries causing resistance to blood flow. A sustained maintenance of such a state through bottled up anger and unforgiveness can lead to high blood pressure. Unforgiveness can lead to poor memory and foggy thinking.

Forgiveness, on the contrary, reduces your sympathetic drive and the consequent release of these chemical substances and consequently blood pressure. Love is the fruit of the recreated spirit of the born again child of God because of the righteousness imputed to us by God. The fruit of righteousness is peace; its effect is quietness and confidence forever. [Isaiah 32:17, NIV] Forgiving others because of the *Agape* love in us enables us to enjoy peace as the fruit of righteousness. Peace means wholeness (or completeness) with nothing missing or broken in our lives (bodies). When you are at peace, your mind is clear and you have clarity of thought with a good memory.

Immunity against Disease

In this section, I delve more into the forgiveness basis of good health by discussing in greater detail the underlying mechanism behind it. Someone once said, "Unforgiveness is like a person taking a poison and hoping that his enemy would die." The truth is that poison kills the person who swallows it. That is what unforgivesness, if not dealt with, can cause. Unforgiveness is an emotional wound that emanates from the heart (spirit). The heart/spirit or soul of man is the seat of emotion. Unforgiveness leads to anger against the one who wronged you. Resentment occurs because you retain the offense, and resentment gives rise to bitterness. Bitterness is like the root of an unwanted herb or plant that can spread over a large area of land. Bitterness defiles others. Resentment and bitterness gives rise to hatred, and hatred gives rise to murder. Here is what the Word says of them:

> [14] Strive to live in peace with everybody and pursue that consecration and holiness without which no one will [ever] see the Lord.
>
> [15] Exercise foresight and be on the watch to look [after one another], to see that no one falls back from and fails to secure God's grace (His unmerited favor and spiritual blessing), in order that no root of resentment (rancor, bitterness, or hatred) shoots forth and causes trouble and bitter torment, and the many become contaminated and defiled by it. [Hebrews 12:14-15, AMP]
>
> [15] Anyone who hates (abominates, detests) his brother [in Christ] is [at heart] a murderer, and you know that no murderer has eternal life abiding (persevering) within him. [1 John 3: 15, AMP]

Unforgiveness, anger because of unforgiveness, bitterness, and hatred are negative emotions that signal to your body to produce fear, fight or flight hormones (chemicals). These are adrenaline and cortisol which the body releases to combat the situation. Adrenaline causes increase in heart rate, and the rate of breathing. It also causes a dilation of the blood vessels to the lungs and muscles, decreases digestion, and decreases blood supply to the brain. Cortisol suppresses the immune system, and converts stored glycogen and fat into blood sugar thereby increasing blood sugar level. The latter can lead to weight gain and diabetes.

Sustained negative emotions caused by unforgiveness result in a sustained state of elevation of these fear hormones, and the effect caused by these hormones generally last longer than the effect of the sympathetic drive of the sympathetic nervous system. Sustained adrenaline level can increase blood pressure and heart rate, cause damage of the blood vessel walls because of the strain it puts on it. Blood flow to the heart and brain can be blocked resulting in heart attack and stroke, respectively.

Science research in HIV patients has correlated forgiveness with lower depression and stress, and greater health satisfaction.

Worry and anxiety can trigger the same hormonal response, the release of adrenaline and cortisol as unforgiveness, resentment, bitterness, and hatred. All of these contribute to chronic stress. When the fight-or-flight response is not "switched" off to allow for the proper balance between fear and relaxation, chronic stress is the result. Stress causes a higher release of cortisol than normal, causing sleep deprivation. High cortisol level has been implicated as the initial trigger of depression in some cases of depression. The fear hormones also suppress the reproductive system.

The fear hormones, adrenaline and cortisol, reduce the production of the body's defense foot soldiers. The body's defense foot soldiers that protect the body against disease are called natural killer cells. These cells defend the body against diseases such as cancer, inflammation, infection, etc. The natural killer cells and other cells (e.g., CD4) that boost our immune system to fight disease are boosted by forgiveness, and forgiveness lowers salivary cortisol levels. [Lawler et al 2003; Lawler et al 2005; Sarinopoulos, 200; Seybold et al 2001; Woods et al 1999; Waltman et al 2009] CD4 cells or T-cells are a type of white blood cells. They play a major function in protecting the body against infection. They alert the body to activate the immune system by sending signals when they detect "invaders" such as bacteria or viruses. Science research in HIV patients has correlated forgiveness with lower depression and stress, and greater health satisfaction. [Temoshok & Chandra 2000; Temoshok & Wald 2005; Wald & Temoshok 2004]. Forgiveness has been shown to boost the immune system of people living with HIV-AIDS [Owen et al 2011]

From the foregoing, you can deduce that forgiveness boosts the immune system, lowers blood pressure, increases glucose conversion to glycogen thereby lowering blood sugar, reduces or eliminates chronic stress or illness, decrease anxiety, reduces or prevents depression and memory loss, and strengthen relationships; and science has confirmed these. Forgiveness deals with the root of the problem, and when a tree is cut off from the root, it dies. It dies because its nutrient supply has been cut off. That is what *Agape* love-based forgiveness does when you forgive the one who wronged you. It also holds true when you forgive yourself.

God's Influence upon the One Who Wronged You

When we forgive our offenders and pray for them, we allow God to work in their lives. This is what Stephen of the early Church did in the Book of Acts. At the point of drawing his last breath when he was being stoned to death, He prayed for those who were responsible for his death and Saul who later became the Apostle Paul was one of them. Let us pick up the tail end of Stephen's speech in Acts 7:

> 51 You stubborn and stiff-necked people, still heathen and uncircumcised in heart and ears, you are always actively resisting the Holy Spirit. As your forefathers [were], so you [are and so you do]!
> 52 Which of the prophets did your forefathers not persecute? And they slew those who proclaimed beforehand the coming of the Righteous One, Whom you now have betrayed and murdered -
> 53 You who received the Law as it was ordained and set in order and delivered by angels, and [yet] you did not obey it!

⁵⁴ Now upon hearing these things, they [the Jews] were cut to the heart and infuriated, and they ground their teeth against [Stephen].
⁵⁵ But he, full of the Holy Spirit and controlled by Him, gazed into heaven and saw the glory (the splendor and majesty) of God, and Jesus standing at God's right hand;
⁵⁶ And he said, Look! I see the heavens opened, and the Son of man standing at God's right hand!
⁵⁷ But they raised a great shout and put their hands over their ears and rushed together upon him.
⁵⁸ Then they dragged him out of the city and began to stone him, and the witnesses placed their garments at the feet of a young man named Saul.
⁵⁹ And while they were stoning Stephen, he prayed, Lord Jesus, receive and accept and welcome my spirit!
⁶⁰ And falling on his knees, he cried out loudly, Lord, fix not this sin upon them [lay it not to their charge]! And when he had said this, he fell asleep [in death]. [Acts 7: 51-60, AMP]

⁸ And Saul was [not only] consenting to [Stephen's] death [he was pleased and entirely approving]. On that day a great and severe persecution broke out against the church which was in Jerusalem; and they were all scattered throughout the regions of Judea and Samaria, except the apostles (special messengers). [Acts 8: 1, AMP]

Stephen prayed for Saul and all those who were responsible for his death as he was about to draw his last breath. He asked the Lord to forgive his killers. What, if Stephen did not pray for Saul? Saul probably would not have surrendered his life to the Lord. Stephen's prayer for Saul and all those responsible for his death enabled God to work in Saul's life leading Saul to repentance and the confession of Jesus as his Lord and Savior. Stephen was doing what the Lord commanded us to do when He said, "But I tell you, love your enemies and pray for those who persecute you." [Matthew 5: 44a, NIV] This is an excellent example for us to emulate, and God rewards us when we do.

Forgive and pray for your enemies. It is their responsibility to respond to God and receive the forgiveness waiting for them in the throne room of God. Paul responded and God changed his life.

> Your past will keep you bound.

Forgive Yourself

Sometimes I find that the devil sells his lies to God's children to the extent that they do not forgive themselves after God had forgiven them. It is important to remember what God has said about our sins. He said, "I, even I, am He Who blots out and cancels your transgressions, for My own sake, and I will not remember your sins." [Isaiah 43: 25, AMP] Know that God Almighty has forgiven you and there is no one mightier than He is. Do not set yourself above God out of ignorance by not forgiving yourself. Receive God's forgiveness for your past sins and forgive yourself.

God has forgotten your past. "Will not remember" means God has forgotten, and He has no record or memory of it because to forget means to lose the remembrance of, and to let go from memory. Why would you try to remind yourself of the sins God has already forgiven you of and forgotten. He removed your sins as far as the east is from the west. [Psalm 103: 12, AMP] God is true to His Word. If you miss it along the way, act upon 1 John 1: 9, "If we confess our sins, he is faithful and just and will forgive us our sins and purify us from all unrighteousness." Once you have done so, move on with God. Do not listen to the devil's lies anymore.

You are a new man in Christ. The old order of things are gone, and the new has come. Get on the new program God has for you. The Apostle Paul wrote as instructed by the Holy Spirit:

> [14] Either way, Christ's love controls us. Since we believe that Christ died for all, we also believe that we have all died to our old life.

¹⁵ He died for everyone so that those who receive his new life will no longer live for themselves. Instead, they will live for Christ, who died and was raised for them.
¹⁶ So we have stopped evaluating others from a human point of view. At one time we thought of Christ merely from a human point of view. How differently we know him now!
¹⁷ This means that anyone who belongs to Christ has become a new person. The old life is gone; a new life has begun! [2 Corinthians 5: 14-17, NLT]

^{13b} but one thing I do, forgetting those things which are behind and reaching forward to those things which are ahead,
¹⁴ I press toward the goal for the prize of the upward call of God in Christ Jesus. [Philippians 3: 13b-14, NKJV]

I do not know about you, but I choose to agree with the Holy Spirit. I choose to let go of my past because I have been redeemed from my past and Jesus remitted my sins through His shed blood at Calvary. Do not let your past keep you bound like Lot's wife who could not make it to safety from Sodom and Gomorrah. Why did she not make it? Her mind did not let go of Sodom which represented her past. Because of that, she disobeyed God's instruction not to look back. She looked back and became a pillar of salt. [Genesis 19: 17, 26, AMP] You are forgiven. Do yourself a favor by forgiving yourself and enjoy the benefits of God's *Agape* love. Let go of your past, otherwise your past will keep you bound.

Guilt and shame are unfriendly friends you do not want to have. They do not right any wrongs. Rather, they are jailers that lock you up in prison. They do not serve you, instead they are destroyers who seek to destroy your health. They come from condemnation. If you sin, God convicts you. Your responsibility is to repent, receive forgiveness and move on with God.

If do not repent when the Holy Spirit has put a finger on your sin, Satan will begin to condemn you. Prolonged condemnation results in shame and guilt. Get rid of them by acting on the Word in 1 John 1: 9 and let the blood of Jesus cleanse you of all righteousness. Move on with God because the Word declares: "Therefore, no condemnation now exists for those in Christ Jesus, because the Spirit's law of life in Christ Jesus has set you free. It made you free from the law that brings sin and death." [Romans 8: 1-2, HCSB]

> Love allows the healing power of God to flow in us and through us.

Science research has shown that difficulty in forgiving oneself has been shown to be related to post traumatic stress disorder symptom (PTSD) severity, anxiety and depression in U.S. veterans. [Witvliet et al 2004] The authors further found that difficulty in forgiving others was not related to anxiety, but associated with depression and PTSD symptom severity. In addition, research has shown that enhanced self-compassion (loving kindness) has been shown to reduce PTSD symptoms and depression. [Kearney et al 2013]

Obey God, act on His Word in 1 John 1: 9 as discussed in the previous paragraph, forgive yourself, be free from depression, guilt and shame, and walk free in the Name of Jesus. Do not only forgive those who wrong you, forgive yourself. Do not be hard on yourself. Do it now, and be free in Jesus Name.

Walking in Love Is not Stupidity

When we walk in love towards those who hate us, we must not be ignorant and unreasonable. We must not cast our pearls to the hogs. We have to listen to God and do as He commands. Walking in love does not mean submitting yourself to someone who does not seek your good. It does not mean submitting yourself to those who hate you. We have to learn from Jesus, our Lord and Savior. He walked this earth as a man, and only hearkened to the Father. He said, "I do nothing of Myself (of My own accord or on My own authority), but I say [exactly] what My Father has taught Me. [John 8: 28, AMP] When Jesus raised Lazarus from the dead some Jews believed in Him, while others went and reported the event to the Pharisees who hated Jesus and wanted Him dead. John recorded thus:

> ⁵³ So from that day on they took counsel and plotted together how they might put Him to death.
>
> ⁵⁴ For that reason Jesus no longer appeared publicly among the Jews, but left there and retired to the district that borders on the wilderness (the desert), to a village called Ephraim, and there He stayed with the disciples.
>
> ⁵⁵ Now the Jewish Passover was at hand, and many from the country went up to Jerusalem in order that they might purify and consecrate themselves before the Passover.
>
> ⁵⁶ So they kept looking for Jesus and questioned among themselves as they were standing about in the temple [area], What do you think? Will He not come to the Feast at all?
>
> ⁵⁷ Now the chief priests and Pharisees had given orders that if anyone knew where He was, he should report it to them, so that they might arrest Him. [John 11: 53-57, AMP]

Jesus must have been instructed by God the Father not to go to Jerusalem for the Passover. This can be deduced from John 8:28 because He did only what the Father told Him to do. "..I do nothing of Myself (of My own accord or on My own authority), but I say [exactly] what My Father has taught Me." [John 8: 23b] He stayed away from the Passover for His protection. He did not say He was the Son of God and no one could dare to touch Him. We have to remember that He walked this earth as any Christian who is baptized in the Holy Spirit. [Philippians 2: 5-8, AMP] If He had disobeyed, He probably would have been killed before it was time for Him to lay down His life. This is very instructive. Stop and think about it. We must listen to the Holy Spirit and not yield ourselves to our enemies to our detriment. Sometimes the Lord may ask you to stay away from some places and people for your protection. Do what He says and do not argue. He is doing it to save your life. Be wise and do not be naïve or stupid. Listen and obey the Lord Who is *Agape* Love, abide in His secret place of protection. It is a benefit of *Agape* love.

4. LOVE'S BENEFITS

There is no fear in love, but perfect love casts out fear. For fear has to do with punishment, and he who fears is not perfected in love. [1 John 4: 18, AMP]

There are many benefits to walking in love, otherwise God would not give us His love and ask us to live a life of love. Therefore, I reiterate some of the points I made previously under the benefits of forgiveness, but approach it with a slightly different bent. Here are some of the benefits of love.

Healing and Wholeness

Healing flows out of God's mercy and loving kindness. It was Love that sent Jesus to Calvary to die for us. Once we learn about His love, He expects us to put His love in us to work in our lives. As discussed under the benefits of forgiveness, one of the benefits of walking in love is divine health. Jesus was the epitome of divine love in manifestation on earth, and He was never sick. Walking in agape love shuts the enemy out of our lives. There is no breach in our defenses for him to penetrate. He cannot lay any claim on us to put sickness and disease on us.

> [30] I will not talk with you much more, for the prince (evil genius, ruler) of the world is coming. And he has no claim on Me. [He has nothing in common with Me; there is nothing in Me that belongs to him, and he has no power over Me.]" [John 14: 30, AMP]

If you are not walking in *Agape* love toward others, it is time to repent and get in line with God's Word. Forgive your offenders and receive your healing in the Name of Jesus. God forgives [every one of] all our iniquities, and heals [each one of] all our diseases. [Psalm 103: 3, AMP]. Do not forget the testimony of the young woman who was healed of arthritis after forgiving her father (see **Good Health** under the **Benefits of Forgiveness**).

Protection, Deliverance, and Promotion

When you walk in love, regardless of what the devil may throw at you, you set yourself up for God to show Himself strong on your behalf. The devil may try to raise hell against you, but God is always there for you. He is there to defend and protect you from harm. He is there to deliver you and promote you. Trouble and crisis from the devil's viewpoint is for your defeat and ultimately destruction because the devil comes to steal, kill, and destroy. However, God sees crisis as an opportunity to show Himself strong on our behalf if we can only trust Him. He sees it as an opportunity to promote us after delivering us from the crisis. For more on crisis, see my book *The Power to Transform.*

We have already seen how Joseph was protected and promoted by God when He chose to forgive his brothers and refused to be bitter against them. God fulfilled the vision He gave Joseph by making him the premier of Egypt, and the brothers bowed to him. We are going to shift our attention to the three Hebrew children (Shadrach, Meshach, and Abednego) who were in the service of the king of Babylon, Nebuchadnezzar, during the Babylonian captivity.

Shadrach, Meshach, and Abednego in the Service of Nebuchadnezzar

King Nebuchadnezzar at the urging of his officials, the peers, of the three Hebrew men promulgated a decree for people to bow down and worship his statue once they heard music played for that purpose. The three Hebrew children who only worshiped the Most High God refused to bow to an idol and chose instead to put their life on the line. In Daniel 3 we read,

> [1] King Nebuchadnezzar made a gold statue ninety feet tall and nine feet wide and set it up on the plain of Dura in the province of Babylon.

[2] Then he sent messages to the high officers, officials, governors, advisers, treasurers, judges, magistrates, and all the provincial officials to come to the dedication of the statue he had set up.

[4] Then a herald shouted out, "People of all races and nations and languages, listen to the king's command!

[5] When you hear the sound of the horn, flute, zither, lyre, harp, pipes, and other musical instruments, bow to the ground to worship King Nebuchadnezzar's gold statue.

[6] Anyone who refuses to obey will immediately be thrown into a blazing furnace."

[7] So at the sound of the musical instruments, all the people, whatever their race or nation or language, bowed to the ground and worshiped the gold statue that King Nebuchadnezzar had set up.

[8] But some of the astrologers went to the king and informed on the Jews.

[9] They said to King Nebuchadnezzar, "Long live the king!

[10] You issued a decree requiring all the people to bow down and worship the gold statue when they hear the sound of the horn, flute, zither, lyre, harp, pipes, and other musical instruments.

[11] That decree also states that those who refuse to obey must be thrown into a blazing furnace.

[12] But there are some Jews—Shadrach, Meshach, and Abednego— whom you have put in charge of the province of Babylon. They pay no attention to you, Your Majesty. They refuse to serve your gods and do not worship the gold statue you have set up." [Daniel 3: 1-2, 4-12, NLT]

The Hebrew children grew up in Babylon in the service of the king and knew the letter of the law. They knew that the law of the land could not be disannulled. However, they also knew that the law of man is subordinate to the law of the Almighty God. They chose to put their trust in God instead of in man. They knew that God would not disappoint them, but man would. They refused to bow to the king's statute and the king was furious.

[13] Then Nebuchadnezzar flew into a rage and ordered that Shadrach, Meshach, and Abednego be brought before him. When they were brought in,

[14] Nebuchadnezzar said to them, "Is it true, Shadrach, Meshach, and Abednego, that you refuse to serve my gods or to worship the gold statue I have set up?

[15] I will give you one more chance to bow down and worship the statue I have made when you hear the sound of the musical instruments. But if you refuse, you will be thrown immediately into the blazing furnace. And then what god will be able to rescue you from my power?" [Daniel 3: 13-15, NLT]

Shadrach, Meshach, and Abednego refused to bow to Nebuchadnezzar's idol, despite the king's threat. They knew that the fear of man is a snare. "The fear of man brings a snare, but whoever leans on, trusts in, and puts his confidence in the Lord is safe and set on high." [Proverbs 29: 25, AMP] That is, a snare set up by Satan to entrap us. They answered the king that the Almighty God, whom they served, was able to deliver them.

[16] Shadrach, Meshach, and Abednego, answered and said to the king, O Nebuchadnezzar, we are not careful to answer thee in this matter.

[17] If it be so, our God whom we serve is able to deliver us from the burning fiery furnace, and he will deliver us out of thine hand, O king.

[18] But if not, be it known unto thee, O king, that we will not serve thy gods, nor worship the golden image which thou hast set up. [Daniel 3: 16-18, KJV]

The three Hebrew children knew God as their Deliverer. They understood from the Word of God thus,

[2] When you pass through the waters, I will be with you, and through the rivers, they will not overwhelm you. When you walk through the fire, you will not be burned or scorched, nor will the flame kindle upon you. [Isaiah 43: 2, AMP]

How could they bow to an idol when they knew that God demonstrated His love to their forebears when He delivered them from the hands of Pharaoh in Egypt? They knew that God parted the Red Sea for the Israelites to pass on dry ground while Pharaoh and his army drowned in the Red Sea. They could not imagine esteeming God lightly and, therefore, bow to Nebuchadnezzar's image. They knew without a doubt that God would deliver them. They knew that "many evils confront the [consistently] righteous, but the Lord delivers him out of them all." [Psalm 34: 19, AMP] They knew that they had to declare their deliverance with their mouths before God could come to their aid.

A miracle cannot manifest unless it is spoken. "The words of the wicked lie in wait for blood, but the mouth of the upright shall deliver them and the innocent ones [thus endangered]. [Proverbs 12: 6, AMP] Shadrach, Meshach, and Abednego understood that once they had declared their faith in the delivering power of God they could not turn around and cancel it. Thus, I quoted Daniel 3: 16-18 from the King James Version [KJV] because of the justice done to the text in this version of the Bible. They stated categorically that God would deliver them. [Daniel 3: 17, KJV] They also made the point to the king that if he did not carry out his threat they would not bow down to worship his golden image. Daniel 3: 18 could be paraphrased as follows, *If you do not carry out your threat, be it known unto you, O king, that we will not serve your gods, nor worship the golden image which you have set up.*

In Daniel 3: 18 the three Hebrew men were reiterating their position that under no circumstance would they bow to and worship other gods. It would be incorrect to state that if God did not deliver them, they would not serve Nebuchadnezzar's gods as it is written in some translations. Here are two of such translations:

> [18] "But even if he does not, we want you to know, Your Majesty, that we will not serve your gods or worship the image of gold you have set up." [Daniel 3: 18, NIV]

> [18] But even if he doesn't, we want to make it clear to you, Your Majesty, that we will never serve your gods or worship the gold statue you have set up." [Daniel 3: 18, NLT]

Think about this closely. How can a dead man bow to an idol when he is no longer living on this earth? It is impossible. Shadrach, Meshach, and Abednego knew their God. They trusted in Him knowing He would not fail them. They did not want to undo their miracle by speaking negatively. Therefore, they could not have said that may be God would not deliver them. There is no uncertainty with our God. He keeps His

Word. Therefore, there is no uncertainty when our faith is in Him and His Word. They believed as King David that the Lord would deliver the righteous from trouble and honor him (Psalm 91: 15), and not just one trouble but every trouble (Psalm 34: 19).

> [15] He shall call upon Me, and I will answer him; I will be with him in trouble, I will deliver him and honor him. [Psalm 91: 15, AMP]

> [19] Many evils confront the [consistently] righteous, but the Lord delivers him out of them all. [Psalm 34: 19, AMP]

They believed what Isaiah believed when he stated in Isaiah 43: 2 that God delivers His children from fire, and they will not even smell smoke. They were saying, in essence, that if they bowed they would burn, but if they did not bow they would not burn. Their bold statement of faith, belief and firm trust in God, infuriated Nebuchadnezzar even more.

Nebuchadnezzar carried out his threat and ordered them to be thrown into the burning fiery furnace.

> [19] Then was Nebuchadnezzar full of fury, and the form of his visage was changed against Shadrach, Meshach, and Abednego: therefore he spake, and commanded that they should heat the furnace one seven times more than it was wont to be heated.
> [20] And he commanded the most mighty men that were in his army to bind Shadrach, Meshach, and Abednego, and to cast them into the burning fiery furnace.
> [21] Then these men were bound in their coats, their hosen, and their hats, and their other garments, and were cast into the midst of the burning fiery furnace.
> [22] Therefore because the king's commandment was urgent, and the furnace exceeding hot, the flames of the fire slew those men that took up Shadrach, Meshach, and Abednego.
> [23] And these three men, Shadrach, Meshach, and Abednego, fell down bound into the midst of the burning fiery furnace.
> [24] Then Nebuchadnezzar the king was astonished, and rose up in haste, and spake, and said unto his counsellors, Did not we cast three men bound into the midst of the fire? They answered and said unto the king, True, O king.

25 He answered and said, Lo, I see four men loose, walking in the midst of the fire, and they have no hurt; and the form of the fourth is like the Son of God.

26 Then Nebuchadnezzar came near to the mouth of the burning fiery furnace, and spake, and said, Shadrach, Meshach, and Abednego, ye servants of the most high God, come forth, and come hither. Then Shadrach, Meshach, and Abednego, came forth of the midst of the fire.

27 And the princes, governors, and captains, and the king's counsellors, being gathered together, saw these men, upon whose bodies the fire had no power, nor was an hair of their head singed, neither were their coats changed, nor the smell of fire had passed on them. [Daniel 3: 19-27, KJV]

Nebuchadnezzar was dumbfounded at what he saw, the Son of God, with the three Hebrew men in the midst of the fiery furnace. The fire did not kindle upon them. He called them out of the furnace. They did not even smell smoke when they came out. The soldiers who threw them into the furnace died instead because of the heat of the furnace. Remember that the soldiers died while carrying out the king's order by just standing near the furnace. This speaks to the incredible delivering power of our God.

The fear of the furnace being heated seven times did not cause Shadrach, Meshach, and Abednego to change their confession. They stood on their confession of faith, which enabled God to raise an invisible shield over them, and deliver them. Jesus said, "Therefore everyone who confesses Me before men, I will also confess him before My Father who is in heaven. [Matthew 10: 32, NASB] God sent His Son as the fourth man into the fiery furnace to deliver them. I believe the fourth man, Jesus, provided a shield of faith (shield of defense) around them that could not be penetrated by the fire. Thus, they came out of the fiery furnace without smelling smoke, and Nebuchadnezzar spoke thus,

28 Then Nebuchadnezzar said, Blessed be the God of Shadrach, Meshach, and Abednego, Who has sent His angel and delivered His servants who believed in, trusted in, and relied on Him! And they set aside the king's command and yielded their bodies rather than serve or worship any god except their own God.

²⁹ Therefore I make a decree that any people, nation, and language that speaks anything amiss against the God of Shadrach, Meshach, and Abednego shall be cut in pieces and their houses be made a dunghill, for there is no other God who can deliver in this way!

³⁰ Then the king promoted Shadrach, Meshach, and Abednego in the province of Babylon. [Daniel 3: 28-30, KJV]

The king was overwhelmed at the awesomeness of God; that He could deliver His servants. He became a defender of the Jewish belief of the true God. [Daniel 3: 29, AMP] He promoted Shadrach, Meshach, and Abednego which was a fulfillment of Psalm 91: 15; God delivers and honors his children and servants.

David in the Service of King Saul

What do you do when someone who felt you had sterling qualities to serve in His organization turns against you? This is what happened to David when he served King Saul, the first king of Israel. Let us pick up the story in 1 Samuel 16,

¹² Jesse sent and brought him. David had a healthy reddish complexion and beautiful eyes, and was fine-looking. The Lord said [to Samuel], Arise, anoint him; this is he.

¹³ Then Samuel took the horn of oil and anointed David in the midst of his brothers; and the Spirit of the Lord came mightily upon David from that day forward. And Samuel arose and went to Ramah.

¹⁴ But the Spirit of the Lord departed from Saul, and an evil spirit from the Lord tormented and troubled him.

¹⁵ Saul's servants said to him, Behold, an evil spirit from God torments you.

¹⁶ Let our lord now command your servants here before you to find a man who plays skillfully on the lyre; and when the evil spirit from God is upon you, he will play it, and you will be well.

¹⁷ Saul told his servants, Find me a man who plays well and bring him to me.

[18] One of the young men said, I have seen a son of Jesse the Bethlehemite who plays skillfully, a valiant man, a man of war, prudent in speech and eloquent, an attractive person; and the Lord is with him.

[19] So Saul sent messengers to Jesse and said, Send me David your son, who is with the sheep.

[20] And Jesse took a donkey loaded with bread, a skin of wine, and a kid and sent them by David his son to Saul.

[21] And David came to Saul and served him. Saul became very fond of him, and he became his armor-bearer.

[22] Saul sent to Jesse, saying, Let David remain in my service, for he pleases me.

[23] And when the evil spirit from God was upon Saul, David took a lyre and played it; so Saul was refreshed and became well, and the evil spirit left him.[1 Samuel 16: 12-23, AMP]

There is no vacuum in the spirit. Once the Spirit of the Lord left Saul, a spirit from the devil took over and filled the void. The Lord did not send an evil spirit to afflict Saul. All He did was to withdraw His Spirit from Saul. [1 Samuel 16: 14-15] Again, the statement in 1 Samuel 16: 15 was made by Saul's servants and not the Lord.

On another note, in 1 Samuel 16: 13 we find that David was anointed by God to be king in the place of Saul, but it was not yet time for him to ascend the throne. David was still a shepherd boy when Saul employed David to play the harp so that the evil spirit that tormented him would depart. David pleased Saul and Saul asked David's father, Jesse, to allow David to remain with him. David had to split his time between serving King Saul and shepherding his father's sheep. Later on things changed.

Things changed after the war with the Philistines. King Saul and the Israelites were afraid of Goliath, the giant champion of the Philistines, who led the Philistines to the battle. The daily (morning and evening) ranting of Goliath at the war front had its desired effect on the Israelites. They were sore afraid, and this was the intent of Goliath. [1 Samuel 17: 11] David took supplies to his senior brothers at the war front, and was stirred up with righteous indignation when he heard Goliath's ranting. He stepped up to the plate and volunteered to take on and take out

Goliath. He slew Goliath and God gave Israel a mighty victory over the Philistines. Let us pick up the narration from 1 Samuel 17:

> [32] David said to Saul, Let no man's heart fail because of this Philistine; your servant will go out and fight with him.
>
> [33] And Saul said to David, You are not able to go to fight against this Philistine. You are only an adolescent, and he has been a warrior from his youth.
>
> [37] David said, The Lord Who delivered me out of the paw of the lion and out of the paw of the bear, He will deliver me out of the hand of this Philistine. And Saul said to David, Go, and the Lord be with you!
>
> [40] Then he took his staff in his hand and chose five smooth stones out of the brook and put them in his shepherd's [lunch] bag [a whole kid's skin slung from his shoulder], in his pouch, and his sling was in his hand, and he drew near the Philistine.
>
> [41] The Philistine came on and drew near to David, the man who bore the shield going before him.
>
> [49] David put his hand into his bag and took out a stone and slung it, and it struck the Philistine, sinking into his forehead, and he fell on his face to the earth.
>
> [50] So David prevailed over the Philistine with a sling and with a stone, and struck down the Philistine and slew him. But no sword was in David's hand.
>
> [51] So he ran and stood over the Philistine, took his sword and drew it out of its sheath, and killed him, and cut off his head with it. When the Philistines saw that their mighty champion was dead, they fled. [1 Samuel 17: 32-33, 37, 40-41, 49-51, AMP]

After the victory, it is interesting to observe that Saul did not recognize David who had served him for some time before the battle with the Philistines. Saul had to ask his general who David was.

> [55] When Saul saw David go out against the Philistine, he said to Abner, the captain of the host, Abner, whose son is this youth? And Abner said, As your soul lives, O king, I cannot tell.
>
> [56] And the king said, Inquire whose son the stripling is.
>
> [57] When David returned from killing Goliath the Philistine, Abner brought him before Saul with the head of the Philistine in his hand.

[58] And Saul said to him, Whose son are you, young man? And David answered, I am the son of your servant Jesse of Bethlehem. [1 Samuel 17: -55-58, AMP]

We notice in verse 58 of 1 Samuel 17 that David had to reintroduce himself to King Saul. From that day King Saul retained David in his army. [1 Samuel 18] David served King Saul well and beat the king's expectations. Wherever you are serving, serve well and beat the expectations of your manager.

Saul was not tormented by an evil spirit when he made the inquiry in 1 Samuel 17: 55. He was in his right mind, otherwise the Holy Spirit would have recorded it for us to read. Why did Saul not recognize David who had contributed greatly to his well-being? How could King Saul, only one chapter later, not recognize someone who was his armor-bearer in 1 Samuel 16? [See 1 Samuel 16: 21.] David served King Saul as unto the Lord and the Lord was with Him always. "And David went out wherever Saul sent him, and he prospered and behaved himself wisely; and Saul set him over the men of war. And it was satisfactory both to the people and to Saul's servants." [1 Samuel 18: 5, AMP]

Things changed drastically when people were heaping more praise on David than on King Saul. Thereafter, King Saul sought to kill David. We read this in 1 Samuel 18:

[6] As they were coming home, when David returned from killing the Philistine, the women came out of all the Israelite towns, singing and dancing, to meet King Saul with timbrels, songs of joy, and instruments of music.

[7] And the women responded as they laughed and frolicked, saying, Saul has slain his thousands, and David his ten thousands.

[8] And Saul was very angry, for the saying displeased him; and he said, They have ascribed to David ten thousands, but to me they have ascribed only thousands. What more can he have but the kingdom?

[9] And Saul [jealously] eyed David from that day forward. [1 Samuel 18: 6-9, AMP]

[10] The next day an evil spirit from God came mightily upon Saul, and he raved [madly] in his house, while David played [the lyre] with his hand, as at other times; and there was a javelin in Saul's hand.
[11] And Saul cast the javelin, for he thought, I will pin David to the wall. And David evaded him twice.
[12] Saul was afraid of David, because the Lord was with him but had departed from Saul. [1 Samuel 18: 6-12, AMP]

It seems the king did not really care about who David was. My deduction is that King Saul may have been more interested in his personal welfare than the welfare of others, at that point in his life. Do not be surprised if a person or an organization you have served whole-heartedly as unto the Lord all of a sudden does not recognize you. Like David, keep your cool and refuse to be bitter. David chose to be better. Although Saul hated him, David refused to entertain offense. When King Saul was pursuing David all over the land of Israel and David had an opportunity to kill him, David would not do it. David said to his men,

[6] ...... "The Lord forbid that I should do such a thing to my master, the Lord's anointed, or lay my hand on him; for he is the anointed of the Lord."
[7] With these words David sharply rebuked his men and did not allow them to attack Saul. And Saul left the cave and went his way. [1 Samuel 24: 6-7, AMP]

Why would God allow David to serve King Saul when He knew that the king would turn against David? God wanted David to learn palace protocol and some things about kingship. If David had gone from being a shepherd boy to kingship, he probably would not have known much about kingly protocol. Although David must have learned palace protocol, he did not learn King Saul's behavior and rebellion against God. The lesson is to learn some things while you are in the "palace," but do not copy the bad behavior or character of the "palace" occupants. Because David forgave King Saul and walked in love towards him, God protected David and the king could not kill him. God delivered and promoted David, and made him king over Israel after King Saul died because of rebellion and idolatry.

Bringing It Home

Why would God allow you to serve a person or an organization that would later turn against you? Learn from David. The Word declares,

> 13 The temptations in your life are no different from what others experience. And God is faithful. He will not allow the temptation to be more than you can stand. When you are tempted, he will show you a way out so that you can endure. [1 Corinthians 10:13, NLT]

You may be treated like David at your place of work. Your manager may not be entirely like King Saul, but God wants us to learn from David's behavior during his service to Saul. Your manager may turn against you and want you fired from work for no justifiable reason. Do not be bitter, but be better. Forgive and pray for him and all those the enemy may be trying to use against you. They are not your enemies, Satan is. They are deceived by Satan to become tools of havoc in His hands. Remember, God delivers and honors.

Pray for those the enemy may raise against you because they do not know what they are doing. They are only responding to their master, the devil. Remember what Jesus did on the cross! He forgave all those who crucified Him. Jesus said, "Father, forgive them, for they do not know what they are doing." [Luke 23: 34a, NIV] In effect, He was saying that they were ignorant of their actions. One would have thought that the Pharisees, the members of the Sanhedrin, and Pilate knew what they were doing. Pilate did not have the guts to release the Lord. When Pilate wanted to release the Lord because he found him innocent, those who wanted the Lord crucified shouted, "His blood is on us and on our children!" [Matthew 27: 25, NIV] We must imitate our Lord and write off offenses committed against us due to ignorance on the part of our offenders.

When confronted with a situation similar to David's, God wants you to be better and not bitter. Remember that your offenders are only tools in the hands of the devil and they do not even know it. They are ignorant.

The enemy wants to use the adversity to defeat you, but God wants to turn it around for your good – your promotion and increase. The Word works. The Lord taught me how to put this to work by forgiving and praying for those who wronged me, and I obtained similar results – deliverance and promotion - as David did.

Being a forgiving person and walking in *Agape* love is important in every area of life, and not just healing and health, protection, deliverance, and promotion. It is important in marriage. It is an important key to a wholesome, successful marriage.

5. A WHOLESOME MARRIAGE

However, each man among you [without exception] is to love his wife as his very own self [with behavior worthy of respect and esteem, always seeking the best for her with an attitude of lovingkindness], and the wife [must see to it] that she respects and delights in her husband [that she notices him and prefers him and treats him with loving concern, treasuring him, honoring him, and holding him dear]. [Ephesians 5: 33, AMP]

You cannot have a wholesome, successful marriage without *Agape* love. Marriage is a God idea, a covenant instituted by God, and He invites us to participate in it. Without understanding the marriage covenant we go into marriage without any revelation of what God expects of us, the right expectations, and what we are to gain from it. If you are married take time and study the marriage covenant in the Bible and ask the Holy Spirit to reveal the Word on marriage to you. Study Ephesians 5: 21-33 and Genesis 2: 19-25 in the Amplified Bible. Using the Amplified Bible aids clarity and you will gain a lot of understanding of what God says about the marriage covenant. A good understanding of the marriage covenant would clear up a lot of misconceptions. There are misconceptions about leaving and cleaving and a host of other issues because some married couples are not making *Agape* love the bedrock of their marriage.

Leave and Cleave
Leaving and cleaving is not for the husbands alone, but for both husband and wife.

[4] Therefore a man shall leave his father and his mother and shall become united and cleave to his wife, and they shall become one flesh. [Genesis 2: 24, AMP]

[10] Hear, O daughter, consider, submit, and consent to my instruction: forget also your own people and your father's house;
[11] So will the King desire your beauty; because He is your Lord, be submissive and reverence and honor Him.
[12] And, O daughter of Tyre, the richest of the people shall entreat your favor with a gift. [Psalm 45: 10-12, AMP]

> To be controlling, manipulating, and intimidating is witchcraft.

The idea here is for the husband and wife to come under God's guardianship, leadership, and direction to form a new home, a new entity, in which they give themselves selflessly to each other. There is a tremendous blessing in doing what the Word says in the Scripture passages quoted above. Although the husband and wife form a new entity apart from their parents, it is a marriage of two families; and you the couple as one are to show *Agape* love to the two families. Love your in-laws.

Husband, you are to focus on loving your wife, the *Agape* way; and wife, you are to focus on reverencing and honoring your husband. You cannot honor, esteem, and reverence your husband if you do not love him with *Agape* love. Sister, as you do what God commands, people will bless you with gifts. My wife and I have put this to work and we are enjoying the blessing of obeying God's Word. Not obeying the Lord's instruction is to court trouble.

When you know that leaving and cleaving is for both parties, a wife cannot complain that her husband is not leaving his family to cleave with her. The latter speaks of selfishness. It is an indication of lack of *Agape* love, and a signal for the desire to control. Wife do not seek to control your husband and vice versa. Such a desire is a recipe for marriage problems that can lead to marriage failure. To be controlling, manipulating, and intimidating is witchcraft. [Galatians 5: 19-21] Witchcraft is a work of the flesh characterized by control, manipulation, and intimidation. Are you looking to turn your husband into a zombie, to do your bidding only? Is that what you want?

Leadership

Wife, do not desire to be the leader in your marital relationship. To be controlling and taking charge in your marital relationship with your husband is an invitation to marital problems and in some cases divorce. This is because when the husband wakes up to his responsibility and desires to provide leadership, the result is a clash.

What, if my husband does not lead or fails to lead, you may ask? Sister, do not usurp your husband's leadership role. Rather, encourage him to lead. Your *Agape* love for him will lead him into what God ordained for him to do. Pray for him. Do not pray for God to change him. Pray Ephesians 1: 17-23 for him and for yourself. Ask God to show you how to be a blessing to your husband. Do not be a thorn in his flesh.

Husband, you are to provide leadership and not be controlling. Exercise of control over your spouse stems from fear. Where *Agape* reigns, fear is cast out.

> [18] There is no fear in love [dread does not exist], but full-grown (complete, perfect) love turns fear out of doors and expels every trace of terror! For fear brings with it the thought of punishment, and [so] he who is afraid has not reached the full maturity of love [is not yet grown into love's complete perfection]. [1 John 4: 18, AMP]

Husband, God's design is for you to love, cherish, and protect your wife. Here is what the Word says of what God expects you to do regarding your wife:

> [21] Be subject to one another out of reverence for Christ (the Messiah, the Anointed One).

[22] Wives, be subject (be submissive and adapt yourselves) to your own husbands as [a service] to the Lord.

[23] For the husband is head of the wife as Christ is the Head of the church, Himself the Savior of [His] body.

[25] **Husbands, love your wives, as Christ loved the church and gave Himself up for her,**

[26] So that He might sanctify her, having cleansed her by the washing of water with the Word,

[27] That He might present the church to Himself in glorious splendor, without spot or wrinkle or any such things [that she might be holy and faultless].

[28] Even so **husbands should love their wives as [being in a sense] their own bodies. He who loves his own wife loves himself.**

[29] **For no man ever hated his own flesh, but nourishes and carefully protects and cherishes it, as Christ does the church,**

[30] Because we are members (parts) of His body.

[31] For this reason a man shall leave his father and his mother and shall be joined to his wife, and the two shall become one flesh.

[32] This mystery is very great, but I speak concerning [the relation of] Christ and the church.

[33] However, **let each man of you [without exception] love his wife as [being in a sense] his very own self; and let the wife see that she respects and reverences her husband [that she notices him, regards him, honors him, prefers him, venerates, and esteems him; and that she defers to him, praises him, and loves and admires him exceedingly].** [Ephesians 5: 25-33, AMP]

"Love" used in Ephesians 5: 25-33 is *Agape* love (the God kind of love), and it means to love, to be full of good-will and exhibit the same, to have a preference for, wish well, and regard the welfare of, and in this case the welfare of the wife. "Husband" is translated from *anér* in Greek which means a male human being; a man, husband. Thus, husband, you are to love your wife, be full of good-will for your wife (*guné* in Greek, which also means woman, and lady) and exhibit the same, have preference for her, wish her well, and her welfare should be your priority. You are to nourish your wife, and most importantly nourish her to maturity in the

Word because that is what the Greek word *ektrephó* translated nourish means.

In addition, you are to cherish (*thalpó* in Greek) your wife, and this means to cherish her with tender love, and protect her. God is not telling you to do what you cannot do. He is saying that you are to treat your wife the way you treat yourself. If you see your wife differently from you, you will not do it. You can only do this with *Agape* love. Husband, you are to provide leadership in the marriage union and the family God has given you. If you are selfish, check yourself because you may be sowing the wrong seed in your marriage.

Wife, you are to be completing to your husband, and encourage him to be who God created him to be. Your *agape* love and respect for him will enable him to lead. When you play your God given role, and not try to reverse it, you will find satisfaction and be able to fulfill God's purpose for your life.

Husband, you are to imitate Christ in your marriage. Give yourself to your wife and marriage the same way Christ gave Himself to us. Lay down your life for your wife. That is, put your wife's interest first before yours. When you love, cherish, nourish, and protect your wife, she has no option but to respect and reverence you. She will notice you, regard you, honor you, prefer you, venerate, and esteem you. She will defer to you, praise you, love, and admire you exceedingly.

Failure to Lead
Husband, make no excuse for yourself by failing to lead. When you fail to lead, by default you fail to:

- provide direction for your family.
- be the authority figure in your home that God ordained and made you to be.
- be a role model for your wife and children.

- be the priest of your home because your lack of leadership is a consequence of your lack of relationship with God or being lukewarm when it comes to fellowshipping with God and His word. If your wife is not Word abiding, you are inadvertently throwing your marriage and children to the dogs – the devil and his gangs to mold them into what you never thought, planned, or expected them to be. Adolescent pregnancy and rebellion are consequences of the husband/father not providing leadership, if he is present in the home. The results are the same if the father is absent in the home.

- be the bread winner of the family. Stop now, repent and do the right thing. A husband/father that does not provide for his family is worse than an infidel. "But if any provide not for his own, and especially for those of his own house, he hath denied the faith, and is worse than an infidel." [1 Timothy 5; 8, KJV]

As you read this and find that you are not providing leadership in your marriage and family, stop reading now. Repent and ask God to forgive you in the Name of Jesus. He will. Now receive His forgiveness and ask the Holy Spirit to help you, and mold you into the leader God created you to be. Do not say, I did not have a father or my father did not care about me. God has a mentor for you. Ask Him to send the Christ-like mentor He has for you into your life. Listen to the mentor God sends into your life as he teaches and models leadership for you. Follow his example as he follows Jesus, and watch God turn your life around.

Do not give yourself sleep. Get out of that laziness and excuses about your past or your upbringing. Take your place of leadership that God has given you. The potential is there in you. All that is needed is for you to yield to God and let Him bring it out as you step into your leadership shoes that He has designed especially for you.

If you are confused because of oppression from the enemy, seek a Holy Spirit filled Bible-based believer to minister to you and set you free. Thereafter, do what God says. Yes, you can because He made you a leader in your marriage and family. Wife, support and pray for your husband as he steps out to do God's will for his life, marriage, and family.

Disrespect - An Evil Under the Sun

I have seen an evil under the sun, where a Christian wife sought to win the love of their child at the expense of her husband, the father of their child. This has happened even when the husband lived in peace with the wife. That is, the husband was not aware that the wife had something against him. The consequence was that the child disrespected the father. Of course, this led to the child rebelling. When that happened the wife equally lost because the rebellion was against both parents.

Wife, if this is what you have been doing, stop now and repent. Ask God to forgive you. What seed are you sowing? The child whose heart you are trying to turn towards you will turn around to hate you, and gravitate toward the father, your husband. Why are you yielding to Satan and working to destroy your marriage and family? Are you ready to reap the harvest of the wrong seeds you are sowing in your marriage? Commit your husband and marriage to God, and ask Him to heal your marital relationship. Seek out a Bible-based Christian counselor, pastor, or believer for help. Selfish love, and not *Agape* love, ruins a marriage.

Dear Christian wife, ask yourself, Am I walking in *Agape* love toward my husband? Husband, ask yourself the same question as regards your relationship with your wife. Where there is selfishness, there is competition. Where there is competition, the two are not one. A house divided against itself cannot stand. The Lord said that the two shall be one. Ask yourself, Am I one with my spouse? Be sincere to yourself in answering the question. The two can only become one if *Agape* love is the basis and foundation of your marriage. The consequences of competition and division between husband and wife is marital problems, and children rebelling. You can agree with me that these consequences are dire.

Wife, you are not one with your husband if your husband's money is yours, but your money is only for you. If your money is yours only, what happens if there is a fortune reversal? At that point you lose whatever little respect you had for your husband because he was the main bread winner for the family. All of a sudden, you find cracks in your relationship because the so-called love for your husband was only cosmetic, and not genuine. It is not genuine because it is not *Agape* love. It was only based on you gaining from your husband, and that is selfishness.

When you disrespect your husband, your children will follow suit. Why should that be? You will eventually act out your disrespect of your husband. When you go to the extent of letting the children know that you are the bread winner of the family, you are sowing seed for your children to disrespect your husband, their father, with rebellion as a consequence. I ask, Is that what you want? Do you not know that when you try to curry your child or children's love at the expense of your husband, you are working at destroying your marriage and your children. What are you modeling for your children? Children copy what parents model and not what they say. Remember that *agape* love does no wrong to one's neighbor. [Romans 13:10]

Paul summarizes our relationship with one another in Roman 13: 8-10, and it also applies to marriage.

> [8] Keep out of debt and owe no man anything, except to love one another; for he who loves his neighbor [who practices loving others] has fulfilled the Law [relating to one's fellowmen, meeting all its requirements].
> [9] The commandments, You shall not commit adultery, You shall not kill, You shall not steal, You shall not covet (have an evil desire), and any other commandment, are summed up in the single command, You shall love your neighbor as [you do] yourself.
> [10] Love does no wrong to one's neighbor [it never hurts anybody]. Therefore love meets all the requirements and is the fulfilling of the Law. [Roman 13: 8-10, AMP]

Seek the welfare of your spouse before yours. This is very important. It is a key to your home being heaven on earth.

Submission

Wife, do what the Word says in Ephesians 5: 33 and see your marriage blossom. Obey the Word and see whether the Lord will not bless you and your marriage. Copy Sarah's example in her relationship with Abraham as Peter describes in his epistle in 1 Peter 3. Apostle Peter lays out for us how a Christian wife and a Christian husband are to conduct themselves. First, we examine the Holy Spirit's advice to the Christian wife.

> [1] In like manner, you married women, be submissive to your own husbands [subordinate yourselves as being secondary to and dependent on them, and adapt yourselves to them], so that even if any do not obey the Word [of God], they may be won over not by discussion but by the [godly] lives of their wives,
>
> [2] When they observe the pure and modest way in which you conduct yourselves, together with your reverence [for your husband; you are to feel for him all that reverence includes: to respect, defer to, revere him—to honor, esteem, appreciate, prize, and, in the human sense, to adore him, that is, to admire, praise, be devoted to, deeply love, and enjoy your husband].
>
> [3] Let not yours be the [merely] external adorning with [elaborate] interweaving and knotting of the hair, the wearing of jewelry, or changes of clothes;
>
> [4] But let it be the inward adorning and beauty of the hidden person of the heart, with the incorruptible and unfading charm of a gentle and peaceful spirit, which [is not anxious or wrought up, but] is very precious in the sight of God.
>
> [5] For it was thus that the pious women of old who hoped in God were [accustomed] to beautify themselves and were submissive to their husbands [adapting themselves to them as themselves secondary and dependent upon them].
>
> [6] It was thus that Sarah obeyed Abraham [following his guidance and acknowledging his headship over her by] calling him lord (master, leader, authority). And you are now her true daughters if you do right and let nothing terrify you [not giving way to hysterical fears or letting anxieties unnerve you]. [1 Peter 3: 1-6, AMP]

Sister, if you believe that God loves you and cares for your welfare, marriage and family, obey His Word. The word "submissive" in AMP or "subject" in KJV in 1 Peter 3: 1 is translated from the Greek word *hupotassó* which means to place or rank under, to subject oneself, to obey; to submit to one's control; to yield to one's admonition or advice. The paraphrase in brackets provided by the AMP conveys the point clearly.

The idea behind submission is that of giving up one's right or will. Submission is not just to a person, but also to the position established by God to ensure order and peace in the marital relationship and family, and avoid chaos. There are four aspects to submission;

- Entrusting oneself to God: We need to follow our Lord Jesus' example on this, and keep our focus on God. "When He was reviled and insulted, He did not revile or offer insult in return; [when] He was abused and suffered, He made no threats [of vengeance]; but he trusted [Himself and everything] to Him Who judges fairly." [1 Peter 2: 23, AMP]
- Respect: Nagging is a disrespectful behavior. Respect your husband.
- Godly character development: This is a major key to submission.
- Doing right: Do what is right because at the end of the day you will answer the Lord on what you did with the Word you know. Submission is an imperative in marriage. Without it there can be no oneness in marriage.

Submission in God's economy is voluntary. It is based on a recognition of God's ordained order. It requires death to pride and a desire to please God by serving the other person. It is based on *Agape* love and not fear. Our perfect example of submission is our Lord Jesus. He submitted Himself to the Father, and humbled Himself to do the Father's will which involved death on Calvary's cross for our redemption. Submitting to God's ordained authority in the case of a wife to her husband, is accepting God's ordained order in marriage for the proper functioning of the marriage covenant between them and peace in the home.

Christian wife, God is saying to submit to the leadership of your husband. Be subject to your husband's authority. [1 Corinthians 11: 10a, AMP] It is voluntary selfless submission. I did not say it, God did and He knows better than we do. Knowing that God is all knowing and just, He is saying it for your best interest and good. If he is not a believing one, your behavior becomes a seed you sow that enables God to give you a harvest of a saved husband.

Wife, your life (behavior, conduct) is the witness that God desires, and not you preaching to or at him. Your preaching may be misconstrued as nagging by an unbelieving husband, hence the Holy Spirit says that he may be won over not by discussion but by your godly life. Thus, the Holy Spirit emphasizes that when the unbelieving husbands observe

> 2 ...... the pure and modest way in which you [*believing wives*] conduct yourselves, together with your reverence [for your husband; you are to feel for him all that reverence includes: to respect, defer to, revere him—to honor, esteem, appreciate, prize, and, in the human sense, to adore him, that is, to admire, praise, be devoted to, deeply love, and enjoy your husband]; [1 Peter 3: 2, AMP]

they have no choice but to surrender their lives to Christ. The beauty of the Christian wife is not so much of external adornment which should be with moderation, but

> 4... the inward adorning and beauty of the hidden person of the heart, with the incorruptible and unfading charm of a gentle and peaceful spirit, which [is not anxious or wrought up, but] is very precious in the sight of God. [1 Peter 3: 4, AMP]

It is this inner beauty, the beauty of character, that is the seed that God works with to give you a harvest of a saved husband.

> 5 For it was thus that the pious women of old who hoped in God were [accustomed] to beautify themselves and were submissive to their husbands [adapting themselves to them as themselves secondary and dependent upon them]. [1 Peter 3: 5, AMP]

Peter concludes his discourse on the beauty and benefit of submission of a wife to her husband by giving us the example of Sarah.

> [6] It was thus that **Sarah obeyed Abraham [following his guidance and acknowledging his headship over her by] calling him lord (master, leader, authority). And you are now her true daughters if you do right and let nothing terrify you** [not giving way to hysterical fears or letting anxieties unnerve you]. [1 Peter 3: 6, AMP; emphasis mine]

The word "obeyed" is translated from the Greek word *hupakouó*. It is a combination of two words, *hupo* (meaning under) and *akoúō* (to obey what is heard). To obey is listen and do, to hearken. Implied in *hupakouó* is an inward attitude of honor and respect coupled with acts of obedience. It is subordinating oneself to a person or what is heard. Thus, Sarah subordinated herself to Abraham's leadership.

The word "lord" is translated from *kurios* in Greek, and it is used to describe a family head in secular Greek. [Precept 2015] It means "he to whom a person or thing belongs, about which he has the power of deciding.' [Thayer 1995] It refers to the one who is "lord" of wife and children. It is important to note that it does not mean that he has the right to 'lord' it over or control them.

As a wifely courtesy, Sarah addressed Abraham as lord as an acknowledgment of her willingly submitting herself to her husband's authority (over her). We can see this in her response to the message from the Lord Who appeared to Abraham to inform him that his wife, Sarah, would bear him a son, the son of promise. "Therefore Sarah laughed to herself, saying, After I have become aged shall I have pleasure and delight, my lord (husband), being old also? [Genesis 18: 12; AMP] Similarly, Ruth addressed Boaz as lord. "Then she said, Let me find favor in your sight, my lord." [Ruth 2: 13a, AMP]

You may say that times have changed, and no wife calls her husband lord these days. That is true, but do not miss the point made by the Holy

Spirit in 1 Peter 3: 6. The point is for the wife to honor and defer to her husband. The message is that of submission.

Sarah's Example

Wife, you become Sarah's true daughter if you follow her example. The word "become" is translated from the Greek word "*ginomai*," and it means to transition from one state into another. Sarah obeyed Abraham calling him lord, indicating that Christian wives should honor and defer to their husbands. As a Christian wife, you become Sarah's true daughter by faith if you continually do what is right without fear of how your husband might behave. That is, you move from not being Sarah's true daughter to being her true daughter by faith. Of Sarah, the Scripture declares:

> 6 Sarah was in the habit of rendering obedience to Abraham, calling him lord, whose children [namely Sarah's] you become if the whole course of your life is in the doing of good, and you are not being caused to fear by even one particle of terror. [1 Peter 3: 6, WUEST]

Sister, if you follow Sarah's example you can be sure of God backing you. The Holy Spirit is saying that you do not need to be terrified and refuse to obey the Word. God has your back covered and He is working behind the scene to reward your labor of love. The reward is clear; a saved, loving, and caring husband who also becomes the priest of the family.

If you say that your husband cannot change, or he is too stubborn to change, check up on yourself. If this is what you say; by your very speech you have blocked God out of your situation. You need to change. Hear the Word of the Lord:

> 2 You are snared with the words of your lips, you are caught by the speech of your mouth. [Proverbs 6: 2, AMP]

20 A man's [moral] self shall be filled with the fruit of his mouth; and with the consequence of his words he must be satisfied [whether good or evil]. [Proverbs 18: 20, AMP]

Have you done what God requires of you in 1 Peter 3: 1-6? Are you telling God that His hand is short that He cannot save (deliver) your husband? [Isaiah 50:2] Are you saying your case is too hard for God? Nothing is too difficult for our God.

> **Any action you take outside of *Agape* is selfishness.**

17 Alas, Lord God! Behold, You have made the heavens and the earth by Your great power and by Your outstretched arm! There is nothing too hard or too wonderful for You.

27 Behold, I am the Lord, the God of all flesh; is there anything too hard for Me? [Jeremiah 32: 17, 27, AMP]

Line up with God's word and see His glory manifested on your behalf. Nothing is too difficult for God. Nothing is impossible for Him, and nothing is impossible to you, if you believe. [Mark 9: 23, AMP] Believe God and stop listening to those unscrupulous friends of yours who are cheering you on to go against God's Word, and divorce your husband because they join you in chorus to say, He can never change. Sister, do not believe that lie from hell. The devil is trying to destroy your marriage and family, and you are falling for his lies

Before you allow selfishness to take you over, I want you to remember that God says that it is *Agape* love that undergirds your marital relationship. It is on it that you build friendship and romantic love with your husband, and not the other way round. Any action you take outside of *Agape* is selfishness. Do not say that you cannot submit to your husband because he is not a Christian. You do not have the Word to support your action. Your husband is sanctified because you are a believing one. "For the unbelieving husband is set apart for God by the wife, and the unbelieving wife is set apart for God by the husband.

Otherwise your children would be corrupt, but now they are set apart for God." [1 Corinthians 7: 14, HCSB] When last did you pray a Word-based prayer of faith for your husband?

In submitting to your husband, I am not asking you to sin against God by agreeing with your husband to do wrong. No, you submit to him in line with God's word and do not go contrary to God's Word. You need God's backing in doing His will. Do not act stupidly, and sin against God. Do God's will (His Word) in your marriage and watch Him transform your life and your husband's.

Wife, appreciate your husband. A friend once said, "What you won't appreciate, you won't celebrate." It is hard to live with someone you just tolerate because if you do not celebrate your husband, you are only tolerating him. How long can you continue in that vein?

Forgiveness

If you want to have a successful marriage, you need to learn how to forgive your spouse. You do not need to carry a grudge and a long face around the house. What point are you trying to make. You may score a point with your spouse, but you become miserable thereafter. You may say, He wronged me and I need to hold out until he asks for forgiveness, and vice versa. You are wrong. You are only shortchanging yourself. You are the one hurting, and not your spouse. What if your spouse did not know that he/she wronged you?

Do not take anything for granted. If you are wronged, let your spouse know. Stop bottling up anger because of entertaining an offense. If you bottle up anger within you because you entertained offense, one day you will explode on a minor issue. Choose to obey God's word. Forgive and let it go. If you do not forgive and let go, you prevent God from answering your prayer.

[25] And whenever you stand praying, if you have anything against anyone, forgive him and let it drop (leave it, let it go), in order that

your Father Who is in heaven may also forgive you your [own] failings and shortcomings and let them drop.

26 But if you do not forgive, neither will your Father in heaven forgive your failings and shortcomings. [Mark 11: 25-26, AMP]

The Lord commands us to forgive and let go of any offense we may have entertained. "Forgive" is present tense in the imperative with active voice. The imperative tense makes a demand on the reader (hearer) to obey the command. Jesus commands us to forgive when we are about to pray. It is a command that we must obey, otherwise God, our Father, will not answer our prayers. Our Lord tells us to examine our hearts before we pray to be sure that there is no unforgiveness in us. Unforgiveness will make your prayer unheard by God the Father. Do you want to pray without getting results?

How can you go to bed without praying with your spouse? If you have not been praying together with your spouse before going to bed, start doing so now. When you do, you need to decide whether you are going to pray with unforgiveness or with a clear conscience towards your spouse because you have forgiven him/her. I believe the latter is what you want so that God can hear and answer your prayer.

Thus, the Holy Spirit admonishes us: "Be angry but do not sin; do not let the sun go down on your anger, and give no opportunity to the devil." [Ephesians 4: 26-27, RSV] Why would you want to let the sun go down on your anger by choosing to entertain offense. God is saying that you should not entertain offense, but if you do, do not go to sleep with it. It is only giving the devil the opportunity/opening to come against you. If you literally practice what the Word says in Ephesians 4: 26-27 and combining it with Mark 11: 25-26, you set yourself up for God to bless your marriage.

I have put this to work in my marriage and I know it works. My wife and I set out to practice this from the first day we got married. Because we pray together before going to sleep, if one of us wronged the other the person in the wrong will ask for forgiveness. Of course, we do so in obedience and out of courtesy. This does not negate Mark 11: 25-26 which we hold dear to our hearts because we want our prayers answered. I believe that this has contributed in no small measure to our friendship which is undergirded with *Agape* love. Heed God's word:

> Love (God's love in us) does not insist on its own rights or its own way, for it is not self-seeking; it is not touchy or fretful or resentful; it takes no account of the evil done to it [it pays no attention to a suffered wrong]. [1 Corinthians 13: 5b, AMP]

We have discussed leadership, submission, and forgiveness as important components of a successful, wholesome marriage, but there is yet a fourth component to it. You may wonder what it is. It is found in 1 Peter 3: 7.

Dwelling with Your Wife According to Knowledge

The admonition of Apostle Peter in 1 Peter 3: 7 is a major key to a successful, wholesome marriage. Although the verse is addressed to husbands, I believe that wives can also learn from the principles presented to us in that verse of Scripture by Apostle Peter.

> [7] In the same way you married men should live considerately with [your wives], with an intelligent recognition [of the marriage relation], honoring the woman as [physically] the weaker, but [realizing that you] are joint heirs of the grace (God's unmerited favor) of life, in order that your prayers may not be hindered and cut off. [Otherwise you cannot pray effectively.] [1 Peter 3: 7, AMP]

> [7] Likewise, ye husbands, dwell with them according to knowledge, giving honour unto the wife, as unto the weaker vessel, and as being heirs together of the grace of life; that your prayers be not hindered. [1 Peter 3: 7, KJV]

The word "dwell" (*sunoikeo*) means to dwell together or live in wedlock with your wife; and according to knowledge means "with an intelligent recognition of the nature of the marriage relation." [Vincent 1887] The word "knowledge" is translated from the Greek word *gnōsis* which is derived from *ginōskō* (to "experientially know"). This knowledge is – functional, working knowledge gained from first-hand (personal) experience, by a direct relationship. Thus, I paraphrase 1 Peter 3: 7 as follows:

> *Husband you are to live in wedlock with your wife with an intelligent recognition of the nature of the marriage relation, coupled with a knowledge gained from first-hand personal experience of your direct relationship with your wife.*

Husband, this means that coming from different backgrounds, there are things you probably expected your wife to do and she could not or did not do. You are to fill that role until your wife who is observing intelligently can take over. She will do it because she loves and cares about you and wants the best for you. I have put this revelation to work, and it works. I am blessed and so is my wife and marriage because I choose to obey God.

As you put this Word to work, you are honoring your wife. The "weaker vessel" in 1 Peter 3: 7 is only referring to the fact that the husband is physically stronger than the woman. There are two reasons why you, as a husband, are to dwell with your wife according to knowledge. They are:

- husband, you and your wife are joint heirs of the grace of life, and
- that your prayers may be answered. If you do not obey the Lord's instruction, your prayers will be hindered and cut off; and you will not be able to pray effectively. That is, you will not be able to pray to get results.

I do not know about you, brother, but I do not want my prayers to go unanswered. I want to be able to see God move on my behalf when I call upon Him. This has to be coupled with Ephesians 5:21: "Be subject to one another out of reverence for Christ (the Messiah, the Anointed One)." "Be subject" is translated from *hupotassó* in Greek which means to yield to one's admonition or advice. Husband, listen to your wife's counsel or advice. Prayerfully consider it and make your decision. The operative words are **prayerfully consider** because your wife may give you a godly counsel and sometimes it may be a counsel that is sight-based (flesh-based). You are the leader in the union, therefore you must take ownership of your decision. The more reason you should pray and seek the Holy Spirit's guidance in making decisions.

Wife, once your husband has taken the decision, stand with him on it because you are one with him. You cannot distance yourself from it. Once you have made your input, pray for your husband, and leave him to decide. You must be comfortable with your husband leading. Wife, I advise you to also dwell with your husband according to knowledge - an intelligent recognition of the nature of the marriage relation. You will be blessed when you put this principle to work.

Husbands you have a key part to play in your marital relationship. Make your wife your best friend. You need to work at it. It is a gradual process, but it is an investment with heavy dividend payments. Let her know about your work, etc. It is important to give her what she can handle emotionally, and not overload her emotionally. Listen to your Helper, the Holy Spirit, and He will direct you on this, You and your wife will find yourselves enjoying marital bliss, experiencing heaven on earth. Equally, wife make your husband your best friend. I pray that God gives you a home that is heaven on earth, a home of peace and love in Jesus' Name.

The Conclusion of the Matter

The conclusion of the matter is to live a life of *Agape* love. When you do, you will be able to love your spouse, and be a dispenser of *Agape* love to others. You will have a home of love and peace; a home to bring up godly children in an atmosphere where they can thrive. The Holy Spirit summarizes this better than I can in Romans 12: 16-21 and 1 Peter 3: 9-13.

> [16] Live in harmony with one another; do not be haughty (snobbish, high-minded, exclusive), but readily adjust yourself to [people, things] and give yourselves to humble tasks. Never overestimate yourself or be wise in your own conceits.

[17] Repay no one evil for evil, but take thought for what is honest and proper and noble [aiming to be above reproach] in the sight of everyone.

[18] If possible, as far as it depends on you, live at peace with everyone.

[19] Beloved, never avenge yourselves, but leave the way open for [God's] wrath; for it is written, Vengeance is Mine, I will repay (requite), says the Lord.

[20] But if your enemy is hungry, feed him; if he is thirsty, give him drink; for by so doing you will heap burning coals upon his head.

[21] Do not let yourself be overcome by evil, but overcome (master) evil with good. [Romans 12: 16-21, AMP]

[9] Never return evil for evil or insult for insult (scolding, tongue-lashing, berating), but on the contrary blessing [praying for their welfare, happiness, and protection, and truly pitying and loving them]. For know that to this you have been called, that you may yourselves inherit a blessing [from God—that you may obtain a blessing as heirs, bringing welfare and happiness and protection].

[10] For let him who wants to enjoy life and see good days [good—whether apparent or not] keep his tongue free from evil and his lips from guile (treachery, deceit).

[11] Let him turn away from wickedness and shun it, and let him do right. Let him search for peace (harmony; undisturbedness from fears, agitating passions, and moral conflicts) and seek it eagerly. [Do not merely desire peaceful relations with God, with your fellowmen, and with yourself, but pursue, go after them!]

[12] For the eyes of the Lord are upon the righteous (those who are upright and in right standing with God), and His ears are attentive to their prayer. But the face of the Lord is against those who practice evil [to oppose them, to frustrate, and defeat them].

[13] Now who is there to hurt you if you are zealous followers of that which is good? [1 Peter 3; 9-13, AMP]

When you walk in *Agape* love, God protects you and your marriage.

With *Agape* love, you can effectively put your faith to work.

6. LOVE: THE KEY TO PREVAILING FAITH

For [if we are] in Christ Jesus, neither circumcision nor uncircumcision counts for anything, but only faith activated and energized and expressed and working through love. [Galatians 5: 6, AMP]

Love, the love of God, is the key to prevailing faith. "Faith is the substance of things hoped for, the evidence of things not seen." [Hebrews 11: 1, KJV] A paraphrase of faith helps to us to have clarity of what faith is. *Faith is the Word of God of things we have earnest expectation of good for, the evidence of things not seen (with our senses).* [See my book, **The Mechanics of Faith**.] Without operating in God's love, you have no guarantee that your faith will produce the desired results. That is why the Apostle Paul, speaking by the unction of the Holy Spirit, declared, "For [if we are] in Christ Jesus, neither circumcision nor uncircumcision counts for anything, but only faith activated and energized and expressed and working through love." [Galatians 5: 6, AMP]

If faith is the Word of God of things we earnest expectation of good for, then faith is love in demonstration.

We cannot separate God from His love because God is Love. [1 John 4: 8, AMP] Since the Word is God (John 1: 1), we can surmise that the Word is Love. If faith is the Word of God of things we have earnest expectation of good for, then faith is love in demonstration. [For more on what faith is, see my book **The Mechanics of Faith**.] Our faith cannot be effective if it is not energized by love. There is no power to our faith if it is not exercised through *Agape* love. Put it another way, the power of God cannot flow through you as you step out in faith if the love of God is not flowing through you.

The faith you are trying to operate is that of Jesus and He is Love. Jesus is God. [John 1: 1, AMP] *Agape* love is a person, and that person is Jesus/God. That is why Paul reminded us that faith is activated, energized, expressed, and operates through the agency of *Agape* love. [Galatians 5: 6, AMP]

> If the Word is God, and God is Love, then the Word is Love.

It is important to note that the faith we are discussing is the God kind of faith. God is the One Who gives us faith by virtue of Him living in us. God our Father has given to every child of His the measure of faith. Thus, the faith we have is not something we earned, but the faith of the Son of God Who lives in us.

> [20] I have been crucified with Christ; it is no longer I who live, but Christ lives in me; and the life which I now live in the flesh I live by faith in the Son of God, who loved me and gave Himself for me. [Galatians 2: 20, KJV]

The love of God has been poured into our hearts through the Holy Spirit Who indwells us. "… For God's love has been poured out in our hearts through the Holy Spirit Who has been given to us." [Romans 5: 5b, AMP] If the Word is God, and God is Love, then the Word is Love. This is akin to the geometric axiom that things equal to the same thing are equal to one another. Thus, we are able to proof that God is the Word and God is Love. [John 1:1; 1 John 4: 8]

If the Word is Love, and faith is the Word of God of things we have earnest expectation of good for, the evidence of things not seen, then we can understand how faith is activated by *Agape* Love. Since our heavenly Father is a faith God, and He is Love, and His love has been poured out in our hearts on the day we confessed Jesus as our Lord and Savior, then we have the love and faith of God.

What is the Faith of God?
The Faith of God

Peter on observing that the fig tree that Jesus cursed a day previously for having leaves without fruit died, drew Jesus'attention to the fact that the fig dried up from its roots. [Mark 11: 13-14, 20] In response to Peter's observation, Jesus said, "Have the faith of God." [Mark 11: 22, YLT] Because Jesus lives is us by His Spirit, we have the faith of God. What, then, is the faith of God?

The Faith of God can best be understood by observing God in action, and there is no better place to start from than the account of creation in Genesis chapter 1.

> ² The earth was without form and an empty waste, and darkness was upon the face of the very great deep. The Spirit of God was moving (hovering, brooding) over the face of the waters. [Genesis 1: 2, AMP]
>
> ³ and God saith, `Let light be;' and light is. [Genesis 1: 3, YLT]
>
> ⁹ And God said, Let the waters under the heavens be collected into one place [of standing], and let the dry land appear. And it was so.
> ¹¹ And God said, Let the earth put forth [tender] vegetation: plants yielding seed and fruit trees yielding fruit whose seed is in itself, each according to its kind, upon the earth. And it was so.
> ¹² The earth brought forth vegetation: plants yielding seed according to their own kinds and trees bearing fruit in which was their seed, each according to its kind. And God saw that it was good (suitable, admirable) and He approved it. [Genesis 1: 9,11-12, AMP]

We find from the above verses in Genesis 1 that whatever God said became and still is. He spoke light and light is. He spoke plants into existence and they are. Thus, the faith of God speaks and it becomes, or it is done. When God commands, it stands fast. King David summarized it for us in Psalm 33 thus:

⁶ By the word of the Lord were the heavens made, and all their host by the breath of His mouth.

⁷ He gathers the waters of the sea as in a bottle; He puts the deeps in storage places.

⁸ Let all the earth fear the Lord [revere and worship Him]; let all the inhabitants of the world stand in awe of Him.

⁹ For He spoke, and it was done; He commanded, and it stood fast. [Psalm 33: 6-9, AMP]

The faith of God speaks and does not look back because God speaks and does not look back. Why? God is Truth, and he cannot lie. Because His word is the word of truth, what He says must come to pass. Since He is the author of integrity and His word is the word of integrity, it has self-fulfilling power. "For with God nothing is ever impossible and no word from God shall be without power or impossible of fulfillment." [Luke 1: 37, AMP] His faith is in us because He lives *in* us by His Spirit. All we have to do is to activate His faith in us by speaking and believing His Word. However, His faith cannot be activated in us if we do not operate in *Agape* love. To operate in Agape Love is to walk in the Spirit. It is to be yielded to the Spirit of God and led by Him.

Faith Is Energized and Operates through Love

God could not have delivered Shadrach, Meshach, and Abednego, which we discussed in Chapter 4 of this book, if they were focused on the offense committed against them by their peers, the king's officials. We gain some insight into why their faith was productive when we read what Paul, by the inspiration of the Holy Spirit, wrote, "For [if we are] in Christ Jesus, neither circumcision nor uncircumcision counts for anything, but only faith activated and energized and expressed and working through love." [Galatians 5:6, AMP] For our faith to work, *Agape* love must be the engine of our lives. We can learn from Shadrach, Meshach, and Abednego how our faith can be energized and expressed through love. Here are the lessons that we can learn from them:

- **None entertainment of offense.** Like Shadrach, Meshach, and Abednego we must refuse to entertain offense. [Luke 17: 1-4, AMP]

- **Forgive and focus on God and not your offender(s).** Shadrach, Meshach, and Abednego did not fix their minds on their accusers. Therefore, when offended/accused we must refuse to focus on our offenders/accusers. Rather, we must forgive our accusers/offenders. [Luke 17: 1-4, AMP]

- **Entrust yourself to God.** Like Shadrach, Meshach, and Abednego we must entrust ourselves to God who judges righteously. [1 Peter 2: 23, AMP]

- **Trust God for your deliverance.** We must trust God to deliver us as He did the three Hebrew brethren. When we do, God will deliver us from every distress and trouble. [Psalm 34: 19, AMP]

- **Operate in faith through love.** We must, like Shadrach, Meshach, and Abednego operate in faith walking through love, and God will not only deliver us, He will promote us. [Psalm 91: 15; Daniel 3: 24-26,30, KJV]

- **Do not doubt.** We must not doubt. Doubting God would make you to change your confession. One of the Greek words translated "doubt" in the New Testament is *diakrino*. [See for example, Mathew 21: 21, AMP] It comes from a combination of two root words *dia* (which means by reason of, for the sake, that, thereby, therefore, through(-out), to, wherefore) and *krino* (which means to call to question or judge) in Greek. The words are combined to form *diakrino* which means to separate thoroughly, withdraw from, oppose, waver, stagger, or hesitate. The word doubt in Hebrew (*tala*) means to suspend, or to be uncertain through hesitation.

When we doubt the Word of God, we oppose ourselves. We become uncertain through hesitation and suspend the Word from working in our lives. When we doubt the Word, we become double minded. The word "double minded" in James 1: 8 (KJV) means to be two-spirited. You cannot yield to the Spirit of God and the devil at the same time. Double mindedness makes you irresolute and unsure of yourself. At that point, you become the enemy's prey because your faith becomes paralyzed by default.

James, by the inspiration of the Holy Spirit, indicated that when we make a request to God, we must do so in faith and refuse to doubt. He gave us an example of asking for wisdom:

> 5 If any of you is deficient in wisdom, let him ask of the giving God [Who gives] to everyone liberally and ungrudgingly, without reproaching or faultfinding, and it will be given him.
> 6 Only it must be in faith that he asks with no wavering (no hesitating, no doubting). For the one who wavers (hesitates, doubts) is like the billowing surge out at sea that is blown hither and thither and tossed by the wind.
> 7 For truly, let not such a person imagine that he will receive anything [he asks for] from the Lord,
> 8 [For being as he is] a man of two minds (hesitating, dubious, irresolute), [he is] unstable and unreliable and uncertain about everything [he thinks, feels, decides]. [James 1: 6-8, AMP]

If the three Hebrew men had changed their statement of faith from "our God whom we serve is able to deliver us from the burning fiery furnace, and he will deliver us out of thine hand, O king" (Daniel 3: 17, KJV) to "But even if he doesn't, we want to make it clear to you, Your Majesty, that we will never serve your gods or worship the gold statue you have set up" (Daniel 3: 18, NLT), they would have perished. If the NLT and NIV translation of Daniel 3: 18 were the most appropriate, it would have meant that the three Hebrew men withdrew their statement of faith, leaving God nothing to work with to bring them out of the crisis situation. They would have opposed themselves. The reason is that the two statements are contrary to each other. They would have doubted God and according to James, they would not have received their deliverance from God. We must stick with our confession of faith, regardless of how the devil may taunt us.

- **Confess Christ before men**. We must confess Christ before men and He will confess us before the Father. [Matthew 10: 32, AMP] This is what Shadrach, Meshach, and Abednego did and God Who could not disappoint their faith will not disappoint ours. Why? Our faith is based on His Word just as the faith of the three Hebrew brethren was based on His Word. The Word is, "You shall not bow down to their gods or serve them or do after their works;" (Exodus 23: 24a, AMP) and "You shall not make yourself any graven image [to worship it] or any likeness of anything that is in the heavens above, or that is in the earth beneath, or that is in the water under the earth." [Exodus 20: 4, AMP]

Love Works by Faith

The miracle that Shadrach, Meshach, and Abednego experienced could not have been possible if their faith was not operating through love. Equally, it took faith for them to choose to forgive their accusers. You may wonder why I believe that was the case. We do not find it stated in Daniel chapter 3 that they pointed fingers at anyone or cursed anyone. It took faith to forgive those who wanted them dead. They understood that if they took a step of faith to forgive their accusers, God would take care of them. There are times we have to step out in faith to love the ones we consider unlovable so that God can work out His will in their lives. Stephen forgiving Saul and all those who killed him just before he breathed his last is another example of love operating through faith.

Love Works through Obedience

Jesus modeled the love of God for us. The love he showed humanity flowed from His love for the Father. He explained to us that His love for the Father was demonstrated by His obedience to the Father.

> [10] If you keep My commandments [if you continue to obey My instructions], you will abide in My love and live on in it, just as I have obeyed My Father's commandments and live on in His love. [John 15: 10, AMP]

> [29] And He Who sent Me is ever with Me; My Father has not left Me alone, for I always do what pleases Him. [John 8: 29, AMP]

His love for the Father and humanity sent Him to the Cross to die for us. Jesus healed the sick, fed the hungry, and set captives free because He had compassion on them when He was on earth. He does not change. Since He mirrored the Father in all things, His love for humanity when He walked the earth was a demonstration of the Father's love for us. It was also a demonstration of His obedience to the Father's will. Obedience is what enabled Him to walk in love. Thus, it is in obeying God that we allow God's love to flow through us to others.

To recap, it is impossible to separate faith from *Agape* love because God is *Agape* love, and our faith is based on the Word. [1 John 4: 8; Romans 10: 17, AMP] *Faith is the rhema Word of God of things we have earnest expectation for, the evidence of things not seen with our physical senses.* The Word is God, hence we cannot separate God from His faith, and neither can we separate Him from His love. [Hebrews 11: 3; 1 John 4: 8, AMP] In addition, we cannot discuss *Agape* love without obedience – obedience to God our Father. Jesus' love for the Father was demonstrated through His obedience to the Father. Equally our love for the Father is demonstrated through our obedience of His voice and Word. Love is not *Agape* love if giving is not involved. It takes faith to give to those who do not merit the gift. God demonstrated His *Agape* love to us through the gift of His only begotten Son.

PART 2: WORSHIPFUL GIVING

7. LOVE DEMONSTRATED THROUGH GIVING

We want to tell you further, brethren, about the grace (the favor and spiritual blessing) of God which has been evident in the churches of Macedonia [arousing in them the desire to give alms]; For in the midst of an ordeal of severe tribulation, their abundance of joy and their depth of poverty [together] have overflowed in wealth of lavish generosity on their part. For, as I can bear witness, [they gave] according to their ability, yes, and beyond their ability; and [they did it] voluntarily. [2 Corinthians 8: 1-3, AMP]

What has love to do with giving? God demonstrated to us that *Agape* love is all about giving.

> [16] For God so greatly loved and dearly prized the world that He [even] gave up His only begotten (unique) Son, so that whoever believes in (trusts in, clings to, relies on) Him shall not perish (come to destruction, be lost) but have eternal (everlasting) life. [John 3: 16, AMP]

Agape love is not agape love without giving.

The word "gave" is from the Greek word *didoomee* which means to give, deliver up, offer, minister, bring forth, smite, and receive. Thus, the implication of John 3: 16 is that God gave up (i.e., delivered or offered up) Jesus His best gift (seed) for us, and as He did the Seed brought (was/is bringing) forth a harvest of sons and daughters which God the Father received and is still receiving. The gift of His Seed smote the devil and he could not stop Him, God's Seed, from bringing forth harvests of sons and daughters. Hallelujah! God said in Genesis 3: 15 that the Seed of the woman (Jesus) would bruise the serpent's head.

God believed the best of us and gave His Son to die for our sins with the expectation that we would respond to His love and come to Him through Christ. *Agape* love is not *Agape* love without giving. [John 3: 16] God loved us so much that while we were yet sinners Christ died for us. The Word declares, "But God demonstrates his own love for us in this: While we were still sinners, Christ died for us." [Romans 5:8, NIV]

Before giving Jesus, God knew His Seed would bruise the enemy's head. He knew that His Seed would strike a deadly blow on the enemy, a blow Satan could never recover from no matter how hard he tried. He knew that His Seed would bring forth much fruit. [John 12: 24] The harvest could not be stopped because the devourer was thoroughly defeated. Thus when God delivered up Jesus to die for our sins, He received His harvest by faith and switched into the expectation mode for the manifestation of the harvest of born again sons and daughters.

John 3: 16 is inextricably tied to John 12:24, "Most assuredly, I say to you, unless a grain of wheat falls into the ground and dies, it remains alone; but if it dies, it produces much grain." [KJV] We need John 12: 24 to gain a full appreciation of John 3: 16. Because of Jesus sacrifice at Calvary, the Father has received and continues to receive much fruit. Much fruit means abundant harvest, harvest with no limits. That is, there is no limit to the number of sons and daughters God is expecting to be born into His Kingdom. God began to reap a harvest of sons and daughters as soon as Jesus began His work here on earth. John records, "... As many as did receive and welcome Him, He gave the authority (power, privilege, right) to become the children of God, that is, to those who believe in (adhere to, trust in, and rely on) His name." [John 1: 12, AMP]

Why did God reap a harvest right from the beginning of Jesus' ministry? How could God reap a harvest when the grain of wheat had not yet fallen to the ground and died as Jesus discussed in John 12:24? Having answers to these questions enable us to understand the law of seedtime and harvest, and how God operates it. When we understand how God gives and receives, we can then set ourselves to operate this spiritual law and become lifetime givers. How did God operate the spiritual law of seedtime and harvest with the gift of His Son?

When God decided to give His only begotten Son to redeem mankind, He offered Him up at that time. Jesus is the Lamb that was slain from the foundation of the world:

> [19] But [you were purchased] with the precious blood of Christ (the Messiah), like that of a [sacrificial] lamb without blemish or spot.
> [20] It is true that He was chosen and foreordained (destined and foreknown for it) before the foundation of the world, but He was brought out to public view (made manifest) in these last days (at the end of the times) for the sake of you. [1 Peter 1: 19-20, AMP]

> [8] And they shall worship Him, all who dwell upon the earth, [everyone] whose name does not stand written in the scroll of the life [the scroll] belonging to the Lamb Who has been slain [in the mind and purpose of God] since the time when the foundations of the universe were laid, and Who is looked upon [by God] as the slain Lamb at present. [Revelation 13: 8, WUEST]

Once God decided to give up Jesus for us, in God's heart and mind it was over. Jesus was a gift already given. The same is true when Abraham offered up Isaac to be sacrificed. God considered Isaac offered up to Him because Abraham had already decided to offer him up to God.

> [17] By faith Abraham, when he was put to the test [while the testing of his faith was still in progress], had already brought Isaac for an offering; he who had gladly received and welcomed [God's] promises was ready to sacrifice his only son,
> [18] Of whom it was said, Through Isaac shall your descendants be reckoned.
> [19] For he reasoned that God was able to raise [him] up even from among the dead. Indeed in the sense that Isaac was figuratively dead [potentially sacrificed], he did [actually] receive him back from the dead. [Hebrews 11; 17-19, AMP]

Jesus came down to earth because the Father had already delivered him up for sacrifice. Since in the mind of God Jesus was already offered as the sacrificial Lamb, God had received His harvest by faith once His Seed left heaven (His hand) and was only waiting for the manifestation. Once Jesus began His ministry, the reaping of the harvest started.

We need to learn from God. Once the Father offered up Jesus (His Seed), He switched into the expectation and receiving/reaping mode, ready to receive us back, and He has not stopped. God coupled His expectation with patience. The Lord is waiting patiently for the harvest of the earth – the salvation of souls.

> Giving without a revelation of the Word on giving will not produce a harvest.
>
> With revelation comes the anointing to perform the Word.

When God lost man, the crown jewel of His creation, to the devil because Adam committed high treason, He decided that He was going to recover His lost creation. The way out was to sow a seed, "a seed of equivalent benefit" as coined by Dr. Oral Roberts, so that He could bring about the restoration of the crown jewel of His creation to Himself. [Roberts 2005] That Seed was His only begotten Son, Jesus. Thus, to experience restoration and, therefore, recover from a loss you need to sow a seed of equivalent benefit. When you do, you are emulating God our Father. You are doing what He did to experience restoration. Our Father is the Author of restoration. When I was studying along these lines few years ago, the Lord ministered the following to me:

> *My ability to have humanity reconciled to Me was there all the time, but it was only released when I sowed My best Seed, My only begotten Son. I did not just release My faith with My sowing; I also released My receiving/reaping capacity with My Seed.*

Emulate God

First, we must remember that the word "gave" translated from *didoomee* in Greek means:

- to deliver or offer up,
- to smite,
- to bring forth, and
- to receive.

To give, deliver or offer up, our seed to God is to give with our hearts totally yielded to Him, withholding nothing. It is to give without looking back, without regrets and that which costs us something. [1 Chronicles 21: 23-24] It is to give cheerfully, promptly, generously and with our whole hearts. [2 Corinthians 9: 6-7, AMP] Our hearts must be in our giving, and that is emulating God. As soon as we are prompted by the Holy Spirit to give, we must agree with God. Once we agree with God, we are to declare our agreement. With this, we settle in our hearts that the gift belongs to the Lord and no longer ours. In our hearts the gift should be offered up to God at this point as Abraham did. We follow throw with prompt obedience. [2 Corinthians 9: 6-9, AMP] This is what the father of our faith, Abraham, did with Isaac.

Our gifts to the Lord reinforces the defeat of the enemy in our lives, rendering him powerless in our finances because he is already smitten. Satan does not like that because he knows the Seed of the woman (Jesus) bruised his head.

As we release the gift from our hands, we should receive our harvest by faith and switch into the expectation mode for the manifestation. As we do, we will see our harvest spring forth because our gifts have been delivered (offered) up to God. We should expect our harvests the same way God expected and is still expecting His harvest so that when our harvests come forth we can take hold of (i.e., receive) them. When God gave, He knew what His harvest would be.

Giving without a revelation of the Word on giving (i.e., a revelation of the Word when you are about to give to God) will not produce a harvest. With revelation comes the anointing to perform the Word. Once you have a revelation from God and act on it, God performs His Word. This is true of giving and all other areas of our relationship with God. When God gave Jesus, He gave with revelation. Jesus revealed that to us when He said that except a grain of wheat falls to the grown and dies, it remain by itself alone; but if it falls to the ground and dies, it brings forth much fruit. [John 12: 24] Your giving must be revelation based; then you can have a basis for expecting and reaping a harvest.

We should, like God, couple our receiving and expectation of our harvests with patience and a pure heart so that we can gain much fruit. The Word declares,

> [15] But as for that [seed] in the good soil, these are [the people] who, hearing the Word, hold it fast in a just (noble, virtuous) and worthy heart, and steadily bring forth fruit with patience. [Luke 8; 15, AMP]

> [11] Our great desire is that you will keep on loving others as long as life lasts, in order to make certain that what you hope for will come true.
> [12] Then you will not become spiritually dull and indifferent. Instead, you will follow the example of those who are going to inherit God's promises because of their faith and endurance. [Hebrews 6: 11-12, NLT]

Combining your prayer with giving out of a heart of love is an explosive force for the manifestation of God's glory in your life. Your harvest is guaranteed by God. [1 Samuel 1: 10-17, AMP] Harvest is part of the seed principle.

Harvest from Giving

You may ask, How can I reap much fruit (harvest) as God does? As we have already discussed, the receiving of your harvest occurs at the point of giving your best to God. First, let us examine closely how we need to go about presenting our offering. It is important to speak or pray the Word of God over your seed (offering, gift) before offering it to the Lord. When Jesus explained the parable of the sower, He said that the sower sowed the Word. In God's economy, Word equals seed. [Mark 4: 14] You must have the seed of the Word to speak over your money seed, or whatever you are offering to the Lord, for it to produce a harvest.

The Seed Principle

A seed is programed to multiply because the life of a seed is in itself. [Genesis 1: 11, AMP] A seed produces after its kind. A seed must be planted before it can grow and multiply. To be able to grow and multiply it must first die. Jesus said,

> ²⁴ I assure you, most solemnly I tell you, Unless a grain of wheat falls into the earth and dies, it remains [just one grain; it never becomes more but lives] by itself alone. But if it dies, it produces many others and yields a rich harvest. [John 12: 24, AMP]

The word "die" means to let go, and the word "into" implies that the seed must first be planted. The Father had to let go of Jesus, and He planted Jesus in the earth because He is the Seed of the woman that smote and bruised the serpent's (devil's) head.

> In God's economy, the Word equals seed.
>
> You must have the seed of the Word to speak over your offering (gift, seed) for it to produce a harvest.

The earth has to bring forth that which is planted in it. Jesus died and resurrected to bring forth many sons and daughters to God. There is no limit to God's multiplying power and He is the only One who can multiply your sown seed. [John 3: 16, AMP] Every seed is programed to multiply when planted in a good soil.

Be the Good Soil

While your seed must be planted in good soil (ministry, church sincerely doing the work of the Lord) to produce a harvest, your heart must also be a good soil too. In Genesis 1:11 God said, "Let the earth bring forth …" and in Hebrews 6: 7 (AMP) He declares, "For the soil which has drunk the rain that repeatedly falls upon it and produces vegetation useful to those for whose benefit it is cultivated partakes of a blessing from God." The soil in this verse is the heart (spirit) of man and rain is the Word. The verse can be paraphrased thus,

> For the heart that has received the Word that is repeatedly fed into it produces a harvest (of the seed sown) to the one for whose benefit it is cultivated and partakes of the blessing (multiplied seed and harvest) from God.

When we speak the Word over our offerings that we present to God, we program them with the Word of God to produce what we have spoken. Every Word, every seed, produces after its kind. The Word of God that we speak over our offerings (seeds) also registers in the soil of our hearts because we are God's garden to be planted. [1 Corinthians 3: 9] The spoken Word makes a demand on our hearts to cause the seeds planted in them to produce after their kind, and bring forth a multiplied harvest. Remember to couple the giving of your gift to God with thanksgiving and praise, and be expectant.

Couple Earnest Expectation with Weeding out Weeds and Thorns

A farmer expecting a good harvest is careful to remove weeds from his farm to keep them from choking his crops to death so that he can have a good harvest. Do not lose hope as far as your harvest is concerned. God does not forget your seed of faith sown. "For God is not unrighteous to forget or overlook your labor and the love which you have shown for His name's sake in ministering to the needs of the saints (His own consecrated people), as you still do." [Hebrews 6: 10, AMP] However, we must be diligent in serving God to enjoy the full assurance of and development of the hope until the end. [Hebrews 6: 11, AMP] The expectation of the righteous cannot be cut off. [Proverbs 24: 14, AMP] Therefore, we must

> 12 ...... not grow disinterested and become [spiritual] sluggards, but imitators, behaving as do those who through faith (by their leaning of the entire personality on God in Christ in absolute trust and confidence in His power, wisdom, and goodness) and by practice of patient endurance and waiting are [now] inheriting the promises. [Hebrews 6: 12, AMP]

A farmer who prepares his field, plants his seed, and waters it does not sit down to worry whether the seed will germinate and yield a harvest. The farmer does not know what happens with the seed in the soil, but he is expectant that the harvest will come. Thus, Jesus said,

> 26 ...The kingdom of God is like a man who scatters seed upon the ground,
> 27 And then continues sleeping and rising night and day while the seed sprouts and grows and increases—he knows not how.
> 28 The earth produces [acting] by itself—first the blade, then the ear, then the full grain in the ear.
> 29 But when the grain is ripe and permits, immediately he sends forth [the reapers] and puts in the sickle, because the harvest stands ready. [Mark 4: 26-29, AMP]

It is important to couple the release of our faith during our giving with expectation. [Hebrews 11: 1, AMP] God believes in the preparation of the field before planting. He had to prepare us for the coming of Jesus. He announced it in Genesis 3: 14–15 and prepared humanity through the years for the arrival of His Son. He used the prophets in the Old Testament to do it and one of those prophets was Isaiah who boldly prophesied of the coming of the Lord and what He was to do. [See Isaiah 9 and 53 as examples.]

God does not know how to worry, and we have to emulate Him by turning our cares over to him. Worry and doubt choke life out of the seed, and prevent a harvest from coming forth. Cast your cares on the

Lord and let Him take care of them for you. [1 Peter 5: 7] Do not worry about how He will meet your needs. That is His business. Your business is to believe Him. He will meet your needs because He is the One Who cares for the birds of the air that do not sow or reap. If He takes care of birds that do not sow, how can He abandon you a sower. It is His good pleasure to give you the Kingdom, all the good that is of the Kingdom. [Luke 12: 32] When devil lies to you to cause you to worry, or be anxious, cast down those thoughts in the Name of Jesus.

Because you are a sower, an instructed seed sower, you know that God is your Source and He cannot abandon you. Let the devil know that God, your Source, has supplied your need according to His riches in Christ Jesus. [Philippians 4: 19] When you do, the weeds of worry, anxiety, and fear cannot grow and choke your planted seeds of faith and prevent your harvests from ripening for you to harvest. Trust God and stand on His Word for provision, and your harvest must surely manifest.

Harvest is by divine instruction and by revelation.

How Harvest Comes

Preparing the soil of your heart before planting your seed of faith (offering) is very important. If you do not sow your seed of faith with revelation, a revelation knowledge of the Word you are standing on, you will probably not get a harvest. With revelation comes the anointing to fulfill the Word that you speak over your offering. When you have revelation knowledge of the Word you are declaring over your offering, you are speaking a *rhema* Word because the faith of God in you has been activated. Because you are speaking out of a state of oneness (union) with God, God's faith is yours. God watches over His Word to perform it. Remember, a *rhema* Word is the Word God quickens (ministers) to you, and God is duty bound to perform His Word. He is

Your harvest is a miracle from God.

the Lord of the harvest, and the performance of His Word causes your harvest to manifest. Your harvest is a miracle from God. [1 Corinthians 3: 6]

You must be sensitive in your spirit to be able to reap your harvest when it is your due season. The Word declares: "And let us not be weary in well doing: for in due season we shall reap, if we faint not." [Galatians 6: 9, KJV] God is a Spirit and He works in us through our spirits to bring His Word to pass in our lives. The same is true of the harvest of the seeds of faith we sow into the Kingdom of God. Harvest comes by divine revelation and instruction. Because most of us do not know this, we miss our harvests and try to blame God or the preacher for it. Your giving is to God and not man. Man is not your Source, God is. Refuse to continue to walk in ignorance and embrace the truth that you are learning in this book. Your days of ignorance on giving and receiving are over in the Name of Jesus. I will share two examples from the Word of God that will help us to understand how harvest comes.

Divine Revelation

Jacob, the father of the 12 tribes of Israel, served Laban for 14 years to marry his daughters, Leah and Rachel. He served seven years for Leah and another seven Rachel. He served Laban for another six years, taking care of his flock. Thus, Jacob served Laban for a total of 20 years and Laban changed his wages 10 times. God did not forget Jacob's vow.

> 20 Then Jacob made a vow, saying, If God will be with me and will keep me in this way that I go and will give me food to eat and clothing to wear,
>
> 21 So that I may come again to my father's house in peace, then the Lord shall be my God;
>
> 22 And this stone which I have set up as a pillar (monument) shall be God's house [a sacred place to me], and of all [the increase of possessions] that You give me I will give the tenth to You. [Genesis 28: 20-22, AMP]

The Lord gave Jacob a divine revelation in a dream of how he was going to reap his harvest. Jacob did not just make a vow to the Lord at Bethel, he also served his father-in-law as unto the Lord. His service was also a seed sown unto the Lord. God did not forget his seed and labor of love. In Genesis 31 we read,

> ⁴ So Jacob sent and called Rachel and Leah to the field to his flock,
>
> ⁵ And he said to them, I see how your father looks at me, that he is not [friendly] toward me as before; but the God of my father has been with me.
>
> ⁶ You know that I have served your father with all my might and power.
>
> ⁷ But your father has deceived me and changed my wages ten times, but God did not allow him to hurt me.
>
> ⁸ If he said, The speckled shall be your wages, then all the flock bore speckled; and if he said, The streaked shall be your hire, then all the flock bore streaked.
>
> ⁹ Thus God has taken away the flocks of your father and given them to me.
>
> ¹⁰ And I had a dream at the time the flock conceived. I looked up and saw that the rams which mated with the she-goats were streaked, speckled, and spotted.
>
> ¹¹ And the Angel of God said to me in the dream, Jacob. And I said, Here am I.
>
> ¹² And He said, Look up and see, all the rams which mate with the flock are streaked, speckled, and mottled; for I have seen all that Laban does to you.
>
> ¹³ I am the God of Bethel, where you anointed the pillar and where you vowed a vow to Me. Now arise, get out from this land and return to your native land.
>
> ¹⁴ And Rachel and Leah answered him, Is there any portion or inheritance for us in our father's house? [Genesis 31: 4-14, AMP]

In Chapter 30 of the book of Genesis we find Jacob using peeled white streaks in rods from poplar, almond, and plane trees as "faith extenders" or "point of contact" to release His faith unto God for the manifestation of his harvest.

37 But Jacob took fresh rods of poplar and almond and plane trees and peeled white streaks in them, exposing the white in the rods.

38 Then he set the rods which he had peeled in front of the flocks in the watering troughs where the flocks came to drink. And since they bred and conceived when they came to drink,

39 The flocks bred and conceived in sight of the rods and brought forth lambs and kids streaked, speckled, and spotted.

Beloved, the godly way to give is to expect to receive.

40 Jacob separated the lambs, and [as he had done with the peeled rods] he also set the faces of the flocks toward the streaked and all the dark in the [new] flock of Laban; and he put his own droves by themselves and did not let them breed with Laban's flock.

41 And whenever the stronger animals were breeding, Jacob laid the rods in the watering troughs before the eyes of the flock, that they might breed and conceive among the rods.

42 But when the sheep and goats were feeble, he omitted putting the rods there; so the feebler animals were Laban's and the stronger Jacob's.

43 Thus the man increased and became exceedingly rich, and had many sheep and goats, and maidservants, menservants, camels, and donkeys. [Genesis 30: 37-43, AMP]

Thus by acting upon the revelation from God, Jacob received his much needed harvest and restoration.

Divine Instruction
This involves receiving a divine instruction from the Lord in your spirit, and following through with obedience to take hold of your harvest. This is what Peter did when he needed money to pay the temple tax. He obeyed the Master's divine instruction on how to get money to pay his temple tax and that of the Master. Jesus instructed Peter in Matthew 17,

27 .....Go down to the sea and throw in a hook. Take the first fish that comes up, and when you open its mouth you will find there a shekel.

Take it and give it to them to pay the temple tax for Me and for yourself. [Matthew 17: 27, AMP]

Peter obeyed the divine instruction and got the coin from the fish's mouth to pay the temple tax. My friend, harvest comes by divine instruction and revelation. We have to be inside (i.e. spirit) minded to receive from God and reap our harvest. God gave His Son expecting a harvest of sons and daughters; emulating him means giving with the expectation of reaping a harvest. Beloved, the godly way to give is to expect to receive.

The Forest Is in the Tree

Sometimes you may be expecting a forest, but the first thing that comes up is a tree. Do not despise the tree because you were looking for a forest. Remember that every forest started from a tree. Do not despise small beginnings. "Your beginnings will seem humble, so prosperous will your future be." [Job 8: 7, NIV] In some cases, you may need to exercise your authority in the Name of Jesus to see your forest manifested. Do not quit. Stand your ground on the authority of the Word to see God's glory manifested in your behalf.

Make yourself the good soil for your harvest to be made manifest. Jesus described the good soil (the good heart) in parable of the sower in Matthew 13:

> 8 But a portion falls upon good ground, and *gives a return, some a hundred for one, some sixty, some thirty. [Matthew 13: 8, WEY]
>
> *Gives] or 'begins to give.' The verbs in the original are all in past tenses, but this one alone is in the imperfect, indicating prolonged action. [Footnote by Weymouth, WEY]

"Gives" in Matthew 13: 8 indicates a prolonged harvest. The imperfect tense in the verse indicates a continued action that is not finished. This is reinforced in the Kenneth Wuest translation of the New Testament of the same verse: "But still other seed fell upon the ground which was good, and **kept on producing fruit**, some on the one hand, one hundred percent, some on the other hand sixty percent, and still some other, thirty percent." [Matthew 13: 8, WUEST] The emphasis is on "kept on producing fruit." Jesus gave us the interpretation of the parable in Matthew 13: 23

> 23 As for what was sown on good soil, this is **he who hears the Word and grasps and comprehends it**; he indeed bears fruit and yields in one case a hundred times as much as was sown, in another sixty times as much, and in another thirty. [Matthew 13: 23, AMP; emphasis added]

> 23 But he who *has received the seed on good ground is he who hears and understands. Such hearers give a return, and yield one a hundred for one, another sixty, another thirty.") [Matthew 13: 23, WEY]

> *Has received seed] Namely, as land receives seed. Literally, 'has been sown,' as we talk not only of sowing wheat, but of sowing a field with wheat. [Footnote by Weymouth, WEY]

It is the heart of the one who gives to God that determines the size of the harvest.

When we sow (give) our seeds we pray/speak the Word over them. As we do, we hear the Word that we speak over our seeds. The Word that we speak over our seeds, programming them to produce harvests are also sown into our hearts (the soil of our hearts). When we receive the Word into our hearts it builds faith in us and enables us to expect our harvests. It is that expectation coupled with patience that enables us to reap our harvests. Love and faith that will not let go of your harvests coupled with expectation and patience are the ingredients that make your heart good soil that produce the desired harvests, or receive the desired harvests from the Lord. Jesus in His interpretation of the parable described the good soil thus:

> 15But that in the good ground, these are the ones who are of such nature that in noble and virtuous heart, having heard the Word are holding it fast and bearing fruit with patience. [Luke 8: 15, WUEST]

¹⁵ But as for that [seed] in the good soil, these are [the people] who, hearing the Word, hold it fast in a just (noble, virtuous) and worthy heart, and steadily bring forth fruit with patience. [Luke 8: 15, AMP]

Manifestation Is Your Responsibility
The responsibility for seeing the manifestation of the harvest is ours. In the parable of the sower in Matthew 13 and Luke 8, excerpts of which are quoted above, the sower sowed the Word and the soil is the heart. [Matthew 13: 19; Luke 8: 12; Mark 4: 14-15; AMP] It is the heart of the one who gives to God that determines the size of the harvest. God wants us to have optimum return on our giving.

Our Father is the Lord of the harvest, and it is His job to determine how your harvest will come and where it will come from.

For us to reap that complete series of returns on our giving we must hold fast the Word we used to sow our seed (give to God) in a noble, virtuous, and worthy heart. A noble, virtuous, and worthy heart is a heart of love. We must couple love with faith and hope (earnest expectation that our harvest will manifest). Everything we receive from the Lord is according to our faith. That is why the good soil in the parable of the sower yielded some hundred, some sixty, and some thirtyfold. The same seed (the Word) was sown in the hearts of the good soil that yielded different sizes of returns (harvests). To keep our faith working, we must be Word abiding. [John 15: 1-7, AMP]

The heart (of the good soil) that yields a hundredfold is the heart that is,
- in right standing with God,
- walking in love,
- fixed on the Word, meditating, declaring, fellowshipping with the Word, and doing what the Word (Lord) commands, and
- patiently and steadily expecting his harvest to manifest.

Such a person expects a complete series of return (a hundredfold), and refuses to limit God. People with this type of heart are constantly expecting miracles on a daily basis, knowing fully well that God puts no limits on blessing His children. They are constantly sowing the seed of the Word in their heart and sowing seeds of faith because they know fully well that the kingdom of God operates by the universal law of seedtime and harvest, sowing and reaping, giving and receiving. They are not weary in well doing because they know that in due season they will reap. [Galatians 6: 9] They hold unto the Word such as Luke 6: 38 with earnest expectation, being fully persuaded that God is able to fulfill His Word.

Harvest Most often Comes from Where You Least Expected

Do not try to figure out where your harvest will come from. Our Father is the Lord of the harvest, and it is His job to determine how your harvest will come and where it will come from. Your job is to believe and expect your harvest from the Lord.

God already knows what to do before you sow your seed and cry out to Him to bless you with a harvest. He already arranged your harvest before you took your step of faith to trust Him with your substance for Him to meet your need. He is our Source of supply and He has no limitation. The Bible abound with examples to buttress this point.

The Examples of Isaac and Elijah

Take the case of Isaac who sowed seed in famine and reaped a hundred-fold the same year. In the natural, it is incomprehensible to plant seeds in a land without rain and expect the seeds to grow, let alone have a bumper harvest. But that is exactly what God did for Isaac because he obeyed Him.

[1] And there was a famine in the land, other than the former famine that was in the days of Abraham. And Isaac went to Gerar, to Abimelech king of the Philistines.

² And the Lord appeared to him and said, Do not go down to Egypt; live in the land of which I will tell you.

³ Dwell temporarily in this land, and I will be with you and will favor you with blessings; for to you and to your descendants I will give all these lands, and I will perform the oath which I swore to Abraham your father.

⁴ And I will make your descendants to multiply as the stars of the heavens, and will give to your posterity all these lands (kingdoms); and by your Offspring shall all the nations of the earth be blessed, or by Him bless themselves.

⁵ For Abraham listened to and obeyed My voice and kept My charge, My commands, My statutes, and My laws.

⁶ So Isaac stayed in Gerar.

¹² Then Isaac sowed seed in that land and received in the same year a hundred times as much as he had planted, and the Lord favored him with blessings. [Genesis 26: 1-6, 12, AMP]

My friend, when you obey God you expect to be blessed. This is what God says in Isaiah 1: 19 (AMP): "If you are willing and obedient, you shall eat the good of the land." I like the Living Bible paraphrase of the verse even better: "If you will only let me help you, if you will only obey, then I will make you rich!"

What would you say of Elijah during the famine in Israel because of lack of rain for three and half years? I do not think that he would have thought that God would use ravens, unclean birds, to get food to him. He knew best to trust God. Because he did, he saw the famine and did not experience it.

² And the word of the Lord came to him, saying,

³ Go from here and turn east and hide yourself by the brook Cherith, east of the Jordan.

⁴ You shall drink of the brook, and I have commanded the ravens to feed you there.

⁵ So he did according to the word of the Lord; he went and dwelt by the brook Cherith, east of the Jordan.

⁶ And the ravens brought him bread and flesh in the morning and bread and flesh in the evening, and he drank of the brook. [1 Kings 17: 2-6, AMP]

Testimony
As a student in Britain, when I needed finances for my upkeep I trusted
God to meet my needs. I did not look to man, but to God. I did not
know where help would come from because that is the Lord's business,
and not mine. God used those I did not think could be of help to bless
me. Like the brethren in 2 Corinthians 8: 1-5, they blessed me out of
their need and God blessed them as they did.

One brother told me that when he was in need, I blessed him by sharing
whatever I had with him. He narrated that my act of kindness, which I
never gave thought to, left an imprint in his heart. He testified that each
time he went to the cash point, the Holy Spirit would minister to him to
get some money to me.

The fact is that I never told anybody that I had a need. God does not
forget our labor of love. Do not be weary in well doing because in due
season you will reap, if you faint not. [Galatians 6: 9, AMP]

Understanding It Is More Blessed to Give Than to Receive
Do not get religious on me by saying, I like to give but I do not like to
receive. It may be so, but it is ignorance; ignorance of the truth of God's
Word on the subject. You may say, What about the Scripture that says,
"It is more blessed to give than to receive." Paul was telling the leaders of
the churches into whose care he, by the Holy Spirit, entrusted the
members not to take advantage of them and milk them dry. The
Scripture states:

> 28 Take care and be on guard for yourselves and the whole flock over
> which the Holy Spirit has appointed you bishops and guardians, to
> shepherd (tend and feed and guide) the church of the Lord or of God
> which He obtained for Himself [buying it and saving it for Himself]
> with His own blood.
> 29 I know that after I am gone, ferocious wolves will get in among you,
> not sparing the flock;

³⁰ Even from among your own selves men will come to the front who, by saying perverse (distorted and corrupt) things, will endeavor to draw away the disciples after them [to their own party].

³¹ Therefore be always alert and on your guard, being mindful that for three years I never stopped night or day seriously to admonish and advise and exhort you one by one with tears.

³² And now [brethren], I commit you to God [I deposit you in His charge, entrusting you to His protection and care]. And I commend you to the Word of His grace [to the commands and counsels and promises of His unmerited favor]. It is able to build you up and to give you [your rightful] inheritance among all God's set-apart ones (those consecrated, purified, and transformed of soul).

³³ I coveted no man's silver or gold or [costly] garments.

³⁴ You yourselves know personally that these hands ministered to my own needs and those [of the persons] who were with me.

³⁵ In everything I have pointed out to you [by example] that, by working diligently in this manner, we ought to assist the weak, being mindful of the words of the Lord Jesus, how He Himself said, It is more blessed (makes one happier and more to be envied) to give than to receive. [Acts 20: 28-35; AMP]

Without understanding the context of the Scripture above, you can deny yourself of God's best for your life. Ignorance will cause you to use a Scripture that was supposed to help church leaders keep themselves in check to keep you from receiving the blessings God has for you. Paul did not tell church leaders not to receive. He was asking them to have a heathy balance and not yield to the carnality of fleshly thinking that their congregations were theirs to bleed dry.

When you give, you are actually making room for God to bless you with more. If you keep giving without receiving, you will eventually have nothing to give. Besides, you would be going against the law of seedtime and harvest, sowing and reaping, giving and reaping. God Who put the law in motion knows better than you. Cooperate with Him by cooperating with the spiritual law of giving and receiving. Do not let ignorance rob you of God's best for you. When you give, expect God to bless you in return. Here is what the richest and wisest man that ever lived said:

> [17] The merciful, kind, and generous man benefits himself [for his deeds return to bless him], but he who is cruel and callous [to the wants of others] brings on himself retribution. [Proverbs 11: 17, AMP]

If you are a good giver, you should be a good receiver. If God, the greatest Giver, Who gave us His Son, refused to receive us, His harvest from His Seed (His Son) that He sowed, where would you/we be. Stop and think about it.

God is altogether consistent. The Scripture you use to put yourself in bondage cannot go against Luke 6: 38 and 2 Corinthians 9.

> [38] For if you give, you will get! Your gift will return to you in full and overflowing measure, pressed down, shaken together to make room for more, and running over. Whatever measure you use to give—large or small—will be used to measure what is given back to you." [Luke 6: 38, TLB]

> [6] [Remember] this: he who sows sparingly and grudgingly will also reap sparingly and grudgingly, and he who sows generously [that blessings may come to someone] will also reap generously and with blessings.

> [7] Let each one [give] as he has made up his own mind and purposed in his heart, not reluctantly or sorrowfully or under compulsion, for God loves (He takes pleasure in, prizes above other things, and is unwilling to abandon or to do without) a cheerful (joyous, "prompt to do it") giver [whose heart is in his giving].

> [8] And God is able to make all grace (every favor and earthly blessing) come to you in abundance, so that you may always and under all circumstances and whatever the need be self-sufficient [possessing enough to require no aid or support and furnished in abundance for every good work and charitable donation].

[9] As it is written, He [the benevolent person] scatters abroad; He gives to the poor; His deeds of justice and goodness and kindness and benevolence will go on and endure forever!

[10] And [God] Who provides seed for the sower and bread for eating will also provide and multiply your [resources for] sowing and increase the fruits of your righteousness [which manifests itself in active goodness, kindness, and charity]. [2 Corinthians 9: 6-10, AMP]

Give with the revelation of the truth you are learning in this book, and expect God to bless you with a harvest. He will cause men to give to you, good measure, pressed down, shaken together to make room for more, and running over. You must be expectant to receive your harvest from the Lord after you have given to Him, or as you bless others because you are doing so as unto the Lord.

What Do You Do with Your Harvest?
The Scripture gives us the answer in Proverbs 3.

[9] Honor the Lord with your capital and sufficiency [from righteous labors] and with the firstfruits of all your income;
[10] So shall your storage places be filled with plenty, and your vats shall be overflowing with new wine. [Proverbs 3: 9-10, AMP]

We are to honor the Lord with the firstfruits of our harvest, tithes, and offerings in appreciation of the fact that He is the Lord of the harvest Who has caused the harvest to come to us in the first place. Take care of your needs and be a blessing. Just as a farmer keeps part of his crop for planting, invest some of your financial harvest. Ask the Holy Spirit to direct you.

Giving, but not Receiving
If you having been giving and not reaping your harvest, it is necessary to examine the Word to know what our Father says about your situation. During the time of Prophet Haggai the returning exiles of the children of

Israel experienced the same problem. They sowed seed and did not reap harvests. The Haggai received this response from the Lord for them.

> 2 Thus says the Lord of hosts: These people say, The time is not yet come that the Lord's house should be rebuilt [although Cyrus had ordered it done eighteen years before].
>
> 3 Then came the word of the Lord by Haggai the prophet, saying,
>
> 4 Is it time for you yourselves to dwell in your paneled houses while this house [of the Lord] lies in ruins?
>
> 5 Now therefore thus says the Lord of hosts: Consider your ways and set your mind on what has come to you.
>
> 6 You have sown much, but you have reaped little; you eat, but you do not have enough; you drink, but you do not have your fill; you clothe yourselves, but no one is warm; and he who earns wages has earned them to put them in a bag with holes in it.
>
> 7 Thus says the Lord of hosts: Consider your ways (your previous and present conduct) and how you have fared.
>
> 8 Go up to the hill country and bring lumber and rebuild [My] house, and I will take pleasure in it and I will be glorified, says the Lord [by accepting it as done for My glory and by displaying My glory in it].
>
> 9 You looked for much [harvest], and behold, it came to little; and even when you brought that home, I blew it away. Why? says the Lord of hosts. Because of My house, which lies waste while you yourselves run each man to his own house [eager to build and adorn it].
>
> 10 Therefore the heavens above you [for your sake] withhold the dew, and the earth withholds its produce.
>
> 11 And I have called for a drought upon the land and the hill country, upon the grain, the fresh wine, the oil, upon what the ground brings forth, upon men and cattle, and upon all the [wearisome] toil of [men's] hands. [Haggai 1: 2-11, AMP]

God made it clear to the Israelites that they did not put Him first in their lives. Because of that the heaven over them became brass. Whatever harvest they reaped, they lost. They lost it because He was not their priority. God does not want us to put Him second in our lives. He must be first in our lives and our all in all. You must first give of yourself to God before you sow your seed for God to give you a harvest. If you do not give of yourself to God, the seed you sow (or your giving) is not out of a heart of love.

Your giving must be out of a heart of love and obedience. If you give out of duty, and not out of a heart of love, you will not reap a harvest. Your giving should be done in faith, as a work of faith, and not as a religious duty. Seed given as a religious duty will not yield fruit. There is no life in it.

When the Israelites heard the Word of the Lord from Haggai, they decided to turn their hearts toward God. They chose to obey the Lord willing and completely.

Agape love is demonstrative.

If we love Jesus, we are to demonstrate it by obeying His commands (Word, precepts, teaching).

> 12 Then Zerubbabel son of Shealtiel and Joshua son of Jehozadak, the high priest, with all the remnant of the people [who had returned from captivity], listened to and obeyed the voice of the Lord their God [not vaguely or partly, but completely, according to] the words of Haggai the prophet, since the Lord their God had sent him, and the people [reverently] feared and [worshipfully] turned to the Lord. [Haggai 1: 12, AMP]

Search yourself, and if your heart is not where it should be with God as regards your giving, repent and line up with His Word and be blessed by the Lord. In addition, check to ensure that you are not scattering your seeds by sowing it in the wrong types of soil; that is, ministries that are unproductive. Listen to God and sow into the ministries that God wants you to sow into and bless those He says you should bless. Do not go outside of God's boundaries. Follow His instructions.

If you are yielded to God and giving because you love Him, but you are not reaping the harvests that are due to you from God, check your expectation level. Are you expecting your harvests, or are you giving without expecting to receive? If you were not giving with the expectation of reaping harvests or you gave but gave up expectation, begin to expect again. No employee works without expecting to be paid. You may say that is not seedtime and harvest. The work you do at your job is a seed you sow, expecting to be paid at the end of the pay period (i.e., harvest time). Remember, God never sowed His best Seed (Jesus) and failed to expect a harvest

> Our love toward God can only be demonstrated by the action it prompts. *Agape* love is demonstrative.

Obedience in Worshipful Giving

Agape love is best understood by the action it prompts. We cannot say that we love God and do not do what He says. If a man says he loves God and does not give his tithes and offerings to God, can he say that he really loves God? Some may say that the tithe (the whole tenth) is under the law. The tithe came into effect before the law. Abraham gave tithe unto Melchizedek.

> [18] Melchizedek king of Salem [later called Jerusalem] brought out bread and wine [for their nourishment]; he was the priest of God Most High,
> [19] And he blessed him and said, Blessed (favored with blessings, made blissful, joyful) be Abram by God Most High, Possessor and Maker of heaven and earth,
> [20] And blessed, praised, and glorified be God Most High, Who has given your foes into your hand! And [Abram] gave him a tenth (*tithe*) of all [he had taken]. [Genesis 14: 18-20, AMP; emphasis mine]

Jesus said that we ought to give of our tithes and be blessing to others, and not do one and leave the other undone.

> [42] You Pharisees are in for trouble! You give God a tenth of the spices from your gardens, such as mint and rue. But you cheat people, and you don't love God. You should be fair and kind to others and still give a tenth to God. [Luke 11: 42, CEV]

To love God is to obey Him.

¹⁵ If you [really] love Me, you will keep (obey) My commands.

¹⁶ And I will ask the Father, and He will give you another Comforter (Counselor, Helper, Intercessor, Advocate, Strengthener, and Standby), that He may remain with you forever—

¹⁷ The Spirit of Truth, Whom the world cannot receive (welcome, take to its heart), because it does not see Him or know and recognize Him. But you know and recognize Him, for He lives with you [constantly] and will be in you.

²¹ The person who has My commands and keeps them is the one who [really] loves Me; and whoever [really] loves Me will be loved by My Father, and I [too] will love him and will show (reveal, manifest) Myself to him. [I will let Myself be clearly seen by him and make Myself real to him.]

²³ Jesus answered, If a person [really] loves Me, he will keep My word [obey My teaching]; and My Father will love him, and We will come to him and make Our home (abode, special dwelling place) with him.

²⁴ Anyone who does not [really] love Me does not observe and obey My teaching. And the teaching which you hear and heed is not Mine, but [comes] from the Father Who sent Me. [John 14: 15-17, 21, 23, 24, AMP]

Jesus explained to us in verses 21 to 23 of John 14 that if we say we love Him and do not do His Word (His commandments), we do not really love him. Our love toward God can only be demonstrated by the action it prompts. *Agape* love is demonstrative. In addition, the Lord Jesus said in John 14: 16-17 that He would send us the Comforter, the Holy Spirit, to in-dwell us. The Holy Spirit, our Helper, is there to help us to do what the Father asks of us. In John 14: 15 Jesus is saying, in essence, if you really love Me, you will demonstrate it by obeying My commands (Word, precepts, teaching).

Giving – A Demonstration of Our Love

Giving of our tithes and offering therefore is a demonstration of our love to God, and not a duty. You cannot give willingly to God unless you have first given of yourself to Him. Jesus has to be the Lord of your life and not just your Savior. We are commanded to make Jesus the Lord of our lives. [Romans 10: 8-11, AMP] The Corinthian church understood this. [2 Corinthians 8: 1-5, AMP] They first gave of themselves to the Lord and then gave willingly to the service of the Lord.

> [1] We want to tell you further, brethren, about the grace (the favor and spiritual blessing) of God which has been evident in the churches of Macedonia [arousing in them the desire to give alms];
>
> [2] For in the midst of an ordeal of severe tribulation, their abundance of joy and their depth of poverty [together] have overflowed in wealth of lavish generosity on their part.
>
> [3] For, as I can bear witness, [they gave] according to their ability, yes, and beyond their ability; and [they did it] voluntarily,
>
> [4] Begging us most insistently for the favor and the fellowship of contributing in this ministration for [the relief and support of] the saints [in Jerusalem].
>
> [5] Nor [was this gift of theirs merely the contribution] that we expected, but **first they gave themselves to the Lord** and to us [as His agents] by the will of God [entirely disregarding their personal interests, they gave as much as they possibly could, having put themselves at our disposal to be directed by the will of God]. [2 Corinthians 8: 1-5, AMP; emphasis added]

It was because they first gave themselves to the Lord that the grace of giving (the giving anointing) came upon them. They were able to give to meet the needs of the saints in Jerusalem over and beyond what could be expected of them. They gave willingly and joyfully out of their need. Paul declared, "Their abundance of joy and their depth of poverty [together] overflowed in wealth of lavish generosity on their part." [2 Corinthians 8: 2, AMP] Meditate upon this. They gave in faith out of a heart of love.

Thus, we can understand why the Holy Spirit declares in 2 Corinthians 9:

> [6] [Remember] this: he who sows sparingly and grudgingly will also reap sparingly and grudgingly, and he who sows generously [that blessings may come to someone] will also reap generously and with blessings.

[7] Let each one [give] as he has made up his own mind and purposed in his heart, not reluctantly or sorrowfully or under compulsion, for God loves (He takes pleasure in, prizes above other things, and is unwilling to abandon or to do without) a cheerful (joyous, "prompt to do it") giver [whose heart is in his giving].

[8] And God is able to make all grace (every favor and earthly blessing) come to you in abundance, so that you may always and under all circumstances and whatever the need be self-sufficient [possessing enough to require no aid or support and furnished in abundance for every good work and charitable donation].

[9] As it is written, He [the benevolent person] scatters abroad; He gives to the poor; His deeds of justice and goodness and kindness and benevolence will go on and endure forever!

[10] And [God] Who provides seed for the sower and bread for eating will also provide and multiply your [resources for] sowing and increase the fruits of your righteousness [which manifests itself in active goodness, kindness, and charity].

[11] Thus you will be enriched in all things and in every way, so that you can be generous, and [your generosity as it is] administered by us will bring forth thanksgiving to God. [2 Corinthians 9: 6-11, AMP]

Our giving must be a demonstration of our love towards God. For it to be a sweet fragrance to God, we must first, of our own volition give ourselves to Him. When we do, we can give willingly, promptly, and joyfully. As we do, God will reward us mightily and in nothing will we lack. He will make sure that we have more than enough to meet our needs and to be a blessing.

Give with Revelation

Do not give without having a revelation of the fact that God the Father wants you blessed. God is not interested in having your money. He is interested in multiplying it back to you. He does not add; He multiplies exponentially. Be sure to speak (pray) the Word over your tithe and your offering. The Word of God brings about the multiplication of your seed for a bountiful harvest. When you obey God with your finance, you will find it easy to obey Him in other areas of your life. Why? Your money represents you. Obey God and expect Him to bless you in return. If we love God because He first loved us, then we demonstrate our love toward Him by obeying Him in all things, and that includes our finances too. There is a blessing in giving.

Blessing in Giving

Every time God speaks of giving in the Bible He always attaches a blessing to it. Always remember that God is not going to ask you to give what He has not already given to you. Your giving must be done in *Agape* love. This is a precondition for receiving a harvest of blessing that God has for you. For instance, you are probably familiar with Luke 6: 38:

> 38 Give, and you will receive. Your gift will return to you in full—pressed down, shaken together to make room for more, running over, and poured into your lap. The amount you give will determine the amount you get back. [Luke 6: 38, NLT]

This is an often-quoted passage when giving our offerings to God. However, the prerequisite for Luke 6: 38 is Luke 6:37:

> 37 Judge not [neither pronouncing judgment nor subjecting to censure], and you will not be judged; do not condemn and pronounce guilty, and you will not be condemned and pronounced guilty; acquit and forgive and release (give up resentment, let it drop), and you will be acquitted and forgiven and released. [Luke 6: 37, AMP]

The Lord is making us to understand that operating in *Agape* love is crucial to the Father receiving our offering. If our offering is not received, we cannot get the expected harvest of multiplied seed sown and the fruits of righteousness from Him. Jesus instructed us to ensure that we have nothing against anyone before we present our offering to God:

> 23 So if when you are offering your gift at the altar you there remember that your brother has any [grievance] against you,
> 24 Leave your gift at the altar and go. First make peace with your brother, and then come back and present your gift. [Matthew 5: 22-24, AMP]

You cannot harbor unforgiveness, resentment, get into strife, entertain offense, break promises and expect your gift to be received by God because they make your gift to have some blemish. [Matthew 5: 22-26, Malachi 2: 10; Mark 11: 25-26; Psalm 15: 4, AMP] Your gift must be without blemish to be acceptable to God. You must give cheerfully and without grudge.

Tithe

The word "tithe" is first mentioned in the Bible in Genesis 14. Abraham went to war against Chedorlaomer and his confederate kings to get back Lot and his family, and God gave him a mighty victory over those kings. Consequently, he took a great spoil. On his return from battle Melchizedek, priest of God Most High met him, had communion with him, and blessed him.

> [18] Melchizedek king of Salem [later called Jerusalem] brought out bread and wine [for their nourishment]; he was the priest of God Most High,
> [19] And he blessed him and said, Blessed (favored with blessings, made blissful, joyful) be Abram by God Most High, Possessor and Maker of heaven and earth,
> [20] And blessed, praised, and glorified be God Most High, Who has given your foes into your hand! And [Abram] gave him a tenth of all [he had taken]. [Genesis 14: 18-20, AMP]

Melchizedek brought out bread and wine, the elements of communion. The bread is a type of the body of Jesus and wine is a type for the blood of Jesus. Melchizedek came to meet Abram just as Jesus came from heaven to meet us. He gave His body and blood for us by laying down His life at Calvary Cross. Melchizedek blessed Abram first. In response to the blessing that Abram received from Melchizedek, Abram gave him a tenth (tithe) of all the spoil he had taken. I believe Abram gave tithe to the Lord through Melchizedek in appreciation for the great victory and deliverance that the Lord wrought for him. Similarly, Jesus blessed us with His body and blood enabling us to have eternal life, be healed, protected, and prospered. We, like Abram, are to give tithes of all to the Lord in response to the blessing He has poured on us.

Abraham gave tithe to the Lord before the law. This is an indication that we need to give tithes to the Lord in appreciation for His goodness in our lives, for prospering us, and giving us power to get wealth. You do not pay your tithe to God, but give it to Him out of a willing and appreciative heart. It is not a debt you owe, but a seed you sow. You cannot repay God for your salvation. It is priceless. Tithes and offerings are different in God's eyes.

In Malachi 3: 8-12 God makes a distinction between tithes and offerings and the blessings that come with the giving of our tithes to Him.

> 8 Will a man rob or defraud God? Yet you rob and defraud Me. But you say, In what way do we rob or defraud You? [You have withheld your] tithes and offerings.
> 9 You are cursed with the curse, for you are robbing Me, even this whole nation.
> 10 Bring all the tithes (the whole tenth of your income) into the storehouse, that there may be food in My house, and prove Me now by it, says the Lord of hosts, if I will not open the windows of heaven for you and pour you out a blessing, that there shall not be room enough to receive it. [Malachi 3: 8-10, AMP]

> 11 "And I will rebuke the devourer for your sakes, So that he will not destroy the fruit of your ground, Nor shall the vine fail to bear fruit for you in the field," Says the Lord of hosts;
> 12 "And all nations will call you blessed, For you will be a delightful land," Says the Lord of hosts. [Malachi 3: 11-12, NKJV)

The tithe and the offering must be given in righteousness. [Malachi 3: 3, AMP] The implication is that we should give our tithes and offerings in faith with love and hope – the expectation of God blessing us in return for our obedience. Whatever is not done out of faith is sin. [Romans 14: 23, AMP] When you withhold the tithe that belongs to the Lord from Him, you withhold God's blessings from your life. To withhold tithes and offerings is to bring a curse upon yourself, and you do not want to do so either willingly or by ignorance.

It is worth noting that God does not curse you, but you are the one who chooses to walk yourself into the curse which is already operating out there in the world. If there is a torrential downpour and you are under an umbrella, you are protected. If you step outside the covering of an umbrella and refuse to be covered, you will be drenched by the rain. An example of walking into the curse is what happened to the children of Israel in the wilderness.

Balak hired Balaam to curse Israel. Balaam told Balak that he could not curse the Israel that God had blessed. However, he advised Balak on how to lure the Israelites to bring the curse upon themselves by letting the women in his kingdom (Moabite women) lure Israeli men into fornication. [Numbers 25: 1, Revelation 2: 14, NKJV]. The components of the curse are described in Deuteronomy 28: 15 – 68. One of them is that the heaven over a person under the curse is brass, making the person's labor to be unproductive.

When Adam and his wife ate of the fruit of the tree of knowledge of good and evil, a type of tithe, which the Lord reserved for Himself in the Garden of Eden, humanity was cursed. [Genesis 3: 1-14, NIV] Another example of someone coming under God's judgment and bringing a whole nation under that judgment for taking the Lord's tithe was Achan. [Joshua 7: 11-26, AMP] Achan defied the Lord's instruction on things that were to be devoted to the Lord and the ones that were to be destroyed (accursed things) during the capture of Jericho. He coveted those things and took them for himself. The Israelites were to destroy everything in Jericho apart from articles of gold, silver, and bronze which were to be devoted to the Lord.

> [18] But you, keep yourselves from the accursed and devoted things, lest when you have devoted it [to destruction], you take of the accursed thing, and so make the camp of Israel accursed and trouble it.

[19] But all the silver and gold and vessels of bronze and iron are consecrated to the Lord; they shall come into the treasury of the Lord. [Joshua 6: 18-19, AMP]

That which were to be devoted to the Lord were the Lord's tithe. Because Achan coveted the Lord's tithe and kept them for himself, the whole nation suffered for his covetousness and disobedience. Israel lost 36 men to a small army of Ai, and was thoroughly discouraged. The consequence of coveting the Lord's tithe was severe. The Lord said to Joshua, Israel's leader,

[11] Israel has sinned; they have transgressed My covenant which I commanded them. They have taken some of the things devoted [for destruction]; they have stolen, and lied, and put them among their own baggage.
[12] That is why the Israelites could not stand before their enemies, but fled before them; they are accursed and have become devoted [for destruction]. I will cease to be with you unless you destroy the accursed [devoted] things among you. [Joshua 7: 11-12, AMP]

The tithe is the Lord's and not yours. It is holy unto the Lord. [Leviticus 27: 30, AMP] It is one-tenth of your gross income. [Malachi 3: 10, AMP] If you withheld the Lord's tithe and wanted to give later (redeem it), you need to add a 20% interest on it. See Leviticus 27: 27. Do not feel uncomfortable about this. That is your flesh at work. God is saying, Can you trust me with your substance so that I can bless you beyond your imagination? [Malachi 3: 10, AMP] "Bring the whole tithe into the storehouse, so that there may be food in My house, and test Me now in this," says the LORD of hosts, "if I will not open for you the windows of heaven and pour out for you a blessing until it overflows." [Malachi 3: 10, AMP]

In addition, God said that He would stop Satan in his tracks and He will not touch the work of your hands and your harvest. [Malachi 3: 11, AMP] If you do not give of the Lord's tithe to the Lord, the devil will have a free reign over your affairs and your family. Remember Achan! God wants to bless us to such an extent that the blessing overflows.

Therefore, we must understand the blessing that God has for us as we tithe. If it is just financial miracles, then we will continue to have room for more. I believe God is serious when He says He wants to bless us to the point where we do not have room for the blessing.

The Blessing of Tithing

To understand the blessing, we must understand when God says to us in Deuteronomy 8,

> 18 But you shall [earnestly] remember the Lord your God, for it is He Who gives you power to get wealth, that He may establish His covenant which He swore to your fathers, as it is this day. [Deuteronomy 8: 18, AMP]

> 18 But remember the Lord your God, for it is he who gives you the ability to produce wealth, and so confirms his covenant, which he swore to your ancestors, as it is today. [Deuteronomy 8: 18, NIV]

The word "power" used in KJV, AMP and other translations of the Bible means ability. Ability is active power, or power to perform. It also means riches, wealth, substance which gives us the power or the wherewithal to be a blessing. God wants you to have the power to be a blessing to others and to give to the spreading of the Gospel. How can you be blessed beyond measure? A closer look at the word ability gives us the answer. Some synonyms of the word ability are ideas, innovations, adroitness, concepts, understanding, talent, wittiness, creativity, inventiveness, giftedness, competency, acumen, and ingeniousness.

God wants to endow you with ideas, concepts, witty inventions, innovations, and creative potentials, etc. which when put to work will generate generational wealth. He wants to prosper us in everything we lay our hands to do beyond our wildest imagination. The word "blessing" in Malachi 3: 10 is from the Hebrew word *berakah* which means blessing, gift, generous, peace (which of course includes prosperity, and gift, among other meanings).

Thus, you can appreciate God giving you a gift such as a talent, a creative idea or concept, a witty invention, or an innovation which, when put to work can create wealth not just for you, but for others that God sends your way or brings into your life. This is the blessing that He wants to convey to those who are diligent in tithing. Linking Deuteronomy 8: 18 with Malachi 3: 10 enables us to understand the harvest we are to expect from the giving of our tithes to the Lord.

Ability is released through the miracle working power of God. Ability to get the blessing or wealth is released through the giving of your tithes and offerings, and the capacity to receive the harvest (the blessing) work together. You must release your faith in the giving of your tithes and offerings, and release your faith to receive at the same time. God determines the how, the when, and the nature of the harvest.

Can God give you financial miracles because you are a tither? Definitely, yes. However, we should not limit God. When you limit Him, you limit the blessing(s) you receive from Him. God is limitless, but you can limit Him in your life. Be open to receive all the blessing He has for you from your tithing because He has no limits to it. Yes, receive the financial miracles and the ideas, concepts, inventions, innovations, etc. that will lead to a lifetime of blessing and generational wealth creation. Not only will He bless you, He said that He would rebuke the devourer, Satan, for your sake. [Malachi 3: 11]

The devourer goes around distributing loss – loss of health (sickness and disease), loss of income or revenue (job or business loss), miscarriage, etc. Moffatt translation of Malachi 3: 11 reads, "I will stop the locust from spoiling your crops, and your vines shall not miscarry (the Lord of host declares)." When combined with Psalm 128: 3 that states, "Your wife shall be like a fruitful vine in the innermost parts of your house; your children shall be like olive plants round about your table;" it can easily be inferred that an end to a tither's wife having miscarriage is what God has promised His tithing children. In addition, the devil will not destroy the harvest of your labor. All people will call you blessed, and you and your family become a people of delight.

Remind God of His Word and resist the devourer and he will not steal from you. God instituted tithing for our benefit and to remind us to put Him first in our lives. The Living Bible paraphrase puts this succinctly, "The purpose of tithing is to put God first in our lives." [Deuteronomy 14: 22, TLB] When you worship God with your tithe, He will bless every work of your hands. "…The Lord your God may bless you in all the work of your hands that you do." [Deuteronomy 14: 29b, AMP]

> Give your tithes (and offerings) to ministries/ churches that exist to minister and not those that minister to exist.

The Floodgates

God said to prove (test) Him by giving Him our tithes if He will not open the windows (floodgates, sluices) of heaven and "pour out so much blessing that there will not be room enough to store it." [Malachi 3: 10, NIV] When the floodgates are open, you cannot stop the water in a dam from pouring out. Therefore, it cannot be said that the tithe opens the floodgates and offering cause the blessing to pour forth. The Hebrew word *aruba* translated windows (floodgates, sluices) in Malachi 3: 10 is the same word translated windows in Genesis 7: 11 where God describes the flooding of the earth during Noah's time: "…. The same day were all the fountains of the great deep broken up, and the windows of heaven were opened." When heaven's windows were opened, the downpour was unstoppable. That is what He is describing to us in Malachi 3: 10. Give your tithe and offering in love and with faith to Jesus to present to the Father for Him to open the windows of heaven and flood you with the blessing. You prove God by your obedience in giving your tithe (and offering) to Him, and He in turn will bless your beyond measure.

Jesus Receives Our Tithes (and Offerings)

Jesus is our High Priest and we present our tithes and offerings to Him. Thus, you cannot have the mistaken notion that you gave your tithe to your pastor. If you do, how do you expect a blessing from God. Yes, we give our tithes and offerings through churches and ministries to the Lord. He is the Lord of the harvest and not the pastor or the ministry you support. Jesus, our High Priest, is the One from Whom we should seek guidance on where to give our tithes (and offerings).

You should give your tithes (and offerings) to the place (church or ministry) that honors the LORD. Do not give your tithe (or offering) to a dead church or ministry. A dead church or ministry is where God's name is not honored – people are not saved into the kingdom, no healing, and captives are not set free. Give your tithes (and offerings) to ministries/churches that exist to minister and are a blessing to you, and not those that minister to exist. In presenting your tithe to the Lord, pattern your prayer after the prayer in Deuteronomy 26: 13–15 and Malachi 3: 10–12. An example of this is at the end of this book for your convenience.

Tithing Works

When I came to the Lord years ago in Nigeria, the country was going through a belt-tightening period of austerity with a high rate of inflation from the implementation of a structural adjustment program recommended by the International Monetary Fund. I said to myself, God's Word must contain some teaching on prosperity. Then I read Kenneth E. Hagin's booklet on *Obedience in Finances* in which he taught about tithing and giving. I checked it out in the Bible and decided to implement what I learnt on tithing. My salary that could only last for two weeks was able to last for a whole month and I had money left over. I said, This program that God put in place for us works. Since then I have not looked back.

If you are not a tither, I challenge you to take God at His Word; prove Him by your obedience and see if He will not surprise you with blessings. Thus, God has the following blessings for you when you give our tithes to Him:

- He will bless all the work of your hands;

- He will give you abundant blessing that you cannot contain;

- He rebukes the devourer on your behalf so that he does not steal/destroy your harvests (the fruits of our labor) and cause miscarriage in your family;

- People will call you blessed (prosperous) because of what God has done in your life; and

- You become a person of delight.

To surmise, we give our tithes to our Father through Jesus our High Priest in appreciation for His goodness in our lives. They are seeds we sow and not debts we owe. Jesus paid it all for us with His blood at Calvary's Cross. Because we sow out of love, we do not do it as a duty. We give in appreciation with a thankful heart, acknowledging like Abraham in Genesis 14: 18-20 that God our Father is:

- the Most High God. There is no one greater or stronger than Him, and to Him alone we bow and worship.

- The Possessor of heaven and earth. "The earth is the Lord's, and the fullness of it, the world, and those who dwell in it." [Psalm 24:1, AMP] "For every beast of the forest is Mine, and the cattle on a thousand hills. I know every bird of the mountains, and everything that moves in the field is Mine." [Psalm 50: 10, AMP] From Him we receive and to Him we give. He is our Source.

- our Protector and Deliverer Who delivers us from our enemies.

- the One Who blesses us. He is the Source of all our blessings. The blessing of tithing is a combination of what is described in Genesis 14: 19-20 and Malachi 3: 10-11.

The tithe is the whole tenth of what God has blessed us with. Ten means a great deal more, and indefinitely. [Webster 1828] Thus, tithing is to enable God pour out a blessing into your life that is a great deal more, and an increase that is indefinite. We are to tithe consistently, promptly, joyfully with a thankful heart, and expect God to pour into our lives a great deal more blessing – ideas, concepts, inventions, innovations, and strategies to implement them - that is indefinite or generational. Do not just worship the Lord with your tithes, worship Him also with your offerings.

8. OFFERINGS – OUR WORSHIP

Honor the Lord with your capital and sufficiency [from righteous labors] and with the firstfruits of all your income; so shall your storage places be filled with plenty, and your vats shall be overflowing with new wine. [Proverbs 3: 9-10, AMP]

Our offerings are a worship unto God. It should not be something done on the side, but taken seriously as a form of worship. God takes our worshipping Him with our substance seriously. When He asked Abraham to offer Isaac, his only (begotten) son, He was asking Abraham to give Him his very best. [Genesis 22: 2] In return, God gave us His only begotten Son (His Seed) as a harvest of Abraham's obedience because of His covenant with Abraham was part of the redemption plan. Our offerings, just like our tithes, trigger the release of God's blessings into our lives. God did not just say give tithes or offerings only, He asks us to give both tithes and offerings. Thus, it is useful for us to study some of the offerings in the Bible.

Many offerings are described in the Bible. We will not discuss all of them, but we will group them into two categories – firstfruits and other offerings (thanksgiving offering, outreach (missionary) offering, benevolence offering, giving to a true prophet of God, giving to your Word teacher and pastor, freewill offering, etc.). The intent is to gain some insight into God's perspective on them, and put the revelation we receive to work for our benefit.

Firstfruits

Firstfruits offering should not be confused with the tithe. The Hebrew word for tithe in the Bible is *ma'aser* (tithes), and *reshith* for firstfruits. I believe that God did not want us to confuse the two. Tithe is not firstfruits, and firstfruits is not tithe. *Reshith* means beginning, choice, choicest, finest, first, first-fruits, or foremost. Firstfruits is the first proceeds of anything. It is the first or earliest of anything. [Webster 1828]

Reason for Firstfruits

Firstfruits offering is given in recognition of our deliverance from Satan's control. [Exodus 13: 11 – 16] It was also an offering commanded by God as a recognition of the fact that the earth and all its products are His gifts to man. The offering was an expression of submission and thankfulness of the Israelites to God for delivering them from Egypt and blessing them with the harvest for their labor. [Exodus 34: 26, Deuteronomy 26: 1-11; Nehemiah 10: 35, AMP] It was to be the best (finest) of their first harvest and not the whole harvest. This is made clear to us in Exodus 34 which I am quoting from two translations for clarity:

> [26a] The first of the firstfruits of your ground you shall bring to the house of the Lord your God [Exodus 34: 26a, AMP]

> [26a] "As you harvest your crops, bring the very best of the first harvest to the house of the LORD your God. [Exodus 34: 26a, NLT]

God left this to man to decide how much he is to give. The implication is that the giver must give out of a heart that is tender towards God and the very best of the first harvest. Even though He left you to decide, He will instruct you on what to give. You have a choice to obey Him or do it your way. The first firstfruits offering was given by Abel in obedience to divine instruction. We gain this insight by examining Hebrews 11: 4 and Genesis 4: 3-4 closely.

> [4] [Prompted, actuated] by faith Abel brought God a better and more acceptable sacrifice than Cain, because of which it was testified of him that he was righteous [that he was upright and in right standing with God], and God bore witness by accepting and acknowledging his gifts.

And though he died, yet [through the incident] he is still speaking. [Hebrews 11: 4, AMP]

³ And in the course of time Cain brought to the Lord an offering of the fruit of the ground.
⁴ And Abel brought of the firstborn of his flock and of the fat portions. And the Lord had respect and regard for Abel and for his offering,
⁵ But for Cain and his offering He had no respect or regard. So Cain was exceedingly angry and indignant, and he looked sad and depressed. [Genesis 4: 3-5, AMP]

³ And it cometh to pass at the end of days that Cain bringeth from the fruit of the ground a present to Jehovah;
⁴ and Abel, he hath brought, he also, from the female firstlings of his flock, even from their fat ones; and Jehovah looketh unto Abel and unto his present. [Genesis 4: 3-4, YLT]

Since faith is the *rhema* Word of God of things hoped for, the evidence of things not seen, Abel responded to the prompting, divine instruction, from God, but Cain did not respond. It is not that Cain delayed giving his offering, because the phrase "in the course of time" which means at the end of days is used for both Cain and Abel because of the conjunction "and" joining the two verses. Abel gave the firstlings (firstborns) of his flock, the very best of his flock, even from the fat ones to God. Obviously Cain did not give his firstfruits accordingly to divine instruction, and God does not stomach disobedience. God warned Cain when He saw him angry because his sacrifice was not accepted, but Cain refused to heed the Lord's warning.

⁶ And the Lord said to Cain, "Why are you so angry? And why do you look annoyed?
⁷ If you do well [believing Me and doing what is acceptable and pleasing to Me], will you not be accepted? And if you do not do well [but ignore My instruction], sin crouches at your door; its desire is for you [to overpower you], but you must master it." [Genesis 4: 6-7, AMP]

Cain did not do well because he did not believe God, ignored His instruction, and, therefore, did not offer a firstfruits offering acceptable to

God. The Scripture did not say that God rejected Cain's offering because it was the fruit of the ground. Cain simply did not give as God instructed Him to give. If his offering was rejected because it was grain offering, how can you explain God accepting Israel's firstfruits offering of the produce of the soil in Deuteronomy 26: 2 and under King Hezekiah in 2 Chronicles 31: 5.

You do not give God your best and He turns a blind eye. When you give Him your firstfruits, He gives you a double portion blessing, the blessing of the firstborn, and He blesses you above all others. When you put God first, He puts you first. God claimed Israel as His firstborn, and blessed her above all other nations. [Exodus 4: 22; Jeremiah 31: 9] We can infer from this that Cain was jealous that Abel would probably enjoy the firstborn blessing which should have been his. Do not be jealous of your brother's blessing; trust God with your firstfruits and see Him bless you with a double portion blessing above all others

Does firstfruits apply to us today? I believe it does. The reason for the firstfruits offering is clarified in Deuteronomy 26:

> [1] When you have entered the land the Lord your God is giving you as an inheritance and have taken possession of it and settled in it,
> [2] take some of the firstfruits of all that you produce from the soil of the land the Lord your God is giving you and put them in a basket. Then go to the place the Lord your God will choose as a dwelling for his Name
> [3] and say to the priest in office at the time, "I declare today to the Lord your God that I have come to the land the Lord swore to our ancestors to give us."
> [4] The priest shall take the basket from your hands and set it down in front of the altar of the Lord your God.
> [5] Then you shall declare before the Lord your God: "My father was a wandering Aramean, and he went down into Egypt with a few people and lived there and became a great nation, powerful and numerous.

⁶ But the Egyptians mistreated us and made us suffer, subjecting us to harsh labor.

⁷ Then we cried out to the Lord, the God of our ancestors, and the Lord heard our voice and saw our misery, toil and oppression.

⁸ So the Lord brought us out of Egypt with a mighty hand and an outstretched arm, with great terror and with signs and wonders.

⁹ He brought us to this place and gave us this land, a land flowing with milk and honey;

¹⁰ and now I bring the firstfruits of the soil that you, Lord, have given me." Place the basket before the Lord your God and bow down before him.

¹¹ Then you and the Levites and the foreigners residing among you shall rejoice in all the good things the Lord your God has given to you and your household. [Deuteronomy 26: 1-11, NIV]

> Abundance is what God has for us when we give tithes and firstfruits and other types of offering to Him.

If the Israelites were to give the firstfruits in recognition of the deliverance God wrought for them in Egypt, are we to be less thankful to God for delivering us from eternal damnation in hell? I believe we should even be more thankful. Similar to the Israelites who were delivered from slavery in Egypt into the Promised Land, we have been delivered from the marketplace of slavery to the devil into the Kingdom of God. Just as He brought them "out of Egypt with a mighty hand and an outstretched arm, with great terror and with signs and wonders," (Deuteronomy 26: 8, NIV) so did He deliver us through Christ Jesus with a demonstration of His awesome power when He raised Christ up from the dead. [Ephesians 1: 19-20, AMP]

The firstfruits offering is given to us for our instruction and encouragement that we should trust God with the best of what He has blessed us, and receive abundant harvest from Him. "For whatever was thus written in former days was written for our instruction, that by [our steadfast and patient] endurance and the encouragement [drawn] from the Scriptures we might hold fast to and cherish hope." [Romans 15: 4, AMP] "If the part of the dough offered as firstfruits is holy, then the whole batch is holy..." [Romans 11: 16a, NIV] We should give our firstfruits offering with joy and thankfulness, patterning our prayer to present the offering after the prayer in Deuteronomy 26: 5–10. See the end of the book for an example of a prayer for offering your firstsfruits. Abundance is what God has for us when we give tithes and firstfruits and other types of offering to Him.

> Selfishness will keep you broke.

Examples of Firstfruits Blessing

We find an example of God blessing the people of Israel and Judah when they heeded king Hezekiah's command to bring their firstfruits and tithes to the Lord:

[4] He commanded the people living in Jerusalem to give the portion due the priests and Levites, that they might [be free to] give themselves to the Law of the Lord.

[5] As soon as the command went abroad, the Israelites gave in abundance the firstfruits of grain, vintage fruit, oil, honey, and of all the produce of the field; and they brought in abundantly the tithe of everything.

[6] The people of Israel and Judah who lived in Judah's cities also brought the tithe of cattle and sheep and of the dedicated things which were consecrated to the Lord their God, and they laid them in heaps.

[7] In the third month [at the end of wheat harvest] they began to lay the foundation or beginning of the heaps and finished them in the seventh month.

[8] When Hezekiah and the princes came and saw the heaps, they blessed the Lord and His people Israel.

[9] Then Hezekiah questioned the priests and Levites about the heaps.

[10] Azariah the high priest, of the house of Zadok, answered him, Since the people began to bring the offerings into the Lord's house, we have

eaten and have plenty left, for the Lord has blessed His people, and what is left is this great store. [2 Chronicles 31: 4-10, AMP]

When the king went to the house of the Lord and saw the heaps from the tithes and firstfruits, he questioned the priests about what he saw. [2 Chronicles 31: 9, AMP] The high priest told the king that the Lord blessed the people abundantly so that they could give to the work of the Lord. This same blessing is for us today. We need to heed God's advice: "Honor the Lord with your capital and sufficiency [from righteous labors] and with the firstfruits (*reshith* [Hebrew for firstfruits] and not *ma'aser* [Hebrew for tithes]) of all your income; so shall your storage places be filled with plenty, and your vats shall be overflowing with new wine." [Proverbs 3: 9-10, AMP; text in brackets added for clarity] Go for it. God keeps His Word. Your blessing is yours and not mine. There is enough for all of us. God does not run short. Selfishness will keep you broke.

Thanksgiving Offering

God is in the delivering business. It is important that when we cry out to God for deliverance and He does, we should return thanks to Him. Noah gave a thanksgiving offering to the Lord for delivering him and his family from the flood that destroyed the earth as it is written in Genesis 8: 20 (AMP), "And Noah built an altar to the Lord and took of every clean [four-footed] animal and of every clean fowl or bird and offered burnt offerings on the altar." As soon as the Lord received the thanksgiving offering offered by Noah, He spoke a blessing on Noah.

> 21 When the Lord smelled the pleasing odor [a scent of satisfaction to His heart], the Lord said to Himself, I will never again curse the ground because of man, for the imagination (the strong desire) of man's heart is evil and wicked from his youth; neither will I ever again smite and destroy every living thing, as I have done.
> 22 While the earth remains, seedtime and harvest, cold and heat, summer and winter, and day and night shall not cease. [Genesis 8: 20-22, AMP]

¹ And God pronounced a blessing upon Noah and his sons and said to them, Be fruitful and multiply and fill the earth.

² And the fear of you and the dread and terror of you shall be upon every beast of the land, every bird of the air, all that creeps upon the ground, and upon all the fish of the sea; they are delivered into your hand.

³ Every moving thing that lives shall be food for you; and as I gave you the green vegetables and plants, I give you everything.

[Genesis 9: 1-3, AMP]

> We need to emulate David and give God our best at all times; that which costs us something.

God blessed Noah with the same blessing He blessed man in the Garden of Eden after man was created. Since God does not change, we should expect the same when we give a thanksgiving offering. Speak the blessing of Genesis 9: 1-3 over your life and God will establish it in your life, and the light of His favor will shine on you.

When Satan moved David to number Israel contrary to God's Word, God allowed the destroying angel to destroy 70,000 men of Israel. [1 Chronicles 21: 1-14, AMP] To stop the plague God commanded David to offer burnt offerings to Him at Ornan's threshing floor.

²⁴ And King David said to Ornan, No, but I will pay the full price. I will not take what is yours for the Lord, nor offer burnt offerings which cost me nothing.

²⁵ So David gave to Ornan for the site 600 shekels of gold by weight.

²⁶ And David built there an altar to the Lord and offered burnt offerings and peace offerings and called upon the Lord; and He answered him by fire from heaven upon the altar of burnt offering.

²⁷ Then the Lord commanded the [avenging] angel, and he put his sword back into its sheath.

²⁸ When David saw that the Lord had answered him at the threshing floor of Ornan the Jebusite, he sacrificed there. [1 Chronicles 21: 24-28, AMP]

David did as the Lord commanded and the plague was stopped. Thereafter, David gave another sacrifice (thanksgiving) offering to the Lord for the deliverance the Lord wrought for Israel. David gave to God that which costs him something. We need to emulate David and give God our best at all times; that which costs us something.

God takes thanksgiving seriously.

Unlike David, King Hezekiah did not offer a thanksgiving offering to the Lord after his healing. This is recorded in second Chronicles 32:

> 24 In those days Hezekiah was sick to the point of death; and he prayed to the Lord and He answered him and gave him a sign.
>
> 25 But Hezekiah did not make return [to the Lord] according to the benefit done to him, for his heart became proud [at such a spectacular response to his prayer]; therefore there was wrath upon him and upon Judah and Jerusalem.
>
> 26 But Hezekiah humbled himself for the pride of his heart, both he and the inhabitants of Jerusalem, so that the wrath of the Lord came not upon them in the days of Hezekiah.
>
> 31 And so in the matter of the ambassadors of the princes of Babylon who were sent to him to inquire about the wonder that was done in the land, God left him to himself to try him, that He might know all that was in his heart. [2 Chronicles 32: 24-26, 31, AMP]

Hezekiah did not return to thank the Lord because of pride in his heart. [2 Chronicles 32: 25, AMP]. God was angry because of Hezekiah's lack of appreciation of His goodness towards him. He humbled himself before the Lord and the wrath of the Lord did not come upon Judah during His reign. However, God left Hezekiah to himself when the Babylonians visited him so that he could know what was in his heart. God already knows our hearts, but He will sometimes leave us to ourselves so that we can discover what we have in our hearts that were not obvious to us. He did a similar thing with the Israelites in the wilderness to reveal their hearts to them. This is recorded in Deuteronomy 8:

² And you shall [earnestly] remember all the way which the Lord your God led you these forty years in the wilderness, to humble you and to prove you, to know what was in your [mind and] heart, whether you would keep His commandments or not." [Deuteronomy 8: 2, AMP]

God takes thanksgiving seriously. Jesus brought home the importance of thanksgiving when one of 10 lepers who were cleansed returned to thank the Lord.

¹² And as He was going into one village, He was met by ten lepers, who stood at a distance.

¹³ And they raised up their voices and called, Jesus, Master, take pity and have mercy on us!

¹⁴ And when He saw them, He said to them, Go [at once] and show yourselves to the priests. And as they went, they were cured and made clean.

¹⁵ Then one of them, upon seeing that he was cured, turned back, recognizing and thanking and praising God with a loud voice;

¹⁶ And he fell prostrate at Jesus' feet, thanking Him [over and over]. And he was a Samaritan.

¹⁷ Then Jesus asked, Were not [all] ten cleansed? Where are the nine?

¹⁸ Was there no one found to return and to recognize and give thanks and praise to God except this alien?

¹⁹ And He said to him, Get up and go on your way. Your faith (your trust and confidence that spring from your belief in God) has restored you to health. [Luke 17: 12-19, AMP]

The thanksgiving offered by the healed man emanated from a faith-filled heart. Jesus confirmed this when He told the man that his faith restored him to health. His faith, trust and confidence that sprung from his belief in God made him whole.

We must humble ourselves before God at all times and be thankful to Him on all occasions. He is not asking us to sacrifice bulls and goats as they did in the Old Testament. He wants us to worship Him with some of what He has blessed us with and not what we do not have. Sometimes our thanksgiving offering can be just a sacrifice of praise, which is the fruit of lips.

Sacrifice of Thanksgiving as the Fruit of Our Lips

You can also give a thanksgiving offering even before the manifestation of the miracle you are expecting from the Lord. The Word calls it a sacrifice of thanksgiving. When you give a sacrifice of thanksgiving, you are saying in effect, My miracle is not yet manifested, but I trust God to fulfill His Word in my life. The Word declares,

> Our praise causes God, our Father, to move on our behalf.
>
> Praise is a key to receiving the manifestation of our miracles.

22 "Consider this, you who forget God, or I will tear you to pieces, with no one to rescue you:
23 Those who sacrifice thank offerings honor me, and to the blameless I will show my salvation." [Psalm 50: 22-23, NIV]

23 He who brings an offering of praise and thanksgiving honors and glorifies Me; and he who orders his way aright [who prepares the way that I may show him], to him I will demonstrate the salvation of God. [Psalm 50: 23, AMP]

As you give God a sacrifice of thanksgiving and walk in the Light as He is Light, you are preparing the way for the manifestation of God's glory in your life. Our Father will surely manifest His glory in your behalf. All you have to do is trust Him because He never fails. God, Who is love, never fails.

Sometimes all that God requires from us is to praise Him. The praise, which is the fruit of our lips, becomes our offering (seed) to Him. We give to him what He requires from us. He is the One Who has given us breath and enables us to speak. Thanksgiving and praise is the protocol for approaching God.

> 4 Enter into His gates with thanksgiving and a thank offering and into His courts with praise! Be thankful and say so to Him, bless and affectionately praise His name!
>
> 5 For the Lord is good; His mercy and loving-kindness are everlasting, His faithfulness and truth endure to all generations. [Psalm 100: 4-5, AMP]

God also commands us to give a sacrifice of thanksgiving and praise at all times.

> 15 Through Him, therefore, let us constantly and at all times offer up to God a sacrifice of praise, which is the fruit of lips that thankfully acknowledge and confess and glorify His name. [Hebrews 13: 15, AMP]

Our Father inhabits our praises. Our praise causes Him to move on our behalf. It was praise that enabled God to set Paul and Silas free from the Philippian jail. Paul and Silas prayed and praised God with bruised bodies, and at the midnight hour God set them free:

> 25 But about midnight, as Paul and Silas were praying and singing hymns of praise to God, and the [other] prisoners were listening to them,
>
> 26 Suddenly there was a great earthquake, so that the very foundations of the prison were shaken; and at once all the doors were opened and everyone's shackles were unfastened.

Whatever your midnight hour may be, emulate Paul and Silas and praise God for your deliverance. He will come through for you. God's Word acted upon God's way, produces God's results.

I have been in many situations where praising God was the only means of having a breakthrough. The Spirit of the Lord would minister to me to praise the Lord, and I would follow through. As I did, God manifested His glory and gave me victory. Praise is a key to receiving the manifestation of our miracles. For more on this, see my book, *The Mechanics of Faith*.

Giving to a True Prophet of God as a Worship of God

I will discuss this with Biblical examples and a testimony. Thus, I will examine the example of the Shunammite giving (ministering) to Elisha, and the Zarephath woman giving [ministering her precious seed (supply of food)] to Elijah. I will then close out this section with a testimony to show that this is applicable to us today.

> You cannot out give God.
>
> God is a no-limit-God, and He puts no limits on the returns He gives to us.

The Shunammite Woman

The Shunammite woman chose to show hospitality to prophet Elisha because she perceived that the prophet who always passed by her home (on ministerial assignments from God) was a man of God. She was sensitive to God and yielded to His promptings. I believe that God nudged her to ask her husband to make a room on the top of their house for Elisha as a place of rest for him. Thus, the man of God always stopped by their home to rest. God blessed them with a son because of her faithful giving. You cannot out give God. The account of how the Shunammite was blessed because of her giving is recorded in 2 Kings 4:

> [8] One day Elisha went on to Shunem, where a rich and influential woman lived, who insisted on his eating a meal. Afterward, whenever he passed by, he stopped there for a meal.
> [9] And she said to her husband, Behold now, I perceive that this is a holy man of God who passes by continually.
> [10] Let us make a small chamber on the [housetop] and put there for him a bed, a table, a chair, and a lamp. Then whenever he comes to us, he can go [up the outside stairs and rest] here.
> [11] One day he came and turned into the chamber and lay there.
> [12] And he said to Gehazi his servant, Call this Shunammite. When he had called her, she stood before him.

¹³ And he said to Gehazi, Say now to her, You have been most painstakingly and reverently concerned for us; what is to be done for you? Would you like to be spoken for to the king or to the commander of the army? She answered, I dwell among my own people [they are sufficient].

¹⁴ Later Elisha said, What then is to be done for her? Gehazi answered, She has no child and her husband is old.

¹⁵ He said, Call her. [Gehazi] called her, and she stood in the doorway.

> God does not forget your seed sown in faith with a heart of love.

¹⁶ Elisha said, At this season when the time comes round, you shall embrace a son. She said, No, my lord, you man of God, do not lie to your handmaid.

¹⁷ But the woman conceived and bore a son at that season the following year, as Elisha had said to her. [2 Kings 4: 8-17, AMP]

Because God does not limit the blessing (the harvest) He has for us, the Shunammite was not just blessed with a son, she also received her dead son restored to life. This is a testimony of a woman's faith, her love for God and God's love for her.

¹⁸ When the child had grown, he went out one day to his father with the reapers.

¹⁹ But he said to his father, My head, my head! The man said to his servant, Carry him to his mother.

²⁰ And when he was brought to his mother, he sat on her knees till noon, and then died.

³² When Elisha arrived in the house, the child was dead and laid upon his bed.

³³ So he went in, shut the door on the two of them, and prayed to the Lord.

³⁴ He went up and lay on the child, put his mouth on his mouth, his eyes on his eyes, and his hands on his hands. And as he stretched himself on him and embraced him, the child's flesh became warm.

[35] Then he returned and walked in the house to and fro and went up again and stretched himself upon him. And the child sneezed seven times, and then opened his eyes. [2 Kings 4: 18-20, 32-35, AMP]

We must never limit God. The Shunammite woman is a good example of someone who knew that God is a no-limit-God, and He puts no limits on the returns He gives to us. Because of her giving (of her seed of faith) which was born out of her relationship with God, God made sure that all that she lost when she left Israel because of famine was returned to her when she returned. God gave her favor with the king and made sure that Gehazi (Elisa's servant) was handy to mention her to the king.

[5] And as Gehazi was telling the king how [Elisha] had restored the dead to life, behold, the woman whose son he had restored to life appealed to the king for her house and land. And Gehazi said, My lord O king, this is the woman, and this is her son whom Elisha brought back to life.
[6] When the king asked the woman, she told him. So the king appointed to her a certain officer, saying, Restore all that was hers, and all the fruits of the field since the day that she left the land even until now. [2 Kings 8: 5-6, AMP]

God does not forget your seed sown in faith with a heart of love. David said, "I have been young and now am old, yet have I not seen the [uncompromisingly] righteous forsaken or their seed begging bread. All day long they are merciful and deal graciously; they lend, and their offspring are blessed." [Psalm 37: 25-26, AMP] It must not be forgotten that although the Shunammite woman blessed the prophet, she was actually giving as a worship to God.

The Zarephath Woman
We have another example of a woman (the Zarephath woman) who gave to a prophet (Elijah) and was richly rewarded by God. In this case, she followed the prophet's instruction. The Word declares, "Believe in the Lord your God and you shall be established; believe and remain steadfast to His prophets and you shall prosper." [2 Chronicles 20: 20, AMP] During the drought in Israel which Elijah had decreed, God sent Elijah

from the brook where he was fed by ravens to Zarephath. The Lord spoke to Elijah thus:

> [9] Arise, go to Zarephath, which belongs to Sidon, and dwell there. Behold, I have commanded a widow there to provide for you.
> [10] So he arose and went to Zarephath. When he came to the gate of the city, behold, a widow was there gathering sticks. He called to her, Bring me a little water in a vessel, that I may drink.
> [11] As she was going to get it, he called to her and said, Bring me a morsel of bread in your hand.
> [12] And she said, As the Lord your God lives, I have not a loaf baked but only a handful of meal in the jar and a little oil in the bottle. See, I am gathering two sticks, that I may go in and bake it for me and my son, that we may eat it—and die.
> [13] Elijah said to her, Fear not; go and do as you have said. But make me a little cake of [it] first and bring it to me, and afterward prepare some for yourself and your son.
> [14] For thus says the Lord, the God of Israel: The jar of meal shall not waste away or the bottle of oil fail until the day that the Lord sends rain on the earth.
> [15] She did as Elijah said. And she and he and her household ate for many days.
> [16] The jar of meal was not spent nor did the bottle of oil fail, according to the word which the Lord spoke through Elijah. [1 Kings 17: 9-16, AMP]

God is the only One who can multiply our resources back to us. All He wants is for us to give Him what we have for Him to multiply back to us.

We find a principle in this story that we need to imbibe. God had a need because Elijah needed to be fed, and the woman had a need because her food supply was running out. For the woman's need to be met, she had to give out of her need to God. God is the only One who can multiply our resources back to us. All He wants is for us to give Him what we have for Him to multiply back to us. All the Zarephath woman needed to do was to obey the prophet of God.

When Elijah arrived at Zarephath he spoke to the widow as recorded in verses 10 and 11 of 1 Kings 17. Before the Zarephath woman could get into doubt and unbelief (see 1 Kings 17: 12), Elijah added:

> [13] ....., Fear not; go and do as you have said. But make me a little cake of [it] first and bring it to me, and afterward prepare some for yourself and your son.
> [14] For thus says the Lord, the God of Israel: The jar of meal shall not waste away or the bottle of oil fail until the day that the Lord sends rain on the earth. [1 Kings 17: 13-14, AMP]

God will not ask us to do something He has not given us the ability to do. Every time He asks us to give, He always rewards our obedience with a blessing. This was the case with the Zarephath woman. The woman's supply did not run out. She was amply supplied throughout the duration of the drought according to the Word of the Lord through Elijah. The return on her giving did not stop at provision, but God also made sure that she received her dead son back to life as recorded below.

> [17] After these things, the son of the woman, the mistress of the house, became sick; and his sickness was so severe that there was no breath left in him.
> [18] And she said to Elijah, What have you against me, O man of God? Have you come to me to call my sin to remembrance and to slay my son?
> [19] He said to her, Give me your son. And he took him from her bosom and carried him up into the chamber where he stayed and laid him upon his own bed.
> [20] And Elijah cried to the Lord and said, O Lord my God, have You brought further calamity upon the widow with whom I sojourn, by slaying her son?
> [21] And he stretched himself upon the child three times and cried to the Lord and said, O Lord my God, I pray You, let this child's soul come back into him.

²² And the Lord heard the voice of Elijah, and the soul of the child came into him again, and he revived.

²³ And Elijah took the child, and brought him down out of the chamber into the [lower part of the] house and gave him to his mother; and Elijah said, See, your son is alive! [1 Kings 17: 17-23, AMP]

God never forgets our seed sown in faith and out of a heart of love. "For God is not unrighteous to forget or overlook your labor and the love which you have shown for His name's sake in ministering to the needs of the saints (His own consecrated people), as you still do." [Hebrews 6: 10, AMP]

Testimony
Several years ago, I was ministering to the Lord and the Lord spoke to me to ask a brother-in-Christ who was looking for a job to bless me. The Lord added, "Tell him that until he gets a job he will not lack." To back it up the Lord gave me 1 Kings 17: 10 – 14. It is important to note that I was not praying for the brother when the Lord ministered to me about him. However, when I told the brother what the Lord told me, he told me that the Lord did not say anything to him. My response to him was that I was not begging him to bless me.

He later called back to say that the Lord had asked him to bless me two weeks previously, and he forgot completely about it. He chose to obey God because He knew it was the right and the best thing for him to do. When he did, I spoke the blessing over him that God would provide for him until he found a job. The Lord did exactly as He promised He would. The brother was without a job for one year and did not lack. God met all his needs.

Now, I did not say I am a prophet, but I believe God and I have chosen to submit to Him and His will for my life. Like Elijah, I had a need. Just as Elijah did not seek out a man to bless him, I did not seek out anybody, not even the brother, to bless me. I trusted God and God took care of me. He does not abandon His own and I am (you are) the apple of God's eye. Trust Him whole-heartedly. He will not forsake or fail you.

Giving for the Spreading of the Gospel and the Lord's Sake

When we give of ourselves and our resources for the spreading of the Gospel, the Lord promised us a hundredfold return on what we have given.

> [29] So Jesus answered and said, "Assuredly, I say to you, there is no one who has left house or brothers or sisters or father or mother or wife or children or lands, for My sake and the gospel's,
>
> [30] who shall not receive a hundredfold now in this time - houses and brothers and sisters and mothers and children and lands, with persecutions - and in the age to come, eternal life. [Mark 10: 29-30, NKJV]

A "hundredfold" is translated from the Greek word *hekatontaplasión* and it is used symbolically to mean all-inclusive (complete, all-encompassing). Hundred means a complete series. [Webster 1828] Thus, a hundredfold return implies a complete series of blessings. The extent to which we enjoy it is determined by us. God does not limit His blessings that He showers on us, we do. Thus, to enjoy God's fullest return on our giving to His work we must be patient and expectant.

Testimony

Several years ago when I was a foreign student in Britain studying for my doctorate, I ran out of money and I did not want to ask man for help. You see, man will disappoint but God will not. One day as I was walking along a street in the Glasgow city center, Scotland when I heard the Spirit of God in my spirit saying to me, "Take that which you have in your account and put in the offering in church tomorrow." This was on a Saturday. At that prompting from the Lord, I walked to my bank and withdrew what I had in my account for offering the next day at church. However, I left a token amount to keep the account open.

The money I had could only last me for two weeks, and I had enough sense to trust God. God provided for me in a way that I cannot describe with words. He did this for nine months that I had not received any remittance from my home country. God blessed me richly and I did not owe. It was a complete series of blessing – a hundredfold. You cannot out-give God.

The Philippian Church

The Philippian church gave in support of Paul's missionary journeys. He told them that it was the right thing to do. Supporting the spreading of the Gospel is the right thing for us to do. There are tremendous benefits that accrue to us from it. Paul by the Holy Spirit declared,

> Supporting the spreading of the Gospel is the right thing for us to do.
>
> When we give to the spreading of the Gospel, we open up a debit and credit account with God in giving and receiving.

14 But it was right and commendable and noble of you to contribute for my needs and to share my difficulties with me.

15 And you Philippians yourselves well know that in the early days of the Gospel ministry, when I left Macedonia, no church (assembly) entered into partnership with me and opened up [a debit and credit] account in giving and receiving except you only.

16 For even in Thessalonica you sent [me contributions] for my needs, not only once but a second time.

17 Not that I seek or am eager for [your] gift, but I do seek and am eager for the fruit which increases to your credit [the harvest of blessing that is accumulating to your account].

18 But I have [your full payment] and more; I have everything I need and am amply supplied, now that I have received from Epaphroditus the gifts you sent me. [They are the] fragrant odor of an offering and sacrifice which God welcomes and in which He delights.

¹⁹ And my God will liberally supply (fill to the full) your every need according to His riches in glory in Christ Jesus. [Philippians 4: 14-19, AMP]

When we give to the spreading of the Gospel, we open up a debit and credit account with God in giving and receiving. "Giving" is translated from the Greek word *dosis*, and it also means gift. The word "receiving" is translated from the Greek word *lépsis*, and it also means receipt. Receiving, therefore is "receipting." Thus, every time we give to the work of the Lord, God gives us a heavenly receipt that we can present to God for withdrawal from the bank of heaven.

Paul had a personal knowledge of Who God is. He knew that God was everything to him. That is why he could say, "And my God will liberally supply ([fill to the full) your every **need** according to His **riches** in **glory** in Christ Jesus." [Philippians 4: 19, AMP, emphasis added] It would be worthwhile studying the bolded words in Philippians 4: 19 closely. The word "need" is translated from the Greek word *chreia,* and it also means employment, requirement, business, necessity, demand, and want. Riches is translated from the Greek word *plootos* which also means wealth (literally money, possessions), and abundance. Glory is translated from *doxa* in Greek. It is used to describe what God is and does when He manifests Himself, especially in the person of Christ, the Anointed One.

The glory of God was demonstrated in the personality and deeds of Jesus our Lord. When Jesus turned water into wine in Cana of Galilee, both the grace and the power of God were in manifestation. [John 2: 11] The combination of the grace (favor, spiritual blessing, anointing) and power of God constitutes God's glory. Philippians 4: 19 can, therefore, be paraphrased thus,

> *And my God will liberally supply (fill to the full) your every need (the employment you need, whatever you require or demand, whatever you need is: whether healing or in your business – contracts, favor, etc., necessity, and wants) according to the wealth of His power, favor, anointing that carries all that He is and does in the Anointed Jesus.*

Is God everything to you? Do you have the personal revelation that Paul had. A revelation that says, No matter what it is and the situation may be, my God will liberally supply (fill to the full) your every need according to His riches in glory in Christ Jesus. Yes, I know Him and I can declare with confidence that He is my Source. Remember that everything He does for us are within the perimeters of His Word.

Thus, when you give to God, do not limit Him. You have receipts from Him to cash in for a harvest that meets your need. This is a return on your giving which our Father guarantees.

Years ago, my wife and I faced a challenging situation and we needed to see God's glory. I told my wife we needed to cash in one of our receipts to see God's

> My God shall supply my requirements, necessity, needs, and wants, according to the wealth of His grace (favor) and power in the Anointed Jesus as He did in Cana of Galilee when He turned water into wine.

glory manifested on our behalf. Our Father never disappoints and He came through for us. The Word works. God's Word acted upon God's way, produces God's results. Glory! Hallelujah! You can understand why the Zarephath woman and Shunammite received their sons back to life because they were involved in the heavenly transaction of giving and receiving (sowing and reaping, seedtime and harvest).

When we give, we are involved in an exciting Kingdom of God adventure of ministering our seeds to the Lord and releasing the power to bring forth harvests and to receive them. Thus, when we are minister our gifts to the Lord, He gives us receipts for our gifts. That is, receipts for our deposits into our heavenly bank accounts. By receiving, it is implied that we have taken hold of our harvests. Hence, my God shall supply my requirements, necessity, needs, and wants, according to the wealth of His grace (favor) and power in the Anointed Jesus as He did in Cana of Galilee when He turned water into wine. As we release our faith with our gift (a seed which is a demonstration of our faith), God gives us the power to receive our harvest right at the point of our giving. We, therefore, need to receive our harvest by faith the moment we release our faith with our seeds that we present to God.

"The merciful, kind, and generous man benefits himself [for his deeds return to bless him],.."

Our reward does not stop here. When you give for the Gospel and the Lord's sake you also have eternal reward. Here is what the Lord will say to those who give for His sake when it is all over and we stand before Him:

32 All nations will be gathered before Him, and He will separate them [the people] from one another as a shepherd separates his sheep from the goats;

33 And He will cause the sheep to stand at His right hand, but the goats at His left.

34 Then the King will say to those at His right hand, Come, you blessed of My Father [you favored of God and appointed to eternal salvation], inherit (receive as your own) the kingdom prepared for you from the foundation of the world.

35 For I was hungry and you gave Me food, I was thirsty and you gave Me something to drink, I was a stranger and you brought Me together with yourselves and welcomed and entertained and lodged Me,

36 I was naked and you clothed Me, I was sick and you visited Me with help and ministering care, I was in prison and you came to see Me.

37 Then the just and upright will answer Him, Lord, when did we see You hungry and gave You food, or thirsty and gave You something to drink?

38 And when did we see You a stranger and welcomed and entertained You, or naked and clothed You?

39 And when did we see You sick or in prison and came to visit You?

[40] And the King will reply to them, Truly I tell you, in so far as you did it for one of the least [in the estimation of men] of these My brethren, you did it for Me. [Matthew 25: 32-40, AMP]

Your reward is the kingdom the Lord has prepared for you from the foundation of the world. What a deal!

Benevolent Giving

Whenever we reach out to bless others, God takes notice. He does not only do that, but He declares that in blessing we are doing ourselves a favor. "The merciful, kind, and generous man benefits himself [for his deeds return to bless him], but he who is cruel *and* callous [to the wants of others] brings on himself retribution." [Proverbs 11: 17, AMP] If we understood this, we would be quick to jump at any opportunity to be a blessing as directed by the Lord. When there is an opportunity to bless those in need, listen to your spirit and do as God commands. The Word declares,

[7] If there is among you a poor man, one of your kinsmen in any of the towns of your land which the Lord your God gives you, you shall not harden your [minds and] hearts or close your hands to your poor brother;
[8] But you shall open your hands wide to him and shall surely lend him sufficient for his need in whatever he lacks.
[9] Beware lest there be a base thought in your [minds and] hearts, and you say, The seventh year, the year of release, is at hand, and your eye be evil against your poor brother and you give him nothing, and he cry to the Lord against you, and it be sin in you.
[10] You shall give to him freely without begrudging it; because of this the Lord will bless you in all your work and in all you undertake.
[11] For the poor will never cease out of the land; therefore I command you, You shall open wide your hands to your brother, to your needy, and to your poor in your land. [Deuteronomy 15: 7-11, AMP]

When you open your hand freely and bless a brother/sister in need God "will bless you in all your work and in all you undertake." [Deuteronomy

15: 11, AMP] In addition, He declares, "When you help the poor you are lending to the Lord – and he pays wonderful interest on your loan." [Proverbs 19: 17, TLB]

The Corinthian Church and Alms Giving
There is a tremendous blessing in giving to brethren in need. Paul, by the Holy Spirit, declared,

> The only way out of their tight financial spot was to give to others in need.

> ¹ We want to tell you further, brethren, about the grace (the favor and spiritual blessing) of God which has been evident in the churches of Macedonia [arousing in them the desire to give alms];
> ² For in the midst of an ordeal of severe tribulation, their abundance of joy and their depth of poverty [together] have overflowed in wealth of lavish generosity on their part.
> ³ For, as I can bear witness, [they gave] according to their ability, yes, and beyond their ability; and [they did it] voluntarily,
> ⁴ Begging us most insistently for the favor and the fellowship of contributing in this ministration for [the relief and support of] the saints [in Jerusalem]. [2 Corinthians 8: 1-4, AMP]

The brethren in Corinth understood that the only way out of their tight financial spot was to give to others in need, and in this case the brethren in Jerusalem. They trusted God and the grace, the anointing for giving came upon them, and they gave (sowed) their way out of lack. They chose to reinforce the bruising of the serpent's head with their gifts. They let the devil understand that in their tribulation, they would give and their seeds of faith would speak for them before God. Because they chose to give despite their tribulation and lack, the joy of the Lord rose up in them and spurred them to trust God with their substance to His glory – their deliverance from tribulation and abundant provision. They gave joyfully and generously, knowing that in giving to help the needy brethren in Jerusalem they were giving to the Lord.

> [6] [Remember] this: he who sows sparingly and grudgingly will also reap sparingly and grudgingly, and he who sows generously [that blessings may come to someone] will also reap generously and with blessings.
>
> [7] Let each one [give] as he has made up his own mind and purposed in his heart, not reluctantly or sorrowfully or under compulsion, for God loves (He takes pleasure in, prizes above other things, and is unwilling to abandon or to do without) a cheerful (joyous, "prompt to do it") giver [whose heart is in his giving]. [2 Corinthians 9: 6-7, AMP]

Paul by the unction of the Holy Spirit told them the blessing the Lord had for them for being cheerful, prompt, and generous givers:

> [8] And God is able to make all grace (every favor and earthly blessing) come to you in abundance, so that you may always and under all circumstances and whatever the need be self-sufficient [possessing enough to require no aid or support and furnished in abundance for every good work and charitable donation].
>
> [9] As it is written, He [the benevolent person] scatters abroad; He gives to the poor; His deeds of justice and goodness and kindness and benevolence will go on and endure forever!
>
> [10] And [God] Who provides seed for the sower and bread for eating will also provide and multiply your [resources for] sowing and increase the fruits of your righteousness [which manifests itself in active goodness, kindness, and charity].
>
> [11] Thus you will be enriched in all things and in every way, so that you can be generous, and [your generosity as it is] administered by us will bring forth thanksgiving to God.
>
> [12] For the service that the ministering of this fund renders does not only fully supply what is lacking to the saints (God's people), but it also overflows in many [cries of] thanksgiving to God.
>
> [13] Because at [your] standing of the test of this ministry, they will glorify God for your loyalty and obedience to the Gospel of Christ which you confess, as well as for your generous-hearted liberality to them and to all [the other needy ones].

[14] And they yearn for you while they pray for you, because of the surpassing measure of God's grace (His favor and mercy and spiritual blessing which is shown forth) in you. [2 Corinthians 9: 8-14, AMP]

You cannot beat such a deal. This same blessing is for us today when we act on the Word in the same way the brethren in Corinth did. God is no respecter of persons. When you give as the brethren in Corinth did, and stand on Corinthians 9: 6-14 God will make sure that

- "all grace (every favor and earthly blessing) come to you in abundance;"

- you are delivered from tribulation;

- you will not lack;

- He provides and multiplies "your [resources for] sowing and increase the fruits of your righteousness, which manifests itself in active goodness, kindness, and charity;"

- you are "enriched in all things and in every way, so that you can be generous;" and

- your generosity "will bring forth thanksgiving to God." [2 Corinthians 9: 8-14, AMP]

Nothing can be compared with the reward that God, our Father, has for us when we give for benevolence. We are not to be tired of being a blessing. "And do not forget to do good and to share with others, for with such sacrifices God is pleased." [Hebrews 13: 16, AMP]

The Feeding of the 5000

The feeding of the 5000 by our Lord Jesus was an example of benevolence. The account of the miracle and the reward for the lad who provided the two fishes and five loaves of bread for Jesus to lift up to the Father for the feeding of the multitude is recorded in John Chapter 6:

[5] Then Jesus lifted up His eyes, and seeing a great multitude coming toward Him, He said to Philip, "Where shall we buy bread, that these may eat?"

6 But this He said to test him, for He Himself knew what He would do.

7 Philip answered Him, "Two hundred denarii worth of bread is not sufficient for them, that every one of them may have a little."

8 One of His disciples, Andrew, Simon Peter's brother, said to Him,

9 "There is a lad here who has five barley loaves and two small fish, but what are they among so many?"

10 Then Jesus said, "Make the people sit down." Now there was much grass in the place. So the men sat down, in number about five thousand.

11 And Jesus took the loaves, and when He had given thanks He distributed them to the disciples, and the disciples to those sitting down; and likewise of the fish, as much as they wanted.

12 So when they were filled, He said to His disciples, "Gather up the fragments that remain, so that nothing is lost."

13 Therefore they gathered them up, and filled twelve baskets with the fragments of the five barley loaves which were left over by those who had eaten. [John 6: 5-13, NKJV]

It was *Agape* love that prompted Jesus to feed the 5000 men, besides women and children. The little boy demonstrated his love for God and His work when he gave all that He had to Jesus to lift up to the Father for multiplication to feed the multitude. Because God always rewards our gift of love, the boy had a multiplied harvest of 12 baskets full of bread and fish.

Giving During Fasting (The Fast of the Lord)

In Isaiah 58, God, our Father, describes to us the blessings He has for us when we give to the poor and the needy. Although the context of the discourse is in connection with fasting (the fast the Lord desires), it is also in line with our discussion here on benevolent giving.

6 [Rather] is not this the fast that I have chosen: to loose the bonds of wickedness, to undo the bands of the yoke, to let the oppressed go free, and that you break every [enslaving] yoke?

7 Is it not to divide your bread with the hungry and bring the homeless poor into your house—when you see the naked, that you cover him,

and that you hide not yourself from [the needs of] your own flesh and blood?

8 Then shall your light break forth like the morning, and your healing (your restoration and the power of a new life) shall spring forth speedily; your righteousness (your rightness, your justice, and your right relationship with God) shall go before you [conducting you to peace and prosperity], and the glory of the Lord shall be your rear guard.

9 Then you shall call, and the Lord will answer; you shall cry, and He will say, Here I am. If you take away from your midst yokes of oppression [wherever you find them], the finger pointed in scorn [toward the oppressed or the godly], and every form of false, harsh, unjust, and wicked speaking,

10 And if you pour out that with which you sustain your own life for the hungry and satisfy the need of the afflicted, then shall your light rise in darkness, and your obscurity and gloom become like the noonday.

11 And the Lord shall guide you continually and satisfy you in drought and in dry places and make strong your bones. And you shall be like a watered garden and like a spring of water whose waters fail not. [Isaiah 58: 6-11, AMP]

To enjoy the blessing described in Isaiah 58 we must do what God says. We must walk in *Agape* love towards others, forgive those who wrong us, and be benevolent. When we meet these conditions, we are assured of prosperity from God, healing and wholeness, and answered prayer. I have put this to work I and reaped the blessing stipulated in Isaiah 58.

Giving is an avenue God has ordained for Him to channel His blessings to us. When you give, you create room for God to fill up your storage places. With every giving God asks us to give, which includes giving to those who teach us the Word, there is a reward He has for us.

Giving to Your Word (Bible) Teacher

The Holy Spirit instructs us to give to those who teach us the Word of God and not faint That is, we must not faint from the reasoning that we have not seen our reward yet. Remember that whatever we give to the Lord must be done in faith and out of a heart of love. When we give to our teachers of the Word in faith and out of a heart of love because we are yielded to the Lord, we can be sure of our rewards from the Lord. The Word instructs as follows,

> 6 Let him who receives instruction in the Word [of God] share all good things with his teacher [contributing to his support].
> 7 Do not be deceived and deluded and misled; God will not allow Himself to be sneered at (scorned, disdained, or mocked by mere pretensions or professions, or by His precepts being set aside.) [He inevitably deludes himself who attempts to delude God.] **For whatever a man sows, that and that only is what he will reap**. [Galatians 6: 6-7, AMP; emphasis added]

> 17 Let the elders who perform the duties of their office well be considered doubly worthy of honor [and of adequate financial support], especially those who labor faithfully in preaching and teaching.
> 18 For the Scripture says, You shall not muzzle an ox when it is treading out the grain, and again, The laborer is worthy of his hire. [1 Timothy 5:17-18, AMP]

Those who minister the Word to us are to reap their harvest from those who receive the teaching of the Word from them. Our Father enunciated this principle which Hezekiah reminded Judah of; and when they obeyed so that the Levites and priests were blessed from the offerings as God stipulated, God prospered them. We also see this in our Lord's ministry

> 1 Soon afterward, [Jesus] went on through towns and villages, preaching and bringing the good news (the Gospel) of the kingdom of God. And the Twelve [apostles] were with Him,
> 2 And also some women who had been cured of evil spirits and diseases: Mary, called Magdalene, from whom seven demons had been expelled;
> 3 And Joanna, the wife of Chuza, Herod's household manager; and Susanna; and many others, who ministered to and provided for Him and them out of their property and personal belongings. [Luke 8: 1-3, AMP]

Paul also reminded the Corinthian church of this principle:

> 11 If we have sown [the seed of] spiritual good among you, [is it too] much if we reap from your material benefits?

¹² If others share in this rightful claim upon you, do not we [have a still better and greater claim]? However, we have never exercised this right, but we endure everything rather than put a hindrance in the way [of the spread] of the good news (the Gospel) of Christ.

¹³ Do you not know that those men who are employed in the services of the temple get their food from the temple? And that those who tend the altar share with the altar [in the offerings brought]?

¹⁴ [On the same principle] the Lord directed that those who publish the good news (the Gospel) should live (get their maintenance) by the Gospel. [1 Corinthians 9: 11-14, AMP]

When you give to your Word teacher, know that you are giving to the Lord, and it is the Lord Who will reward you. This holds true for every giving that you do as a demonstration of your love for God. Remember that our Father is the Lord of the harvest. [Luke 10: 2]

Breakthrough Giving (Giving on Purpose)

You can give to God on purpose which means that you can receive from Him on purpose. Your gift releases your blessing. This is what happened to Hannah the mother of Samuel, the prophet. Hannah desired to have a child for years, but she did not see the manifestation of God's glory in her life. She decided to couple her prayer with giving and it became a memorial before God.

¹⁰ And [Hannah] was in distress of soul, praying to the Lord and weeping bitterly.

¹¹ **She vowed, saying, O Lord of hosts, if You will indeed look on the affliction of Your handmaid and [earnestly] remember, and not forget Your handmaid but will give me a son, I will give him to the Lord all his life; no razor shall touch his head.**

¹² And as she continued praying before the Lord, Eli noticed her mouth.

¹³ Hannah was speaking in her heart; only her lips moved but her voice was not heard. So Eli thought she was drunk.

¹⁴ Eli said to her, How long will you be intoxicated? Put wine away from you.

¹⁵ But Hannah answered, No, my lord, I am a woman of a sorrowful spirit. I have drunk neither wine nor strong drink, but I was pouring out my soul before the Lord.
¹⁶ Regard not your handmaid as a wicked woman; for out of my great complaint and bitter provocation I have been speaking.
¹⁷ Then Eli said, Go in peace, and may the God of Israel grant your petition which you have asked of Him.
¹⁸ Hannah said, Let your handmaid find grace in your sight. So [she] went her way and ate, her countenance no longer sad. [1 Samuel 1: 10-18, AMP; emphasis added]

When Hannah told Eli that she was not drunk but praying, Eli came into agreement with her and asked God to grant her request. Hannah received her miracle because it is recorded that she said, "Let your handmaid find grace in your sight." Mary the mother of our Lord said similar words in agreement with the Word of the Lord through angel Gabriel to her. [Luke 1: 38, AMP] We note in 1 Samuel 1: 18 that Hannah went home different, "her countenance was no longer sad."

Hannah moved the hand of God with giving (a vow) coupled with her prayer. "Elkanah knew Hannah his wife, and the Lord remembered her. Hannah became pregnant and in due time bore a son and named him Samuel [heard of God], Because, she said, I have asked him of the Lord." [1 Samuel 1: 19b-20, AMP] When she gave birth to Samuel, she fulfilled her vow by returning him to the Lord. [1 Samuel 1: 24-28, AMP] The lesson here is that when we vow to the Lord we must pay our vows. "Offer to God the sacrifice of thanksgiving, and pay your vows to the Most High, and call on Me in the day of trouble; I will deliver you, and you shall honor and glorify Me." [Psalm 50: 14-15, AMP]

Do not rush to make a vow to the Lord if you will not make good on your promise to the Lord. King Solomon, by the Spirit of the Lord, warned us of the consequences of not paying vows we have made to the Lord,

⁴ When you vow a vow or make a pledge to God, do not put off paying it; for God has no pleasure in fools (those who witlessly mock Him). Pay what you vow.
⁵ It is better that you should not vow than that you should vow and not pay.
⁶ Do not allow your mouth to cause your body to sin, and do not say before the messenger [the priest] that it was an error or mistake. Why should God be [made] angry at your voice and destroy the work of your hands?[Ecclesiastes 5: 4-6, AMP]

The bottom line is, do not make a vow to God if you will be unwilling to pay after you have received the Lord's blessing.

You can give to God on purpose and not necessarily as a vow. Please remember that you are not buying a blessing from God. Your giving must proceed out of a realization that all that you are and have come from the Lord. [1 Chronicles 29:13-14, AMP] You cannot bribe God or buy His blessing. King David gave the offering in 1 Chronicles 21: 24-27 [AMP] in acknowledgement of God's mercy and love.

Characteristics of Breakthrough Offering

- The offering must be offered in faith, and must be Word-based. For it to be given in faith, it must be given with a heart of love.

- Give what stretches your faith.

- Give out of your need (and not surplus), and aim your gift (seed) at your need.

- You are able to do all of the above because you have first given yourself to God. [2 Corinthians 8: 1-5, AMP]

Testimonies

Here are some present day testimonies which were harvests of giving that will encourage your faith. I will share them under two broad categories. These are employment and promotion, and debt cancelation.

Employment and Promotion
One day a brother asked me to pray for him to get a job. I told him I could only pray for God to give him a job that was commensurate with the skills and qualification God had given him, and not anything less. What he was going for was beneath his skills set, experience, and qualification. I challenged him to look for a job that was commensurate with the skills and qualification God had given him. In addition, I asked him to sow a seed (give an offering to God) for the job. I advised him to pray over the offering in agreement with his wife, specifically telling the Lord that he was sowing the seed for an excellent

> The key is to obey God at whatever state you are and He will bring you to the desired destination, the best that He has for you.

job. He did as I advised him and in no time, he had the exact job we had asked for from the Lord.

The testimony from the couple has been very humbling to me. They told me that what I did not know was that they had to scrape whatever they had in their house to give to the Lord in obedience to His Word through me. They said that because of their obedience, God prospered them and their lives and family changed for the better from that day. Hallelujah, you cannot out-give God.

Debt Cancellation
Years ago a sister who came to the Lord in our fellowship gave me a frantic phone call when I was about to leave for work in the morning. I told her to speak with my wife, and I promised to call her when I returned from work. When I called her back, I learnt from her that she had credit card debt of $110,000. She was a baby Christian, and I taught

her the importance of tithing and offering in God's economy. I advised her to give of her tithes to the Lord. In addition to the tithes, she should give offerings. She was to give her offerings specifically for debt cancellation.

In addition, I taught her how to pray over her tithe and her offering. I told her to take the offering and pray a simple prayer like this, *Lord I release my faith with this seed which I am sowing for the cancellation of my debt in Jesus' Name.* Thereafter, she was to give subsequent offerings in thanksgiving for the cancellation of her debt. Within three weeks, God cancelled her debt. God gave her favor with her creditors who reduced her debt drastically, and her father who had never blessed her with money visited her and gave her $50,000 without her asking. She used the money to pay off some of her debts. The key is to obey God at whatever state you are, and He will bring you to the desired destination, the best that He has for you.

Freewill Offering

The freewill offering was instituted before the law. We first learn about it from the relationship between Abraham and God. Thereafter, there are many examples in the Bible.

Abraham

God told Abraham to offer Isaac to Him as a freewill offering.

> [2] [God] said, Take now your son, your only son Isaac, whom you love, and go to the region of Moriah; and offer him there as a burnt offering upon one of the mountains of which I will tell you.
> [3] So Abraham rose early in the morning, saddled his donkey, and took two of his young men with him and his son Isaac; and he split the wood for the burnt offering, and then began the trip to the place of which God had told him.

⁹ When they came to the place of which God had told him, Abraham built an altar there; then he laid the wood in order and bound Isaac his son and laid him on the altar on the wood.

> **God will never ask you to give Him what you do not have.**

¹⁰ And Abraham stretched forth his hand and took hold of the knife to slay his son.

¹¹ But the Angel of the Lord called to him from heaven and said, Abraham, Abraham! He answered, Here I am.

¹² And He said, Do not lay your hand on the lad or do anything to him; for now I know that you fear and revere God, since you have not held back from Me or begrudged giving Me your son, your only son.

¹⁵ The Angel of the Lord called to Abraham from heaven a second time

¹⁶ And said, I have sworn by Myself, says the Lord, that since you have done this and have not withheld [from Me] or begrudged [giving Me] your son, your only son,

¹⁷ In blessing I will bless you and in multiplying I will multiply your descendants like the stars of the heavens and like the sand on the seashore. And your Seed (Heir) will possess the gate of His enemies, [Genesis 22: 2-3, 9-12, 15-17, AMP]

Abraham obeyed God without hesitation because he knew that he was in covenant with God. He knew that all he had, including Isaac, was from the Lord and the Lord's. He also knew that all God has was his. Thus, when he received the *rhema* word, the faith instruction, to offer Isaac as a freewill offering, he obeyed promptly. He believed that God who gave Isaac would raise him up. He did it by faith energized by *Agape* love for God. Of this, it is recorded in Hebrews 11:

> ¹⁷ By faith Abraham, when he was put to the test [while the testing of his faith was still in progress], had already brought Isaac for an offering; he who had gladly received and welcomed [God's] promises was ready to sacrifice his only son,
>
> ¹⁸ Of whom it was said, Through Isaac shall your descendants be reckoned.

[19] For he reasoned that God was able to raise [him] up even from among the dead. Indeed in the sense that Isaac was figuratively dead [potentially sacrificed], he did [actually] receive him back from the dead. [Hebrews 11; 17-19, AMP]

Because Abraham obeyed God and offered Isaac as his freewill offering to the Lord, God blessed him beyond measure. He spoke the blessing over him, and it was a generational blessing.

[15] The Angel of the Lord called to Abraham from heaven a second time
[16] And said, I have sworn by Myself, says the Lord, that since you have done this and have not withheld [from Me] or begrudged [giving Me] your son, your only son,
[17] In blessing I will bless you and in multiplying I will multiply your descendants like the stars of the heavens and like the sand on the seashore. And your Seed (Heir) will possess the gate of His enemies, [Genesis 22: 15-17, AMP]

The same blessing is for you when you give freely to the Lord. Give what He tells you to offer to Him.

Building of the Ark of the Tabernacle

God commanded Moses to take a freewill offering in the wilderness for the building of the ark of the tabernacle. God had given them wealth on their departure from Egypt by transferring the wealth of the Egyptians to them. [Exodus 12: 35-36, AMP] Thus, He was asking them to offer to Him out of what He had given them. God will never ask you to give Him what you do not have. He will always give you a seed to sow.

[4] And Moses said to all the congregation of the Israelites, This is what the Lord commanded:
[5] Take from among you an offering to the Lord. Whoever is of a willing and generous heart, let him bring the Lord's offering: gold, silver, and bronze;
[6] Blue, purple, and scarlet [stuff], fine linen; goats' hair;
[7] And rams' skins tanned red, and skins of dolphins or porpoises; and acacia wood;

⁸ And oil for the light; and spices for anointing oil and for fragrant incense;

⁹ And onyx stones and other stones to be set for the ephod and the breastplate.

¹⁰ And let every able and wise hearted man among you come and make all that the Lord has commanded:

¹¹ The tabernacle, its tent and its covering, its hooks, its boards, its bars, its pillars, and its sockets or bases;

²⁹ The Israelites brought **a freewill offering to the Lord, all men and women whose hearts made them willing and moved them to bring anything for any of the work which the Lord had commanded by Moses** to be done. [Exodus 35: 4-11, 29, AMP; emphasis mine]

The people responded as their hearts prompted them. More appropriately, they responded as they yielded their hearts to the Lord in obedience to the Lord's command through Moses.

³ And they received from Moses all the freewill offerings which the Israelites had brought for doing the work of the sanctuary, to prepare it for service. And they continued to bring him freewill offerings every morning.

⁴ And all the wise and able men who were doing the work on the sanctuary came, every man from the work he was doing,

⁵ And they said to Moses, The people bring much more than enough for doing the work which the Lord commanded to do.

⁶ So Moses commanded and it was proclaimed in all the camp, Let no man or woman do anything more for the sanctuary offering. So the people were restrained from bringing,

⁷ For the stuff they had was sufficient to do all the work and more. [Exodus 36: 3-7, AMP]

They trusted God as their Source (Provider). That is why they could give beyond measure.

Offering for the Building of the First Temple for the Lord in Israel

The Lord did not allow King David to build Him a temple because He said that King David was a warrior and had blood on his hands. Rather, He told King David that Solomon would build Him the temple. That did not stop David from making provision for the building of the temple. He led by example in giving freely for the building of the temple and asked his people to give freely to the Lord, starting from his leaders. King David gave out of a heart of love and not selfishness. He knew that the blessing would accrue to generations after him, starting from Solomon.

¹ And King David said to all the assembly, Solomon my son, whom alone God has chosen, is yet young, tender, and inexperienced; and the work is great, for the palace is not to be for man but for the Lord God.

² So **I have provided with all my might for the house of my God** the gold for things to be of gold, silver for things of silver, bronze for things of bronze, iron for things of iron, and wood for things of wood, as well as onyx or beryl stones, stones to be set, stones of antimony, stones of various colors, and all sorts of precious stones, and marble stones in abundance.

³ Moreover, **because I have set my affection on the house of my God, in addition to all I have prepared for the holy house, I have a private treasure of gold and silver which I give for the house of my God:**

⁴ It is 3,000 talents of gold, gold of Ophir, 7,000 talents of refined silver for overlaying the walls of the house,

⁵ Gold for the uses of gold, silver for the uses of silver, and for every work to be done by craftsmen. **Now who will offer willingly to fill his hand [and consecrate it] today to the Lord [like one consecrating himself to the priesthood]?**

⁶ **Then the chiefs of the fathers and princes of the tribes of Israel and the captains of thousands and of hundreds, with the rulers of the king's work, offered willingly**

⁷ And gave for the service of the house of God—of gold 5,000 talents and 10,000 darics, of silver 10,000 talents, of bronze 18,000 talents, and 100,000 talents of iron.

⁸ And whoever had precious stones gave them to the treasury of the house of the Lord in the care of Jehiel the Gershonite.

⁹ Then **the people rejoiced because these had given willingly, for with a whole and blameless heart they had offered freely to the Lord. King David also rejoiced greatly.** [1 Chronicles 29: 1-9, AMP; emphasis mine]

Because David set his affection on the house of my God, he was able to give willingly to the building of the Lord's temple. He led by example and His people followed suit.

David's Freewill Offering Prayer

In giving his freewill offering to the Lord, King David gave us an example of how to pray over our freewill offering. I have reproduced the whole text below because it is an excellent example for us to use in patterning our prayers for presenting our freewill offerings to the Lord.

> [10] Therefore David blessed the Lord before all the assembly and said, Be praised, adored, and thanked, O Lord, the God of Israel our [forefather], forever and ever.
>
> [11] Yours, O Lord, is the greatness and the power and the glory and the victory and the majesty, for all that is in the heavens and the earth is Yours; Yours is the kingdom, O Lord, and Yours it is to be exalted as Head over all.
>
> [12] Both riches and honor come from You, and You reign over all. In Your hands are power and might; in Your hands it is to make great and to give strength to all.
>
> [13] Now therefore, our God, we thank You and praise Your glorious name and those attributes which that name denotes.
>
> [14] But who am I, and what are my people, that we should retain strength and be able to offer thus so willingly? **For all things come from You, and out of Your own [hand] we have given You.**
>
> [15] For we are strangers before You, and sojourners, as all our fathers were; our days on the earth are like a shadow, and there is no hope or expectation of remaining.
>
> [16] **O Lord our God, all this store that we have prepared to build You a house for Your holy Name and the token of Your presence comes from Your hand, and is all Your own.**
>
> [17] **I know also, my God, that You try the heart and delight in uprightness. In the uprightness of my heart I have freely offered all these things. And now I have seen with joy Your people who are present here offer voluntarily and freely to You.**

¹⁸ O Lord, God of Abraham, Isaac, and Israel, our fathers, keep forever such purposes and thoughts in the minds of Your people, and direct and establish their hearts toward You.
¹⁹ And give to Solomon my son a blameless heart to keep Your commandments, testimonies, and statutes, and to do all that is necessary to build the palace [for You] for which I have made provision. [1 Chronicles 29: 10-19, AMP; emphasis mine]

The bolded text contains what we need in framing our prayers for presenting our freewill offerings to God. Out of His hand we have received, and we give willingly and freely to Him. Like David, we ask God to keep His thoughts in our hearts, and direct and establish our hearts toward Him.

Restoration of the Worship of Eternal God in Judah under Hezekiah

When King Hezekiah restored the worship of the Lord in Judah and commanded the people to give their tithes, firstfruits, and offerings, God prospered His people beyond measure.

³ In the first year of his reign, in the first month, he opened the doors of the house of the Lord [which his father had closed] and repaired them.
⁴ He brought together the priests and Levites in the square on the east
⁵ And said to them, Levites, hear me! Now sanctify (purify and make free from sin) yourselves and the house of the Lord, the God of your fathers, and carry out the filth from the Holy Place.
¹⁵ They gathered their brethren and sanctified themselves and went in, as the king had commanded by the words of the Lord, to cleanse the house of the Lord.
²⁰ Then King Hezekiah rose early and gathered the officials of the city and went up to the house of the Lord. [2 Chronicles 29: 3-5,15,20, AMP]

Before asking the people to worship the Lord and give to Him, King Hezekiah asked the Levites and the priests to first sanctify themselves. He also asked God to forgive the sins of his people.

[17] For many were in the assembly who had not sanctified themselves [become clean and free from all sin]. So the Levites had to kill the Passover lambs for all who were not clean, in order to make them holy to the Lord.

[18] For a multitude of the people, many from Ephraim, Manasseh, Issachar, and Zebulun, had not cleansed themselves, yet they ate the Passover otherwise than Moses directed. For Hezekiah had prayed for them, saying, May the good Lord pardon everyone

[19] Who sets his heart to seek and yearn for God—the Lord, the God of his fathers—even though not complying with the purification regulations of the sanctuary.

[20] And the Lord hearkened to Hezekiah and healed the people. [2 Chronicles 30: 17-20, AMP]

For King Hezekiah, worship of the true God was paramount. Thus, he provided for the burnt offerings in the Lord's house so that the Lord could be worshipped as He had commanded them in the Law.

[2] And Hezekiah appointed the priests and the Levites after their divisions, each man according to his service, the priests and Levites for burnt offerings and for peace offerings, to minister, to give thanks, and to praise in the gates of the camp of the Lord.

[3] King Hezekiah's personal contribution was for the burnt offerings: [those] of morning and evening, for the Sabbaths, for the New Moons, and for the appointed feasts, as written in the Law of the Lord. [2 Chronicles 31: 2-3 , AMP]

Having led by example and I believe he knew what Moses said that we should not go before the Lord empty handed, he commanded the people to give the portion due the Levites and the priests. The priests and the Levites were to receive their harvests of ministering in the temple, the reward of their labor of love, from the offerings of the people. The people understood what the Lord expected of them; that is, to give of their firstfruits and tithes. They gave freely to the Lord.

[4] He commanded the people living in Jerusalem to give the portion due the priests and Levites, that they might [be free to] give themselves to the Law of the Lord.

⁵ As soon as the command went abroad, the Israelites gave in abundance the firstfruits of grain, vintage fruit, oil, honey, and of all the produce of the field; and they brought in abundantly the tithe of everything.

⁶ The people of Israel and Judah who lived in Judah's cities also brought the tithe of cattle and sheep and of the dedicated things which were consecrated to the Lord their God, and they laid them in heaps.

⁷ In the third month [at the end of wheat harvest] they began to lay the foundation or beginning of the heaps and finished them in the seventh month.

⁸ When Hezekiah and the princes came and saw the heaps, they blessed the Lord and His people Israel.

⁹ Then Hezekiah questioned the priests and Levites about the heaps.

¹⁰ Azariah the high priest, of the house of Zadok, answered him, Since the people began to bring the offerings into the Lord's house, we have eaten and have plenty left, for the Lord has blessed His people, and what is left is this great store. [2 Chronicles 31: 4-10 , AMP]

When the people gave freely to the Lord of their firstfruits and tithes, God blessed them abundantly. Their giving released their blessing. For that to happen, they first gave of themselves, and then gave freely to the Lord. As the Lord blessed them, they gave more and theirs was an overflow of the blessing of the Lord.

Rebuilding of the Temple

Those who returned from Babylonian captivity gave freely for the rebuilding of the Lord's temple. "After they arrived at the Lord's house in Jerusalem, some of the family leaders gave freewill offerings for the house of God in order to have it rebuilt on its original site. [Ezra 2:68, HCSB] Because they gave freely to the rebuilding of the house of the Lord, God prospered them. When we give for a church building project to glorify our Lord, expect to be blessed as the Israelites were.

In summary, we have examined different instances where people gave freely to the Lord. The freewill offering is God originated, and it has some uniqueness about it. What are those things that make freewill offering unique? They are:

- First, give yourself to the Lord.
- The Lord will minister to you what to offer to Him.
- Obey Him. It is your choice.

When you obey the Lord by doing what are listed above, He commands His blessing on you the same way He did on Abraham and the Israelites as we have read in His Word. In blessing He will bless you, and in multiplying He will multiply you. The Lord will prosper you as you give freely and willingly of what you have to Him.

Sowing in Famine

A time of famine is a time of no rain. When there is no rain, a seed planted cannot grow. It is the rain that causes what is sown in the soil to grow because the rain makes a demand on the soil to produce. Equally, the Word will make your seed of faith to produce after its kind.

> [10] For as the rain and snow come down from the heavens, and return not there again, but water the earth and make it bring forth and sprout, that it may give seed to the sower and bread to the eater,
>
> [11] So shall My word be that goes forth out of My mouth: it shall not return to Me void [without producing any effect, useless], but it shall accomplish that which I please and purpose, and it shall prosper in the thing for which I sent it. [Isaiah 55: 10-11, AMP]

Isaac's Example

It is in the setting of famine in Gerar where people were running to Egypt that the Lord appeared to Isaac and gave him some instructions.

> [2] And the Lord appeared to him and said, Do not go down to Egypt; live in the land of which I will tell you.
>
> [3] Dwell temporarily in this land, and I will be with you and will favor you with blessings; for to you and to your descendants I will give all

these lands, and I will perform the oath which I swore to Abraham your father.

⁴ And I will make your descendants to multiply as the stars of the heavens, and will give to your posterity all these lands (kingdoms); and by your Offspring shall all the nations of the earth be blessed, or by Him bless themselves,

⁵ For Abraham listened to and obeyed My voice and kept My charge, My commands, My statutes, and My laws.

⁶ So Isaac stayed in Gerar. [Genesis 26: 2-6, AMP]

> God was with Isaac in the famine, but the famine was not in the Eternal.

God was with Isaac in the famine, but the famine was not in the Eternal. That is why He instructed Isaac to go against rational thinking and dwell in Gerar. Isaac trusted the Lord and obeyed His command. It is important to note that every word from God is a command. He had seen his father (Abraham) obey God and how God blessed him for his obedience; he, therefore, knew that it was in his best interest to obey God. Thus Isaac stayed in Gerar, and sowed seed in a land that was in famine. Why did he have the gumption to sow seed in famine? He knew he had God's backing. God had spoken to him and that was enough for him. For our benefit God says,

> ¹¹ So shall My word be that goes forth out of My mouth: it shall not return to Me void [without producing any effect, useless], but it shall accomplish that which I please and purpose, and it shall prosper in the thing for which I sent it. [Isaiah 55: 11, AMP]

He knew God performs His word, and He also knew God as his Provider. Consequently, Isaac sowed seed in famine and God prospered him abundantly. The same year, he reaped a hundredfold what he sowed and the Lord favored him with blessings. He was so blessed that the Philistines envied him.

¹² Then Isaac sowed seed in that land and received in the same year a hundred times as much as he had planted, and the Lord favored him with blessings.
¹³ And the man became great and gained more and more until he became very wealthy and distinguished;
¹⁴ He owned flocks, herds, and a great supply of servants, and the Philistines envied him. [Genesis 26: 12-14, AMP]

A word from God obeyed plus a seed of faith sown produces a financial miracle. Obedience of God's command carries with it great reward. It was true for Isaac, and it is true for us.

> A word from God obeyed plus a seed of faith sown produces a financial miracle.
>
> Obedience of God's command carries with it great reward.

¹⁹ If you willingly obey me, the best crops in the land will be yours. [Isaiah 1: 19, CEV]

¹⁹ If you consent and obey, You will eat the best of the land; [Isaiah 1: 19, NASB]

¹⁹ If you will only let me help you, if you will only obey, then I will make you rich! [Isaiah 1: 19, TLB]

Isaac did not just have the best crops in the land, he had the only crops in the land of Gerar, and became the envy of the heathen Philistines. Why, you may ask? Isaac was operating God's economy that is based on seedtime and harvest, and harvest comes by divine instruction and revelation.

When you are under financial pressure, a time of your personal famine listen to God and not your circumstance that the enemy speaks through. Sow seed and do not hold back. Sow with the revelation you have gained in reading this section and the whole of this chapter and see whether God will not prosper you.

The Widow Who Gave All She Had to God

The widow in Mark 12 gave of her last to God and the Lord noticed it.

> Trust God, doubt the devil, your feelings and circumstance, and see God show Himself strong on your behalf.

> ⁴¹ And He sat down opposite the treasury and saw how the crowd was casting money into the treasury. Many rich [people] were throwing in large sums.
>
> ⁴² And a widow who was poverty-stricken came and put in two copper mites [the smallest of coins], which together make half of a cent.
>
> ⁴³ And He called His disciples [to Him] and said to them, Truly and surely I tell you, this widow, [she who is] poverty-stricken, has put in more than all those contributing to the treasury.
>
> ⁴⁴ For they all threw in out of their abundance; but she, out of her deep poverty, has put in everything that she had—[even] all she had on which to live. [Mark 12: 41-44, AMP]

God does not abandon His own. Although there is no mention of her harvest, the fact that the Lord commented on it speaks volumes. She gave her best, and out of her need, her famine. I believe that our Father Who put in motion the law of seedtime and harvest, sowing and reaping, giving and receiving must have given her a bountiful harvest.

In Psalm 126 the Spirit of God makes me to understand that when you sow out of your need (personal famine), you will definitely reap a bountiful harvest that will make you to be full of joy.

> ⁵ They who sow in tears shall reap in joy and singing.
>
> ⁶ He who goes forth bearing seed and weeping [at needing his precious supply of grain for sowing] shall doubtless come again with rejoicing, bringing his sheaves with him. [Psalm 126: 5-6, AMP]

God does not change, and He does not violate His word. What He did in the Old Testament, I believe He did for the widow in Mark 12. He will do it for you too, if you believe Him the way the widow did.

God goes contrary to the world system. In God's economy, there is no seed or crop failure because as long as the earth remains, seedtime and harvest will not fail. Why, you may ask? It is a spiritual law that God put in place in Genesis 8:22 and He watches over His word to perform it. Trust God, doubt the devil, your feelings and circumstance, and see God show Himself strong on your behalf. It works. I know it works.

Offering that Brings Generational Blessing

We have already seen how Abraham received generational blessing through freewill offering because of his obedience to divine instruction. David did too when he gave for the building of the first temple by King Solomon in Jerusalem. Tithing can also bring generational blessing. Generational blessing is not just limited to tithing and freewill offering.

An offering to the Lord is not just money gift. It is anything you have to worship the Lord with a heart of faith and love. It could be hospitality which is what Rahab, the prostitute, offered the Israeli spies Joshua sent to spy out Jordan. It resulted in her being saved from death when Jericho was destroyed. In fact, the salvation was for her entire family. We read the this in Joshua 2:

> [1] Joshua son of Nun sent two men secretly from Shittim as scouts, saying, Go, view the land, especially Jericho. And they went and came to the house of a harlot named Rahab and lodged there.
>
> [2] It was told the king of Jericho, Behold, there came men in here tonight of the Israelites to search out the country.
>
> [3] And the king of Jericho sent to Rahab, saying, Bring forth the men who have come to you, who entered your house, for they have come to search out the land.
>
> [4] But the woman had taken the two men and hidden them. So she said, Yes, two men came to me, but I did not know from where they had come.

⁵ And at gate closing time, after dark, the men went out. Where they went I do not know. Pursue them quickly, for you will overtake them.

⁶ But she had brought them up to the roof and hidden them under the stalks of flax which she had laid in order there.

⁷ So the men pursued them to the Jordan as far as the fords. As soon as the pursuers had gone, the city's gate was shut.

⁸ Before the two men had lain down, Rahab came up to them on the roof,

⁹ And she said to the men, I know that the Lord has given you the land and that your terror is fallen upon us and that all the inhabitants of the land faint because of you.

¹⁰ For we have heard how the Lord dried up the water of the Red Sea for you when you came out of Egypt, and what you did to the two kings of the Amorites who were on the [east] side of the Jordan, Sihon and Og, whom you utterly destroyed.

¹¹ When we heard it, our hearts melted, neither did spirit or courage remain any more in any man because of you, for the Lord your God, He is God in heaven above and on earth beneath.

¹² Now then, I pray you, swear to me by the Lord, since I have shown you kindness, that you also will show kindness to my father's house, and give me a sure sign,

¹³ And save alive my father and mother, my brothers and sisters, and all they have, and deliver us from death.

¹⁴ And the men said to her, Our lives for yours! If you do not tell this business of ours, then when the Lord gives us the land we will deal kindly and faithfully with you. [Joshua 2: 1-14, AMP]

Rahab protected the Israeli spies from being killed by the king of Jericho. In concert with God's Word that when we are kind, merciful, and generous, we are blessing ourselves because our gifts return to bless us, Rahab blessed herself by providing shelter and a hiding place for the spies. Rahab was not only saved, but her entire family, her father's house, was saved. Thus we find that when the Lord gave Israel the mighty victory over Jericho with the implosion of Jericho's wall, Joshua ensured that Israel kept her promise with Rahab saving her and her father's house. Thus, we read from Joshua 6:

¹⁶ And the seventh time, when the priests had blown the trumpets, Joshua said to the people, Shout! For the Lord has given you the city.

¹⁷ And the city and all that is in it shall be devoted to the Lord [for destruction]; only Rahab the harlot and all who are with her in her house shall live, because she hid the messengers whom we sent.

¹⁸ But you, keep yourselves from the accursed and devoted things, lest when you have devoted it [to destruction], you take of the accursed thing, and so make the camp of Israel accursed and trouble it.

¹⁹ But all the silver and gold and vessels of bronze and iron are consecrated to the Lord; they shall come into the treasury of the Lord.

²⁰ So the people shouted, and the trumpets were blown. When the people heard the sound of the trumpet, they raised a great shout, and [Jericho's] wall fell down in its place, so that the [Israelites] went up into the city, every man straight before him, and they took the city.

²¹ Then they utterly destroyed all that was in the city, both man and woman, young and old, ox, sheep, and donkey, with the edge of the sword.

²² But Joshua said to the two men who had spied out the land, Go into the harlot's house and bring out the woman and all she has, as you swore to her.

²³ So the young men, the spies, went in and brought out Rahab, her father and mother, her brethren, and all that she had; and they brought out all her kindred and set them outside the camp of Israel.

²⁴ And they burned the city with fire and all that was in it; only the silver, the gold, and the vessels of bronze and of iron they put into the treasury of the house of the Lord.

²⁵ **So Joshua saved Rahab the harlot, with her father's household and all that she had; and she lives in Israel even to this day, because she hid the messengers whom Joshua sent to spy out Jericho.** [Joshua 6: 17-25, AMP; emphasis mine]

Rahab and her father's family were not just delivered from death, but Rahab was saved. We find that she was grafted into the nation of Israel, a foreshadow of today's Church or Kingdom of God, if you will. She became mother of Boaz who married Ruth, and Ruth was the great grandmother of King David. Our Lord Jesus, of course, came into this world through the lineage of David.

⁵ Salmon the father of Boaz, whose mother was Rahab, Boaz the father of Obed, whose mother was Ruth, Obed the father of Jesse,
⁶ Jesse the father of King David, King David the father of Solomon, whose mother had been the wife of Uriah. [Matthew 1: 5-6, AMP]

Rahab did not know what God had in store for her when she gave to God's people. All she knew was to do good. She did her very best. We are commanded to do good to all men, especially those of the household of God. When we do, God rewards us handsomely; and in some cases the blessing becomes generational. Here is the Holy Spirit's admonish to us on this:

⁹ And let us not lose heart and grow weary and faint in acting nobly and doing right, for in due time and at the appointed season we shall reap, if we do not loosen and relax our courage and faint.
¹⁰ So then, as occasion and opportunity open up to us, let us do good [morally] to all people [not only being useful or profitable to them, but also doing what is for their spiritual good and advantage]. Be mindful to be a blessing, especially to those of the household of faith [those who belong to God's family with you, the believers]. [Galatians 6: 9-10, AMP]

¹ Let love for your fellow believers continue and be a fixed practice with you [never let it fail].
² Do not forget or neglect or refuse to extend hospitality to strangers [in the brotherhood—being friendly, cordial, and gracious, sharing the comforts of your home and doing your part generously], for through it some have entertained angels without knowing it.
³ Remember those who are in prison as if you were their fellow prisoner, and those who are ill-treated, since you also are liable to bodily sufferings. [Hebrews 13; 1-3, AMP]

Please do not give out of selfishness, thinking whether what you are about to give will result in a generational blessing. Let your heart be after God, to please Him in all you do. In giving, you are to give your very best. Give out of a heart of love, and the Lord of the harvest has a sure reward of a bountiful harvest for you. Rahab was not looking for a financial harvest. She was expecting deliverance from physical death, but her act of faith did not go unnoticed by God. God does not forsake your work of faith, your labor of love. God calls what Rahab did faith.

> [31] [Prompted] by faith Rahab the prostitute was not destroyed along with those who refused to believe and obey, because she had received the spies in peace [without enmity]. [Hebrews 11: 31, AMP]

> [24] You see that a man is justified (pronounced righteous before God) through what he does and not alone through faith [through works of obedience as well as by what he believes].
> [25] So also with Rahab the harlot—was she not shown to be justified (pronounced righteous before God) by [good] deeds when she took in the scouts (spies) and sent them away by a different route?
> [26] For as the human body apart from the spirit is lifeless, so faith apart from [its] works of obedience is also dead. [James 2: 24-26, AMP]

Seed money is a seed you sow into a person's life to trigger the release of a much needed blessing into the person's life.

Thus, our giving is our faith working through love, and God honors faith. God pronounced her righteous by her work of faith. Thus, she was grafted into God's family and the royal line of David through which our Lord Jesus came.

Seed Money

Jesus in John 6: 1-13 needed to feed the 5000 men besides women and children, but He had no food at hand. A little boy gave what he had, two fish and five loaves, to Jesus for the purpose of feeding the multitude. Jesus, in turn, presented the seed (two fish and five loaves) to the Father to multiply for the feeding of the multitude. Note that the seed of two fish and five loaves were not enough to feed the multitude, but it became the seed that Jesus offered to the Father to multiply back to Him to meet the need of the hungry multitude.

Years ago a friend needed $5000. The Lord ministered to me to give $500, and as soon as he received the money he should take it and give thanks to our Father based on John 6: 11. "Jesus took the loaves, and when He had given thanks, He distributed to the disciples and the disciples to the reclining people; so also [He did] with the fish, as much as they wanted." [AMP] The Lord told me that once he obeyed, he would receive the remaining $4500. I did as the Lord commanded me, and the brother did and in a few weeks the Lord miraculously provided him with the $5000 he needed.

I asked the Lord to explain to me what He meant by this type of giving. He told me it was seed money. Seed money is a seed you sow into a person's life to trigger the release of a much needed blessing into the person's life. I have since put this to work by sowing into the lives of those who seek to raise funds for missionary trips and we have seen God meet their budget over and beyond our expectations.

The Importance of Speaking The Word over Your Offering
The offering you give has no life by itself. It is the Word that you speak over your offering that programs it for multiplication. It is the Word that contains the "DNA" of what you want produced. This is what God did at creation in Genesis 1, and Genesis 1: 11 is a good example of this. "And God said, Let the earth put forth [tender] vegetation: plants yielding seed and fruit trees yielding fruit whose seed is in itself, each according to its kind, upon the earth. And it was so." [Genesis 1: 11, AMP] In that Word that God spoke was the genetic material to produce different plants and vegetables.

Thus, when you pray the Word over your offering, you program it to produce after the Word of God you spoke over it in faith. Every time we give to the Lord, we are involved in the operation of the spiritual law of seedtime and harvest, sowing and reaping, giving and receiving. The seed you sow may not be money alone; it could be time, a life changing word you speak to somebody, praying for others, or ministering to others. It is whatever the Lord has blessed you with that you can use to be a blessing to others, and give to the service of the Lord.

> The offering you give has no life by itself. It is the Word that you speak over your offering that programs it for multiplication.

You Benefit Yourself When You Give

Finally, remember that when you give, you are actually blessing yourself. Your gift releases your blessing. They actually return to bless you. Here is what the Word says of a generous person:

> [17] The merciful, kind, and generous man benefits himself [for his deeds return to bless him], but he who is cruel and callous [to the wants of others] brings on himself retribution.
>
> [24] There are those who [generously] scatter abroad, and yet increase more; there are those who withhold more than is fitting or what is justly due, but it results only in want.
>
> [25] The liberal person shall be enriched, and he who waters shall himself be watered.
>
> [28] He who leans on, trusts in, and is confident in his riches shall fall, but the [uncompromisingly] righteous shall flourish like a green bough.
>
> [30] The fruit of the [uncompromisingly] righteous is a tree of life, and he who is wise captures human lives [for God, as a fisher of men - he gathers and receives them for eternity]. [Proverbs 11: 17, 24-25, 28, 30, AMP]
>
> [8] And God is able to make all grace (every favor and earthly blessing) come to you in abundance, so that you may always and under all

circumstances and whatever the need be self-sufficient [possessing enough to require no aid or support and furnished in abundance for every good work and charitable donation].

9 As it is written, He [the benevolent person] scatters abroad; He gives to the poor; His deeds of justice and goodness and kindness and benevolence will go on and endure forever! [2 Corinthians 9: 8-9, AMP]

Do whatever the Lord tells you to do. Just do it.

7 If there is among you a poor man, one of your kinsmen in any of the towns of your land which the Lord your God gives you, you shall not harden your [minds and] hearts or close your hands to your poor brother;

8 But you shall open your hands wide to him and shall surely lend him sufficient for his need in whatever he lacks.

10 You shall give to him freely without begrudging it; because of this the Lord will bless you in all your work and in all you undertake. [Deuteronomy 15: 7-8,10, AMP]

17 Not that I seek or am eager for [your] gift, but I do seek and am eager for the fruit which increases to your credit [the harvest of blessing that is accumulating to your account].

19 And my God will liberally supply (fill to the full) your every need according to His riches in glory in Christ Jesus. [Philippians 4: 17,19, AMP]

You cannot give to God and lack. Rather, our heavenly Father ensures that abundance is your portion because you cannot out give Him.

What Do You Give?

In this section, I will discuss this important question in detail. You may ask what do I give? Is it only money? No, not just money! You give what you have to the Lord, out of a willing heart as He prompts you to give. It could be your time, *agape* love, favor, hospitality, a word of encouragement, kindness, influence used the right way, talent, money, prayer, or praise which is the fruit of your lips.

When it comes to giving, there are two points you have to address. These are:

> God will never ask you to give what you do not have. He always leaves us with a seed to sow.

- Lord, what would you have me do (give)? This follows after the pattern that the Holy Spirit used Saul (later called Paul) to illustrate for us at the point of His conversion. "Trembling and astonished he asked, Lord, what do You desire me to do? The Lord said to him, But arise and go into the city, and you will be told what you must do." [Acts 9: 6, AMP] Saul obeyed the Lord, and later the Holy Spirit used him to write most of the New Testament for us.
- Do whatever the Lord tells you to do. Just do it. [John 2: 5] It is a response to the question raised in the first point.

You give whatever God ministers to you to give as a worship unto Him. It is what you give that God multiplies and there are no limits to His blessing. On your part, do not limit Him. He told Abraham to offer Isaac as a freewill offering to Him. When Abraham obeyed, God said to him,

> [17] In blessing I will bless you and in multiplying I will multiply your descendants like the stars of the heavens and like the sand on the seashore. And your Seed (Heir) will possess the gate of His enemies,
> [18] And in your Seed [Christ] shall all the nations of the earth be blessed and [by Him] bless themselves, because you have heard and obeyed My voice. [Genesis 22: 17-18, AMP]

God will never ask you to give what you do not have. He always leaves us with a seed to sow. Through Elisha, He asked the widow of the son of the prophets what she had of sale value that she could give for Him to multiply back to her.

¹ Now the wife of a son of the prophets cried to Elisha, Your servant my husband is dead, and you know that your servant feared the Lord. But the creditor has come to take my two sons to be his slaves.

² **Elisha said to her, What shall I do for you? Tell me, what have you [of sale value] in the house? She said, Your handmaid has nothing in the house except a jar of oil.**

³ Then he said, Go around and borrow vessels from all your neighbors, empty vessels—and not a few.

⁴ And when you come in, shut the door upon you and your sons. Then pour out [the oil you have] into all those vessels, setting aside each one when it is full.

⁵ So she went from him and shut the door upon herself and her sons, who brought to her the vessels as she poured the oil.

⁶ When the vessels were all full, she said to her son, Bring me another vessel. And he said to her, There is not a one left. Then the oil stopped multiplying.

⁷ Then she came and told the man of God. He said, Go, sell the oil and pay your debt, and you and your sons live on the rest. [1 Kings 4: 1-7, AMP; emphasis mine]

When the widow obeyed God, she was blessed beyond her wildest imagination. God did not just cancel her debt, but He gave her a generational business. Notice what Elisha said to her after she had poured the oil into all the vessels she had borrowed: "Go, sell the oil and pay your debt, and you and your sons live on the rest." [For a detailed discussion of this miracle of debt cancellation and generational business see my book, *The Timeless Zone*.] God always wants to increase us, and our obedience is an important key to receiving God's prosperity. David said:

¹² The Lord has been mindful of us, He will bless us: He will bless the house of Israel, He will bless the house of Aaron [the priesthood],

¹³ He will bless those who reverently and worshipfully fear the Lord, both small and great.

¹⁴ May the Lord give you increase more and more, you and your children.

¹⁵ May you be blessed of the Lord, Who made heaven and earth! [Psalm 115: 12-15, AMP]

Trust the Lord with your life, your substance, and obey Him in all things, and see if He will not prosper you beyond your wildest dreams. He keeps record of your giving so that He can reward you as at and when needed.

God Keeps Record of Your Giving

Our God is the best Banker, Accountant, and Financial Comptroller you could ever wish to have. He never forgets your giving (seed sown). He rewarded Jacob 20 years after Jacob made a vow to Him. Jacob made a vow to the Lord after he encountered Him at Bethel:

> ²⁰ Then Jacob made a vow, saying, If God will be with me and will keep me in this way that I go and will give me food to eat and clothing to wear,
> ²¹ So that I may come again to my father's house in peace, then the Lord shall be my God;
> ²² And this stone which I have set up as a pillar (monument) shall be God's house [a sacred place to me], and of all [the increase of possessions] that You give me I will give the tenth to You. [Genesis 28: 20-22, AMP]

Twenty years later God appeared to Jacob in a (prophetic) dream to restore to Jacob over and above all the wages that Laban, his father-in-law, withheld from him. Laban changed Jacob's wages 10 times. The Angel of the Lord reminded Jacob of the vow He made to the Lord 20 years earlier, letting him, I believe, know that God did not forget Jacob's vow, hence the restoration.

> ¹⁰ And I had a dream at the time the flock conceived. I looked up and saw that the rams which mated with the she-goats were streaked, speckled, and spotted.
> ¹¹ And the Angel of God said to me in the dream, Jacob. And I said, Here am I.

¹² And He said, Look up and see, all the rams which mate with the flock are streaked, speckled, and mottled; for I have seen all that Laban does to you.

¹³ I am the God of Bethel, where you anointed the pillar and where you vowed a vow to Me. Now arise, get out from this land and return to your native land. [Genesis 31: 10-13, AMP]

The Apostle Paul drove home the point that God our Father keeps accurate records of our banking transactions in our heavenly bank accounts. Each time you give for the Lord's sake and the Gospel's sake (used here in a general sense to cover all types of giving) you open up a debit and credit account with the bank of Heaven, the Central Bank of Heaven (Heaven's Reserve Bank).

¹⁵ And you Philippians yourselves well know that in the early days of the Gospel ministry, when I left Macedonia, **no church (assembly) entered into partnership with me and opened up [a debit and credit] account in giving and receiving except you only.**

¹⁷ Not that I seek or am eager for [your] gift, but I do seek and **am eager for the fruit which increases to your credit [the harvest of blessing that is accumulating to your account].** [Philippians 4: 15,17, AMP; emphasis mine]

Without a debit and credit account in giving and receiving, you have no harvest to reap. To reap where you do not sow would be stealing, and God is against thievery. To enable Him to bless us, He sent Jesus to Calvary to win the victory for us, opening up the channel for us to have reserves in Heaven to draw from as at and when needed.

9. THE PRINCIPLE OF RELEASE

[Remember] this: he who sows sparingly and grudgingly will also reap sparingly and grudgingly, and he who sows generously [that blessings may come to someone] will also reap generously and with blessings. [2 Corinthians 9: 6, AMP]

The principle of release is this: you release your best into the hands of God, and He in turn gives you His best. The principle of release sets in motion the wheel of the law of seedtime and harvest in your life the way God has ordained it. To be able to release your best into the hands of the Lord, you must do it in faith with a pure heart. To give in faith is to give what God instructs you to give, and not what you think.

> ⁴ [Prompted, actuated] by faith Abel brought God a better and more acceptable sacrifice than Cain, because of which it was testified of him that he was righteous [that he was upright and in right standing with God], and God bore witness by accepting and acknowledging his gifts. And though he died, yet [through the incident] he is still speaking. [Hebrews 11: 4, AMP]

Abel hearkened to God's divine command and gave God his firstfruits offering, but Cain did not hearken to the divine command. God said to Cain:

> ⁷ If you do well [believing Me and doing what is acceptable and pleasing to Me], will you not be accepted? And if you do not do well [**but ignore My instruction**], sin crouches at your door; its desire is for you [to overpower you], but you must master it." [Genesis 4: 7, AMP; emphasis mine]

Cain did not understand the law of release. Instead of following through with divine instruction, he disobeyed and became jealous of his brother.

He understood that God's acceptance of his brother's sacrifice would translate into blessing.

When God accepts what you release into His hand, He responds by blessing you. He releases the blessing that He has for you into your life.

Heaven responds to earth. Heaven moves in response to a move made from earth. The law of seedtime and harvest is the basis for the principle of release. "While the earth remains, Seedtime and harvest, Cold and heat, Winter and summer, And day and night Shall not cease." [Genesis 8: 22, AMP] Seedtime is the season proper for sowing.

Prophecy of the Coming of Jesus

In Genesis 3:15 God prophesied the coming of Jesus and the defeat of Satan after Satan had deceived the woman resulting in she and her husband Adam sinning against God. The result was the fall of man and loss of his dominion to Satan. Then God said, "And I will put enmity (open hostility) between you and the woman, and between your seed (offspring) and her Seed; He shall [fatally] bruise your head, and you shall [only] bruise His heel." [Genesis 3: 15, AMP] In this verse God prophesied the coming of Jesus our Lord. However, for God to send Jesus he had to use man to trigger the coming ("release") of Jesus from heaven to earth. How did He do it?

Abraham's Offering and the Gift of Jesus

God raised up Abram (later Abraham), a man He could relate and do business with. In Abraham, God found a man who could trust Him and do His will for his life. Abraham is called the friend of God. "…. Abraham believed in (adhered to, trusted in, and relied on) God, and this was accounted to him as righteousness (as conformity to God's will in thought and deed), and he was called God's friend." [James 2: 23, AMP] In fact, the Scripture declares that the Lord could not destroy Sodom and Gomorrah without first letting Abraham know.

¹⁷ The Lord said, "Shall I keep secret from Abraham [My friend and servant] what I am going to do,
¹⁸ since Abraham is destined to become a great and mighty nation, and all the nations of the earth will be blessed through him?
¹⁹ For I have known (chosen, acknowledged) him [as My own], so that he may teach and command his children and [the sons of] his household after him to keep the way of the Lord by doing what is righteous and just, so that the Lord may bring upon Abraham what He has promised him." [Genesis 18: 17-19, AMP]

Abraham was God's friend and servant through whom the whole world was to be blessed. This is because of the blessing of the covenant God made with Abraham. When God called Abraham, then Abram, in Genesis 12, He said:

² And I will make you a great nation,
And I will bless you [abundantly],
And make your name great (exalted, distinguished);
And you shall be a blessing [a source of great good to others];
³ And I will bless (do good for, benefit) those who bless you,
And I will curse [that is, subject to My wrath and judgment] the one who curses (despises, dishonors, has contempt for) you. And in you all the families (nations) of the earth will be blessed." [Genesis 12: 2-3, AMP]

When God wanted to activate the plan of redemption here on earth which was already consummated in heaven, He asked Abraham to release what he had to him. He did not just ask for anything, He asked for Abraham's most treasured or beloved possession, his only son Isaac; or as the Douay-Rheims Bible put it, "… thy only begotten son Isaac." [Genesis 22: 2] It is important to note that Abraham was God's blood covenant partner because God had earlier cut a covenant with him in Genesis 15: 9-21. That meant that God lived for Abraham and vice versa.

Thus, to "release" Jesus from heaven to come down to earth and redeem us, He needed to start the move from the earth. He, therefore, asked Abraham to give Him his only begotten son Isaac. Isaac was Abraham's only begotten son because he was birthed as a consequence of a covenant relationship between Abraham and Sarah who were in covenant with God. Ishmael was not a covenant son, but a son of a bond woman born of the flesh. "But what does the Scripture say? "Cast out the bondwoman [Hagar] and her son [Ishmael], For never shall the son of the bondwoman be heir and share the inheritance with the son of the free woman.""

> A miracle does not manifest unless it is spoken.

God asked Abraham to give him his best, his only son.

> ² God said, "Take now your son, your only son [of promise], whom you love, Isaac, and go to the region of Moriah, and offer him there as a burnt offering on one of the mountains of which I shall tell you." [Genesis 22: 2, AMP]

God's intent was that through Abraham's obedience, He could send His beloved Son to the earth to die and redeem us from Satan's dominion and control. Although Abraham did not know the ramification of God's request, all that God needed from Abraham was obedience out of full trust and confidence in Him – a heart of love for God. The Word declares that in asking for Abraham to offer Isaac to Him, "God did prove Abraham,…" [Genesis 22: 1, ASV] I like the word "prove" because to prove is to make certain; to show; or to evince. To evince is to show in a clear manner or unmistakable terms; to prove beyond any reasonable doubt; to manifest; to make evident. God wanted to make evident to the devil that Abraham is a man He could partner with on earth.

Because of Abraham's relationship with God which made him to have a listening heart, Abraham made some statements of faith which were prophetic. When they got to close to Mount Moriah he told his servants to wait for him and Isaac while they went to the mountain to worship the Lord. When Isaac asked where the sacrificial lamb was, Abraham told him that the Lord would provide for Himself a lamb for sacrifice. "Abraham said, "My son, God will provide for Himself a lamb for the burnt offering." So the two walked on together." This statement had two dimensions to it.

First, it indicated that God would miraculously provide a lamb for the burnt offering at Mount Moriah where they were to worship God, instead of sacrificing Isaac. Secondly, he prophesied of Jesus Who was the sacrificial Lamb for our redemption. A miracle does not manifest unless it is spoken. God in His economy considered Isaac offered to Him as a burnt offering – a sacrifice of faith.

> [17] By faith Abraham, when he was tested, offered up Isaac, and he who had received the promises was offering up his only begotten son; [Hebrews 11: 17, NASB]

> [17] The one it had been said about, Your seed will be traced through Isaac. [Hebrews 11: 18, HCSB]

> [19] For he considered [it reasonable to believe] that God was able to raise Isaac even from among the dead. [Indeed, in the sense that he was prepared to sacrifice Isaac in obedience to God] Abraham did receive him back [from the dead] figuratively speaking. [Hebrews 11: 19, AMP]

Abraham gave God his best, his only begotten son through whom his Seed, Jesus, was to come. Because he did, he enabled God to send Jesus to us. This is the principle of release. Abraham gave God his best, Isaac, God released His best, Jesus, to us. This is why we have John 3: 16. When Abraham raised his hand to kill Isaac for the burnt offering at Mount Moriah God said:

> [12] ..... "Do not reach out [with the knife in] your hand against the boy, and do nothing to [harm] him; for now I know that you fear God [with reverence and profound respect], since you have not withheld from Me your son, your only son [of promise]." [Genesis 22: 12, AMP]

God, Who abhors human sacrifice did not want Isaac sacrificed to him as a burnt offering because that is what the worshippers of Baal were doing. It was for that same reason, among others, that the inhabitants of the Promised Land were to be driven out and the Land given to Abraham's descendants. Thus, God provided a ram for sacrifice as Abraham had spoken.

> 13 Then Abraham looked up and glanced around, and behold, behind him was a ram caught in a thicket by his horns. And Abraham went and took the ram and offered it up for a burnt offering (ascending sacrifice) instead of his son.].” [Genesis 22: 13, AMP]

A place of obedience is a place of vision.

God is always particular in what He says and does. He chose Mount Moriah for Abraham to offer him a burnt offering. Moriah is from from two Hebrew words *ra'ah* and *Yahh* which means seen and Jah, respectively. Combining the two words yields the meaning seen of Jah – seen of the Lord. Moriah, therefore, is a place of vision. A place of vision is a place of obedience. Put another way, a place of obedience is a place of vision.

Obedience to God enables us to hear from him and to see what He is showing us. Thus, Abraham was able to see the ram God provided for the sacrifice. In fact, Douay-Rheims Bible calls the region of Moriah in Genesis 22: 2, the land of vision. It was there that Abraham knew God as Jehovah Jireh. “So Abraham named that place The Lord Will Provide. And it is said to this day, “On the mountain of the Lord it will be seen and provided.””

When Abraham released his best, his son Isaac, to God willingly with no hesitation, God had to pronounce a blessing on Abraham and further affirmed the coming of Jesus to redeem man.

> 15 The Angel of the Lord called to Abraham from heaven a second time 16 and said, “By Myself (on the basis of Who I Am) I have sworn [an oath], declares the Lord, that since you have done this thing and have not withheld [from Me] your son, your only son [of promise],
> 17 indeed I will greatly bless you, and I will greatly multiply your descendants like the stars of the heavens and like the sand on the

seashore; and **your seed shall possess the gate of their enemies** [as conquerors]. [Genesis 22: 15-17, AMP; emphasis mine]

> To receive the best from God, we must give Him your best.

Thus from the offering of Isaac by Abraham to God at God's request, God shows us how the law of seedtime and harvest operates through the principle of release. Without a release on earth, there is no release from heaven. God used His covenant partner to show us how the blessing of God can be released into our lives if we follow the example of Abraham.

God only pronounced the blessing on Abraham after Abraham had willingly obeyed Him. This is very instructive. It clearly shows that the principle of release puts into motion, the law of seedtime and harvest. The lesson is that to receive the best from God, we must give Him our best. Abraham gave that which cost him something. In fact, it cost him all that he lived for. We can learn the following from Abraham:

- Abraham spoke the provision of the ram prophetically into a existence. His statement to his servants was not just a statement of faith. "Abraham said to his servants, "Settle down and stay here with the donkey; the young man and I will go over there and worship [God], and we will come back to you."" Abraham believed God Who promised that the posterity of Isaac was to inherit the promises He made to him in Genesis 12: 2.
- Based on his prophetic statement to Isaac, Abraham expected God to provide a lamb for sacrifice. Isaac, of course, was a most expressive type of Jesus.
- Abraham loved God and took more pleasure in God than in Isaac. It is very important for us to learn this from Abraham, our father of faith. Here is what Jesus had to say about our love for our parents or our children. "He who loves father or mother more than Me is not worthy of Me; and he who loves son or daughter

more than Me is not worthy of Me." [Matthew 10: 37, AMP] Our commitment to our Lord Jesus should take precedence over everyone and everything else.

- When you release to God what He asks of you and not hold back, you prove to God that you fear and revere Him. This is what Abraham proved.

> [12] The Lord said, "Do not reach out [with the knife in] your hand against the boy, and do nothing to [harm] him; for now I know that you fear God [with reverence and profound respect], since you have not withheld from Me your son, your only son [of promise]." [Genesis 22: 12, AMP]

- It is only after releasing to God what He asked of you that you can hear from Him and see the blessing as we learn from Abraham.

> [13] Then Abraham looked up and glanced around, and behold, behind him was a ram caught in a thicket by his horns. And Abraham went and took the ram and offered it up for a burnt offering (ascending sacrifice) instead of his son.
> [14] So Abraham named that place The Lord Will Provide. And it is said to this day, "On the mountain of the Lord it will be seen and provided."
> [15] The Angel of the Lord called to Abraham from heaven a second time
> [16] and said, "By Myself (on the basis of Who I Am) I have sworn [an oath], declares the Lord, that since you have done this thing and have not withheld [from Me] your son, your only son [of promise],
> [17] indeed I will greatly bless you, and I will greatly multiply your descendants like the stars of the heavens and like the sand on the seashore; and your seed shall possess the gate of their enemies [as conquerors].
> [18] Through your seed all the nations of the earth shall be blessed, because you have heard and obeyed My voice." [Genesis 22: 13-18, AMP]

Thus, we can understand when God says, ""I will bless those in every nation who trust in me as you do." And so it is: all who trust in Christ share the same blessing Abraham received." [Galatians 3: 9, TLB]

David understood the principle of release. Because he loved God whole heartedly, he knew that he could always run to God no matter the situation. In his lowest moments, he knew that it was only God he could run to; and that was the case when he disobeyed God and conducted a census in Israel.

> Always give God that which costs you something. It causes Him to arise on your behalf and bless you with a miracle or the blessing that you need.

David's Offering Stayed the Plague

David gave God that which cost him something, and God stayed the plague that killed 70,000 Israelites because of David's disobedience which God called arrogance. He numbered God's children when God had said that His chosen people were to be numberless. [1 Chronicles 21: 1-17] David refused to accept the items of the sacrifice that he was to offer to the Lord free of charge from Ornan.

> [24] But King David said to Ornan, "No, I will certainly pay the full price; for **I will not take what is yours for the Lord, nor offer a burnt offering which costs me nothing.**"
> [25] So David gave Ornan 600 shekels of gold by weight for the site. [1 Chronicles 21: 24-25, AMP; emphasis mine]

David knew that if God did not stop the plague, no one could. Abraham knew that if God did not provide a lamb (a ram) for sacrifice, no one could. That which costs you something is what would put in motion the principle of release of God's blessing in your life because it is what gets the law of seedtime and harvest working for you. Always give God that which costs you something. It causes Him to arise on your behalf and bless you with a miracle or the blessing that you need.

The Rest of Us

What would stretch your faith for a financial blessing or any other blessing you need from God? What do you have of value like the widow in 2 Kings 4: 1-7 that you can give God to multiply back to you as a harvest that meets your need? Release your seed to God and let God release the much needed blessing to you right now according to Mark 11: 23-24. If you already have a receipt because you gave your best to God, you can order your harvest now. Command the devil to take his hands off your harvest, and dispatch ministering angels to go forth and bring your harvest to you now in the Name of Jesus Christ our Lord.

In this chapter the Spirit of the Lord has shown us the principle behind the worshipful giving we discussed in the previous chapters. The principle of release that God taught us through Abraham and practiced by saints of old should govern all your giving. Here is a summary of examples to encourage your faith.

- Hannah vowed to give her all, the only son she asked of God, to God. God opened her womb, and she had Samuel. When she fulfilled her vow by giving Samuel back to the Lord (1 Samuel 1: 24-28), the Lord blessed her with three more sons and two daughters. [1 Samuel 2: 21]
- The Zarephath woman gave the first portion of her last cake to God because Elijah was sent by God to her, and God sustained her and her household throughout the famine. [1 Kings 17: 13-14]
- The widow of one of the son of the prophets turned over her jar of oil to God by following through with divine instructions from Elisha. God cancelled her debt and made her an oil merchant – something she was not expecting. [2 Kings 4: 1-7] We serve a

God Who does exceeding superabundantly above our highest prayers, hopes, dreams, and desires. [Ephesians 3: 20, AMP]

- The Corinthian Church gave out of their lack, and God caused them to be self-sufficient, requiring no aid, but abounding in good works. [2 Corinthians 9: 6-11, AMP]
- The Philippian Church gave their best to God, and Paul, by the Holy Spirit, said that they opened up a debit and credit account with God. That is, through their giving they put into motion the principle of release; thereby enabling the cardinal law of seedtime time and harvest to work for them. Because they, by their giving, put into motion the principle of release, Paul, prompted by the Holy Spirit, declared, "And my God will liberally supply (fill to the full) your every need according to His riches in glory in Christ Jesus." [Philippians 4: 19, AMP]

No matter your need, give God your very best out of a pure, willing, and obedient heart. Aim your seed at your need, and see God bless you beyond limits. If you do not give with a pure heart that is willing and totally yielded to God, you are wasting your time. God does not hear the prayer of sinners or that of believers who are not working in obedience to Him. John, the apostle, wrote, "We know that God does not listen to sinners, but **if anyone is a worshiper of God and does his will, God listens to him.**" [John 9: 31, AMP, emphasis mine] Our Father wants you blessed and walking in victory all the time.

What Does the Principle of Release Govern?

The principle of release governs every area of our lives and our walk with God. Here are some examples.

- It governs giving and receiving in a general sense as seen in the examples discussed above and Abraham's offering of Isaac which I have discussed in detail.

- It is the key to breakthrough. When Hannah coupled her prayer with a vow to release the son that God was to give to her to God, God remembered her and gave her Samuel. [1 Samuel 1] It governs breakthrough in employment and (job) promotion. In chapter 8 of this book I narrated a testimony of a brother and his wife who released all that they had, their all, into the hands of the Lord, and the Lord blessed the brother with an excellent job that carried with it a promotion. He combined his prayer for a job with his giving, releasing all into the hands of the Lord. This enabled God to release the excellent job He had for him into his hands.

- It is the key to debt cancellation and financial prosperity. An excellent Bible example is the widow of the son of the prophets in 2 Kings 4: 1-7 discussed in the previous section. I also narrated a testimony of the sister whose $110,000 credit card debt was cancelled as she released what she had to God for Him to multiply back in the form of cancellation of her debt.

- It governs our confession (speech) and prayer. Without releasing your words of acknowledgement that Christ was raised from the dead and confessing Him as your Lord and Savior, you cannot be saved. [Romans 10: 8-11] It brings possession because by releasing your words toward God to acknowledge that Christ died for you, God rewards you with salvation. It enabled the woman who had the issue of blood in Mark 5 to receive her healing. "For she kept saying, If I only touch His garments, I shall be restored to health." {Mark 5: 28, AMP]

Jesus said that if you say, believe and do not doubt that what you say takes place, the Father makes it good (releases) to you.

> [23] For verily I say to you, that whoever may say to this mount, Be taken up, and be cast into the sea, and may not doubt in his heart, but may believe that the things that he saith do come to pass, it shall be to him whatever he may say.

²⁴ Because of this I say to you, all whatever -- praying -- ye do ask, believe that ye receive, and it shall be to you. [Mark 11: 23-24, YLT]

It governs prayer because Jesus said that the same principle that governs speech governs prayer as you see from Mark 11: 23-24 above. When you speak, you release words; and when you pray you put forth words.

- It governs the exercise of authority. See Mathew 16: 19 and Matthew 18: 18. It is only what you bind on earth that God gives you backing by ensuring that the demons in the stellar heaven (the second heaven) cannot operate either. The third heaven is where God resides. Satan and his demons have no access there anymore. They were cast out. [Luke 10: 18] For more on binding and loosing, see my book, ***Dominion Power.*** If you do not bind the demons, God will not do anything. [James 4: 7; 1 Peter 5: 8-9]

- It governs repentance, forgiveness, love, favor, and blessing. When we repent of our sins, God forgives us. [1 John 1: 9] If we do not repent, we short change ourselves and become open target for the enemy. Lack of repentance is harboring sin in your life. The adversary will come for what is because sin by any name is his. Sin makes the devil have a claim on you. When he comes to exact payment for having what is his, he is merciless. Do not let the devil have any claim on you. Because you are not a sinner whose nature is to practice sin, if you sin be quick to repent and let the blood of Jesus cleanse you from all unrighteousness.

The adversary tried his worst against our Lord Jesus, but he could not have access to Him. Why, you may ask? Jesus was without sin. That is why He said in John 14:

³⁰ I will not talk with you much more, for the prince (evil genius, ruler) of the world is coming. And he has no claim on Me. [He has nothing in common with Me; there is nothing in

Me that belongs to him, and he has no power over Me.] [John 14: 30, AMP]

You must not let the devil have access to you.

When you forgive others, God forgives you. [Mark 11: 25-26] Whatever good you do to others, God will repay you with good. "Remember, the Lord will pay you for each good thing you do, whether you are slave or free." [Ephesians 6: 8, TLB] It is the basis of our victory over the enemy. When you pray for those who seek your hurt, God gives you victory in the situation and blesses you in addition. [1 Peter 3; 9-14, AMP]

When you shower favor and loving kindness on others, God ensures that you are blessed in return. "The merciful, kind, and generous man benefits himself [for his deeds return to bless him], but he who is cruel and callous [to the wants of others] brings on himself retribution." [Proverbs 11: 17, AMP]

- It governs deliverance from anxiety and worry which precede panic attack and hypertension, respectively. When you cast your cares on the Lord, He takes care of you and solves your problems.

> [22] Cast your burden on the Lord [release it] and He will sustain and uphold you; He will never allow the righteous to be shaken (slip, fall, fail). [Psalm 55: 22, AMP]

> [7] Casting all your cares [all your anxieties, all your worries, and all your concerns, once and for all] on Him, for He cares about you [with deepest affection, and watches over you very carefully]. [1 Peter 5: 7, AMP]

God has told us that He cares for us, and we need not worry about the things unbelievers spend their lives worrying about. [Luke 12: 32] Take God at His Word; do what He says and watch Him take care of your needs for you.

- It is the basis of intercession for the deliverance of others from danger, and the salvation of souls into the Kingdom of God. It is the basis of deliverance from the jaws of death. A good example is Jonah in the belly of the fish. He sacrificed thanksgiving to God and made a vow, probably that he will go to Nineveh to preach if God gave him life again. Although the Bible does not state it categorically, I believe it is implied as we read below.

> 7 When my soul fainted within me I remembered the Lord: and my prayer came in unto thee, into thine holy temple.
> 8 They that observe lying vanities forsake their own mercy.
> 9 But I will sacrifice unto thee with the voice of thanksgiving; I will pay that that I have vowed. Salvation is of the Lord.
> 10 And the Lord spake unto the fish, and it vomited out Jonah upon the dry land. [Jonah 2: 7-10, KJV]

It was only after his thanksgiving and vow that God ordered the fish to spew him out. Jonah's thanksgiving and vow triggered, activated, his release from the fish's belly. Without Jonah doing his part, God would not have ordered the fish to release him. In your adversity, lift up your voice to God. Sacrifice thanksgiving to Him, and see if He will not deliver you. He did it for Jonah. He did for Paul and Silas as they praised Him with bruised bodies in a Philippian jail in Acts 16. He set them free because they chose to praise Him in their adversity.

What miracle or breakthrough do you need? Whether it is financial or otherwise, couple your prayer with your giving. Release your very best into the hands of the Lord, and let Him release the very best harvest that he has for you into your hands.

If it is finances, as you lift up your seed to God decree the financial harvest you need according to Mark 11: 23 (YLT) and Job 22: 28 (AMP). Bind Satan, and dispatch ministering angels to go forth and bring you your financial harvest. Believe it is done according to Mark 11; 23 and switch over into the expectation mode. Keep your eyes on the Lord of the harvest and His Word, and not on what you released into His hands. Whatever else you need, decree it and God will make it good unto you. Stay in thanksgiving and you will see the manifestation of your harvest. Because you have released your best to God, He in turn releases His best harvest into your hands. The principle of release will bring you victory in every situation. Jesus' victory at Calvary's Cross enables us to be partakers of the blessings the Father has for us through the principle of release.

PART 3: THE VICTORY OF LOVE

10. LOVE IS THE VICTORY

When He was reviled and insulted, He did not revile or offer insult in return; [when] He was abused and suffered, He made no threats [of vengeance]; but he trusted [Himself and everything] to Him Who judges fairly. [1 Peter 2: 23, AMP]

It was *Agape* love that won the victory for us at Calvary's Cross. The devil was dethroned at the Cross of Christ. Paul records in 1 Corinthians 2:

> [6] We do discuss 'wisdom' with those who are mature; only it is not of this world or of the dethroned Powers who rule this world." [1 Corinthians 2: 6, MOFFATT]

> [6] Howbeit we speak wisdom among them that are perfect: yet not the wisdom of this world, nor of the princes of this world, that come to nought. [1 Corinthians 2: 6, KJV]

The word "nought" used in the passage above in the KJV is translated from the Greek word *katargeo*. It means "to bring to nought, to be rendered entirely useless, to destroy, to make of no effect, fail, put down , and make void." Thus, I paraphrase 1 Corinthians 2: 6 thus:

> *We do discuss wisdom with those who are spiritually mature. Only, it is not the wisdom of this world, nor of the princes of this world (the powers) who have been dethroned, rendered entirely useless, made of no effect, brought to nought, put down, and (their powers) made void (ineffective, useless, and inoperative).*

Thus, the wisdom of the Gospel is that the devil has been dethroned. How did our Lord do this? The answer is found in Colossians 2:

> [15] "And then having drawn the sting of all the powers ranged against us, he exposed them, shattered, empty and defeated, in his final glorious triumphant act!" [Colossians 2: 15, PHILLIPS]

[15] And the hostile princes and rulers He shook off from Himself, and boldly displayed them as His conquests, when by the Cross He triumphed over them. [Colossians 2: 15, WEY]

[15] [God] disarmed the principalities and powers that were ranged against us and made a bold display and public example of them, in triumphing over them in Him and in it [the cross]. [Colossians 2: 15, AMP]

[15] On that cross he discarded the cosmic powers and authorities like a garment, he made a public spectacle of them and led them as captives in his triumphal procession. [Colossians 2: 15, NEB]

> Jesus demonstrated to us that *agape* love would always produce victory.
>
> Love triumphed over evil and hatred at Calvary's Cross.

Our Lord drew the sting of the devil and his gang that were ranged against us at His crucifixion on the cross. He drew the sting of sin, the devil's accusations and condemnation, sickness, disease, and poverty. He took them upon Himself. He drew the sting of all the attacks the enemy would ever lunch against us. After taking them all on our behalf, our Lord Jesus took His eyes off those the devil used to crucify Him unto the Father and prayed, "Father, forgive them, for they know not what they do." [Luke 23: 34a, AMP] I believe that at that moment Satan's defeat was sealed.

In the face of all that Satan could hurl against our Lord, the Son of Love, He demonstrated to us that *Agape* love would always produce victory. The Lord forgave His accusers and those who killed Him just a few moments before He breathed His last breath; moments before He laid down His life. What would have been Satan's possible argument against God (i.e. unforgiveness) was debunked. Jesus, the Son of God, the Son of Love, forgave those who crucified Him, and at that point Satan and his retinue of demons were stripped of their power. They have no power against God's elect. They were dethroned, shattered, made empty, rendered useless, brought to nought, put down, and their powers made null and void against God's elect. Hallelujah!

It was moments after the prayer of forgiveness that our Lord declared, "It is finished." [John 19: 30, AMP] Our Lord Jesus triumphed over Satan on the Cross. Love triumphed over evil and hatred at Calvary's Cross. Jesus, the Son of Love, discarded the cosmic powers like a garment. He shook them off from Himself on the cross through a demonstration of the power

> This is the glorious Gospel: that the powers of this world have been dethroned, we are forgiven and our sins remitted.

of *Agape* love, the power of forgiveness. Once He asked the Father to forgive His accusers/killers, the contest with the devil was over. Therefore, He declared, "It is finished." The victory of love was demonstrated for all to see at Calvary.

To the undiscerning it looked like a defeat because Jesus was crucified, but to the discerning God (Love) demonstrated His triumph over Satan and His cohorts. Through the power of love, Jesus completely stripped the devil and his cohorts of their power against us, and the Father openly displayed to the whole world Christ's triumph at the cross where our sins were forever washed away. The Father concurred with the Son by demonstrating His power through the tearing of the curtain of the temple into two from top to bottom, and splitting open rocks.

> 50 And Jesus cried again with a loud voice and gave up His spirit.
> 51 And at once the curtain of the sanctuary of the temple was torn in two from top to bottom; the earth shook and the rocks were split.
> 52 The tombs were opened and many bodies of the saints who had fallen asleep in death were raised [to life]; [Matthew 27: 50-52, AMP]

By implication, we can understand what John wrote in Revelation 12:

[10] Then I heard a loud voice saying in heaven, "Now salvation, and strength, and the kingdom of our God, and the power of His Christ have come, for the accuser of our brethren, who accused them before our God day and night, has been cast down.

[11] And they overcame him by the blood of the Lamb and by the word of their testimony,…. [Revelation 12: 10, NKJV]

We have overcome Satan because of the blood of Jesus. Nothing can stop us from having access to the Father. Through Christ, the Anointed One, we now have access to the Father. Glory! This is the glorious Gospel: that the powers of this world have been dethroned, we are forgiven and our sins remitted. We are not only forgiven, we are also enthroned with the Lord at the Father's right hand. [Ephesians 2: 4-6, WEY] Hallelujah! We are forever redeemed. [Hebrews 9:12, AMP] We must deploy the power of *Agape* love (forgiveness) to our benefit.

Be ready and willing to forgive and pray the same prayer Jesus prayed on the Cross for those the enemy uses against you. "Father, forgive them, for they know not what they do." When we do this, the enemy is paralyzed and his defeat reinforced. His powers become ineffective against us, and we maintain the triumph of Jesus in our lives.

Love Dealt with Fear at Calvary
We can understand why John, the apostle of *Agape* love, wrote in 1 John 4:

[16] And we know (understand, recognize, are conscious of, by observation and by experience) and believe (adhere to and put faith in and rely on) the love God cherishes for us. God is love, and he who dwells and continues in love dwells and continues in God, and God dwells and continues in him.

[17] In this [union and communion with Him] love is brought to completion and attains perfection with us, that we may have confidence for the day of judgment [with assurance and boldness to face Him], because as He is, so are we in this world.

¹⁸ There is no fear in love [dread does not exist], but full-grown (complete, perfect) love turns fear out of doors and expels every trace of terror! For fear brings with it the thought of punishment, and [so] he who is afraid has not reached the full maturity of love [is not yet grown into love's complete perfection] [1 John 4: 16-18, AMP]

John saw and heard when love triumphed over evil at the Cross of Calvary. Thus, John declared, "There is no fear in love [dread does not exist], but full-grown (complete, perfect) love turns fear out of doors and expels every trace of terror!" Peter described it this way: "When He was reviled and insulted, He did not revile or offer insult in return; [when] He was abused and suffered, He made no threats [of vengeance]; but he trusted [Himself and everything] to Him Who judges fairly." [1 Peter 2: 23, AMP]

Our speech controls our actions. Let us emulate Jesus and walk in love, and as we do, we become imitators of our Father Who is love. It is good to heed the admonition of the Holy Spirit in Ephesians 4: 29–5: 2.

> ²⁹ Let no foul or polluting language, nor evil word nor unwholesome or worthless talk [ever] come out of your mouth, but only such [speech] as is good and beneficial to the spiritual progress of others, as is fitting to the need and the occasion, that it may be a blessing and give grace (God's favor) to those who hear it.
> ³⁰ And do not grieve the Holy Spirit of God [do not offend or vex or sadden Him], by Whom you were sealed (marked, branded as God's own, secured) for the day of redemption (of final deliverance through Christ from evil and the consequences of sin).
> ³¹ Let all bitterness and indignation and wrath (passion, rage, bad temper) and resentment (anger, animosity) and quarreling (brawling, clamor, contention) and slander (evil-speaking, abusive or blasphemous language) be banished from you, with all malice (spite, ill will, or baseness of any kind).
> ³² And become useful and helpful and kind to one another, tenderhearted (compassionate, understanding, loving-hearted), forgiving one another [readily and freely], as God in Christ forgave you. [Ephesians 4: 29-32, AMP]

¹ Therefore be imitators of God [copy Him and follow His example], as well-beloved children [imitate their father].

² And walk in love, [esteeming and delighting in one another] as Christ loved us and gave Himself up for us, a slain offering and sacrifice to God [for you, so that it became] a sweet fragrance. [Ephesians 5:1-2, AMP]

When we are established in righteousness, which connotes the possession of the attributes of faith, love, and hope, we do not fear; and we become far from oppression and terror is removed from us. [Isaiah 54: 14, AMP]

God is love and you as His child are in Him. Because He is love, you are love. There is no fear in love because there is no fear in God. Consequently, there is no fear in you. Perfect love casts out fear. Fear brings torment (punishment).

No Condemnation

Condemnation is a weapon of the enemy that carries with it the thought of punishment. Because condemnation is a form of fear, it opens you up to the attack of the enemy. Notice what the Holy Spirit says in Romans 8:

¹Therefore, [there is] now no condemnation (no adjudging guilty of wrong) for those who are in Christ Jesus, who live [and] walk not after the dictates of the flesh, but after the dictates of the Spirit.

² For the law of the Spirit of life [which is] in Christ Jesus [the law of our new being] has freed me from the law of sin and of death. [Romans 8: 1-2, AMP]

Jesus set you free forever from every condemnation the devil may bring against you because He paid for it all at Calvary. After He did that He disarmed the devil and rendered him powerless against you, child of God.

¹³ And you who were dead in trespasses and in the uncircumcision of your flesh (your sensuality, your sinful carnal nature), [God] brought to life together with [Christ], having [freely] forgiven us all our transgressions,

¹⁴ Having cancelled and blotted out and wiped away the handwriting of the note (bond) with its legal decrees and demands which was in force and stood against us (hostile to us). This [note with its regulations, decrees, and demands] He set aside and cleared completely out of our way by nailing it to [His] cross.

¹⁵ [God] disarmed the principalities and powers that were ranged against us and made a bold display and public example of them, in triumphing over them in Him and in it [the cross]. [Colossians 2; 13-15, AMP]

> Without walking in love, you are an open target for the enemy.

> Do not yield yourself anymore to the bondage of fear through condemnation, worry, anxiety, or any of the devil's wiles.

Take hold of this truth and do not let go of it. That is why Paul, the apostle, wrote in Romans 8:

³³ Who shall bring any charge against God's elect [when it is] God Who justifies [that is, Who puts us in right relation to Himself? Who shall come forward and accuse or impeach those whom God has chosen? Will God, Who acquits us?]

³⁴ Who is there to condemn [us]? Will Christ Jesus (the Messiah), Who died, or rather Who was raised from the dead, Who is at the right hand of God actually pleading as He intercedes for us?

³⁵ Who shall ever separate us from Christ's love? Shall suffering and affliction and tribulation? Or calamity and distress? Or persecution or hunger or destitution or peril or sword? [Romans 8: 33-35, AMP]

Jesus has set you free forever from fear and the fear of death.

¹⁴ Since, therefore, [these His] children share in flesh and blood [in the physical nature of human beings], He [Himself] in a similar manner partook of the same [nature], that by [going through] death He might

bring to nought and make of no effect him who had the power of death—that is, the devil—

15 And also that He might deliver and completely set free all those who through the [haunting] fear of death were held in bondage throughout the whole course of their lives. [Hebrews 2: 14-15, AMP]

Therefore, do not yield yourself anymore to the bondage of fear through condemnation, worry, anxiety, or any of the devil's wiles.

> Love will reject every lie of the enemy that will bring unforgiveness, and any thought that will bring us again under Satan's bondage.

Fear, Health, and Famine

Fear (the spirit of fear) depresses your immune system, and allows the enemy to attack you with sicknesses and diseases such as irritable bowel syndrome, cancer, hypertension, and the like. Hypertension is the fear of that which is not. Worry is a form of fear that can result in hypertension. Anxiety is fear that can lead eventually to panic attack, if it is not dealt with at the onset. This is why Peter wrote,

> To stay healthy and victorious in every area of life, walk in agape love.

7 Casting the whole of your care [all your anxieties, all your worries, all your concerns, once and for all] on Him, for He cares for you affectionately and cares about you watchfully.

8 Be well balanced (temperate, sober of mind), be vigilant and cautious at all times; for that enemy of yours, the devil, roams around like a lion roaring [in fierce hunger], seeking someone to seize upon and devour.

9 Withstand him; be firm in faith [against his onset—rooted, established, strong, immovable, and determined], ... [1 Peter 5: 7-9a, AMP]

We must cast our cares, worries, anxieties on the Lord. Our bodies are not meant to carry them. Resist fear, worry, and anxiety from the onset so that the enemy will not use them as openings to oppress you with sickness and disease. The spirit of fear is a door opener for other spirits of oppression to come against you. Stop the spirit of fear in its tracks before you become his hostage. "…Be subject to God. Resist the devil [stand firm against him], and he will flee from you." [James 4; 7, AMP] To be effective in resisting the devil, you must be submitted to Love (God). When you do, the devil cannot stand before you because *Agape* love renders him totally powerless. To stay healthy and victorious in every area of life, walk in *Agape* love. When you do, you will be successful in all you do. [Psalm 1: 1-3, AMP]

In the area of finance, you will be successful. You will not be afraid to invest under the Lord's direction, unlike the wicked servant who refused to invest the money the master gave him for investment because he was afraid. [Luke 19: 12-24, AMP] When you trust God Who is love, and are yielded to Him, you seek His guidance in everything you do. Because you decide to be Spirit-led and not flesh-led, you prosper in everything you do. In addition, you are protected by our Father Who is Love.

The Protective Covering of the Shield of Faith

Love activates the covering shield of faith. You see, the weapons of our warfare are not carnal but mighty through God (Love) to the pulling down of strongholds. Love will reject every lie of the enemy that will bring unforgiveness, and any thought that will bring us again under Satan's bondage that we were delivered from when we confessed Christ. A stronghold is a negative thought or lie that you believe to be true. Replace the lie that nobody loves you; nobody cares for you; or somebody can kill you with the truth that God, Who is Love, loves and cares for you watchfully, therefore nobody can kill you. Receive His love; declare it over yourself and be a dispenser of *Agape* love. Forgive others so that Satan does not take advantage of you.

You cannot war a good warfare if you do not operate in love because the spiritual armor that God has given us is the whole armor of Love. The Holy Spirit commands us to "Put on God's whole armor [the armor of a heavy-armed soldier which God supplies], that you may be able successfully to stand up against [all] the strategies and the deceits of the devil." [Ephesians 6: 11, AMP] Since God is love, the Holy Spirit is telling us to put on the whole armor of Love. The shield of faith will not be activated when you need it if you do not walk in love because faith is activated and energized through love. Without walking in love, you are an open target for the

> When you cast down contrary thoughts, you are casting down the spirit (evil spirit(s)) behind the thoughts because words generate thoughts.

enemy. To keep the devil at bear and walk in perpetual victory, decide to walk in love no matter the circumstance or situation. *Agape* love is the victory.

Cast Down Negative Thoughts

Cast down every thought that is contrary to God's Word and will for you in the Name of Jesus. The Scripture states in 2 Corinthians 10:

> [3] For though we walk (live) in the flesh, we are not carrying on our warfare according to the flesh and using mere human weapons.
>
> [4] For the weapons of our warfare are not physical [weapons of flesh and blood], but they are mighty before God for the overthrow and destruction of strongholds,
>
> [5] [Inasmuch as we] refute arguments and theories and reasonings and every proud and lofty thing that sets itself up against the [true] knowledge of God; and we lead every thought and purpose away captive into the obedience of Christ (the Messiah, the Anointed One). [2 Corinthians 10: 3-5, AMP]

When you cast down contrary thoughts, you are casting down the spirit (evil spirit(s)) behind the thoughts because words generate thoughts. [John 5:38, AMP] Replace the wrong (negative) thoughts with the Word of God. Fix your mind on what God says about you and think on those things that are excellent, admirable, and worthy of praise.

> [8] For the rest, brethren, whatever is true, whatever is worthy of reverence and is honorable and seemly, whatever is just, whatever is pure, whatever is lovely and lovable, whatever is kind and winsome and gracious, if there is any virtue and excellence, if there is anything worthy of praise, think on and weigh and take account of these things [fix your minds on them]. [Philippians 4: 8, AMP]

When you do Philippians 4: 8, the devil cannot have your thought life or hold you in the arena of reason where he operates. Rather, you whip him and put him under your feet with the Word, the sword of the Spirit, which is energized by *Agape* love. If you let him hold you in the arena of reason where he can control you, he has you whipped.

The Love Walk

Our Lord Jesus gave us a new commandment, "I give you a new commandment: that you should love one another. Just as I have loved you, so you too should love one another." [John 13: 34, AMP]. It is by loving one another that we demonstrate to the world that we are God's children. "By this shall all [men] know that you are My disciples, if you love one another [if you keep on showing love among yourselves]." [John 13:35, AMP]. You may ask, How can I keep this commandment? I am glad you asked.

You cannot love others if you have not first received God's love into your life. The way to do that is to accept and confess Jesus as the Lord of your life. if you are not born again, pray the **Prayer of Salvation** at the end of this book, and receive Christ Jesus as your Lord and Savior. When you receive Christ you receive the love of God, you can then release that love in you towards Him. You will then be able to love yourself, and others as you love yourself.

> [30] And you shall love the Lord your God out of and with your whole heart and out of and with all your soul (your life) and out of and with all your mind (with your faculty of thought and your moral understanding) and out of and with all your strength. This is the first and principal commandment.
> [31] The second is like it and is this, You shall love your neighbor as yourself. There is no other commandment greater than these. [Mark 12: 30-31, AMP]

You cannot speak badly of someone you pray for sincerely.

Remember that *Agape* love is a peacemaker, and does only good.

A person who is selfish does not even love himself; therefore, he has no capability of loving others. When you receive Jesus, you receive the love of God poured into your heart through His Spirit Who lives in you. Thereafter, you can love as God has commanded. This does not happen overnight. Once you accept God's love, decide to love yourself. You cannot love others if you do not love yourself. Decide, as an act of your will, to love others as you love yourself. What do you do with those who you may describe as unlovable?

First, you must decide that you will do God's Word concerning the love walk. Second, based on 1 Corinthians 13: 4 -8 continually, confess that you are a love child of a love God and whatever *Agape* love is that is who you are. If someone says something nasty to you, you declare, *I forgive you. I am not unforgiving, resentful, or touchy.* Third, decide to look past the person you see always provoking you. Realize that the person's behavior is reflection of the person's ignorance. [Luke 23:34, AMP] Choose to believe the best of the person. That is, believe to see the real person God created that person to be to become manifest. You have a part to play in this. Pray for the person and speak well of the person. You cannot speak badly of someone you pray for sincerely. Fourth, decide to be a blessing to those the devil uses against you, as the Lord directs you. As you do these things, you will find yourself growing in love. Choose to be a giver of your time, resources, etc. to be a blessing to others. Remember that agape love is a peacemaker, and does only good.

"Whereas the spirit yields a harvest of love, joy, peace, patience, kindness, generosity, forbearance, gentleness, faith, courtesy, temperateness, purity. No law can touch lives such as these." [Galatians 5: 22, KNOX] Since *agape* love in us is a harvest (fruit) of the spirit, it will grow as it receives nourishment from the Vine. Feed on the Word on *Agape* love and put it to work and see it grow. A fruit grows on a branch and not the stem. Jesus said, "I am the Vine; you are the branches. Whoever lives in Me and I in him bears much (abundant) fruit. However, apart from Me [cut off from vital union with Me] you can do nothing." [John 15: 5, AMP]. The fruit of the spirit in Galatians 5: 22 is referring to the fruit that the recreated spirit bears because the recreated spirit is nourished with the Word. Reading the verse in context helps to clarify this:

> [17] The impulses of nature and the impulses of the spirit are at war with one another; either is clean contrary to the other, and that is why you cannot do all that your will approves.
> [18] It is by letting the spirit lead you that you free yourselves from the yoke of the law.
> [22] Whereas the spirit yields a harvest of love, joy, peace, patience, kindness, generosity, forbearance,
> [23] gentleness, faith, courtesy, temperateness, purity. No law can touch lives such as these;
> [24] those who belong to Christ have crucified nature, with all its passions, all its impulses. [Galatians 5: 17-18, 22-24, KNOX]

It is clear from Galatians 5:17-18 that God is talking about the recreated human spirit which is at war with the flesh and vice versa. Therefore, verse 22 which is part of the same discourse cannot be talking about the

Holy Spirit. Studying these verses in conjunction with John 15: 5 help to clarify what spirit is referred to in Galatians 5:22.

If you do not choose to walk in love, you will find yourself coming short when it comes to joy, peace, patience, kindness, generosity, forbearance, gentleness, and purity. You will find that your faith is not operating as it should. You may say I have been doing just fine. That may have been so, but now you have learnt the truth about operating in *Agape* love, and God will hold you responsible for what you now know. There is no law against love. When you operate in love, you are walking in the Spirit, and you will not gratify the desires of the flesh.

> [19] Now the doings (practices) of the flesh are clear (obvious): they are immorality, impurity, indecency,
> [20] Idolatry, sorcery, enmity, strife, jealousy, anger (ill temper), selfishness, divisions (dissensions), party spirit (factions, sects with peculiar opinions, heresies),
> [21] Envy, drunkenness, carousing, and the like. I warn you beforehand, just as I did previously, that those who do such things shall not inherit the kingdom of God. [Galatians 5: 19-20, AMP]

Testimony

A few decades ago I was leading a fellowship in Glasgow, Britain. The fellowship began to grow. As it did, I found that a brother would ask me of another brother instead of speaking to that brother directly. I talked with the Lord about it, and He told me to teach on *Agape* love. When I taught on it the first time, there was a lot of crying and repenting. Two meetings later, the Lord asked me to go back and teach on love. I said, Lord, I already did . He replied that I should go back and teach it one more time. I obeyed and it changed the dynamics of the fellowship. Brethren began to love and care for each other.

When one person needed a miracle, it became the need of the whole fellowship and all would join in prayer and stand in faith to see the miracle manifested. I cannot remember a miracle we needed that we did not receive from the Lord. People were calling in prayer requests from different parts of Britain for us to lift up before God for miracles. It was glorious.

When we choose to line up with God and walk in love, our love will grow exceedingly just like our faith and cause us to walk in perpetual victory. It also enables us to believe God and walk in the authority that we have in Christ Jesus. Hallelujah!

Finally, I want to state categorically that *Agape* love makes the important difference in every situation we face. *Agape* love is the difference between bondage and freedom, and the difference between victory and defeat. It is the difference between dominion power (authority) and oppression (subjugation); the difference between your command of faith being executed and not being executed, Choose liberty and walk free as you put the dynamics of *Agape* love you have learned in this book to work in your life.

REFERENCES

Ette, E. I. (2014). *The Mechanics of Faith*. Alaythace Publishing. Natick, U.S.A.

Ette, E. I. (2014). *The Power to Transform*. Alaythace Publishing. Natick, U.S.A.

Kearney, D. J., Malte, C. A., McManus, C., Martinez, M. E., Felleman, B., & Simpson, T. L. Loving-Kindness Meditation for Posttraumatic Stress Disorder: A Pilot Study. *Journal of Traumatic Stress*. 2013, 26, 426–434).

Hagin, K. E. (1979). *Obedience in Finances*. Kenneth Hagin Ministries. Tulsa, OK, U.S.A.

Lawler, K. A., Younger, J. W., Piferi, R. L., Billington, E., Jobe, R., Edmondson, K., et al. (2003). A change of heart: Cardiovascular correlates of forgiveness in response to interpersonal conflict. *J Behavioral Medicine*, 26(5), 373-393.

Lawler, K. A., Younger, J. W., Piferi, R. L., Jobe, R. L., Edmondson, K. A., Jones, W. H. (2005). The unique effects of forgiveness on health: An exploration of pathways. *Journal of Behavioral Medicine*, 28(2), 157-167.

Owen, A. D., Hayward, R. D., Toussaint, L. L. (2011). http://www.sbm.org/meeting/2011/presentations/saturday/paper_sessions/Paper%20Session%2021%20-%20Forgiveness%20and%20immune%20functioning.pdf. Accessed 2015

Precept Ministries. (2015). http://www. http://www.preceptaustin.org/. Accessed 2015.

Roberts, O. (2005). *When You See the Invisible, You Can Do the Impossible*. Destiny Image Publishers, Shippensburg, PA., U.S.A.

Sarinopoulos, I. (2000). Forgiveness and physical health. Unpublished doctoral dissertation, University of Wisconsin-Madison.

Seybold, K. S., Hill, P. C., Neumann, J. K., Chi, D. S. (2001). Physiological and psychological correlates of forgiveness. *Journal of Psychology and Christianity* 20, 250–259.

Strong, J. (2010) Strong's Exhaustive Concordance. Accessed through http://biblehub.com/strongs.htm.

Temoshok, L. R., & Chandra, P. S. (2000). The meaning of forgiveness in a specific situational and cultural context: Persons living with HIV/AIDS in India. In: McCullough, M. E., Pargament , K. I., Thoresen, C. E. (Eds.), Forgiveness: Theory, research, and practice (pp. 41-64). New York: Guilford Press.

Temoshok, L. R., Wald, R. L. (2005). Forgiveness and health in persons living with HIV-AIDS. In: Worthington, E. L. (Ed.), Handbook of forgiveness (pp. 335-348). New York: Routledge.

Thayer, J. & Strong, J. (1995) *Thayer's Greek Lexicon, Electronic Database.* Copyright © 2002, 2003, 2006, 2011 by Biblesoft, Inc. Accessed from http://biblehub.com/greek/3588.htm 2015

Toussaint, L., Williams, D. R. (2003). Physiological correlates of forgiveness: Findings from a racially and socioeconomically diverse sample of community residents. Presented at A Campaign for Forgiveness Research Conference, Atlanta, GA.

Vincent, M. R. (1887). Vincent Word Studies of the New Testament. Charles Scribner's Sons, New York. Accessed online through https://www.studylight.org/commentaries/vnt.html 2016.

Wald, R. L., & Temoshok, L. R. (2004). Spirituality, forgiveness, and health in a U.S. inner-city HIV clinic. Proceedings, XV International AIDS Conference, Bangkok, Thailand (pp. 55-58). Bologna, Italy: Medimond.

Waltman, M. A., Russell, D. C., Coyle, C. T., Enright, R. D., Holter, A. C., Swoboda, C. M. (2009). The effects of a forgiveness intervention on patients with coronary artery disease. *Psychology and Health*, 24(1), 11-27.

Webster, N. (1828). *Dictionary of the English Language.* http://machaut.uchicago.edu/websters. Accessed 2015

Woods, T. E., Antoni, M. H., Ironson, G. H., & Kling, D. W. (1999). Religiosity is associated with affective and immune markers in symptomatic HIV infected gay men. *Journal of Psychosomatic Research*, 46, 165-176

Witvliet, C. V., Phipps ,K. A., Feldman, M. E., Beckham, J. C. Posttraumatic mental and physical health correlates of forgiveness and religious coping in military veterans. *Journal of Trauma Stress*. 2004; 17(3):269-73.)

CONFESSIONS AND PRAYERS

I am a son of my heavenly Father and co-heir with Christ, the Anointed One. Father God, You have given me the guarantee that I am Yours. You are my Father, and I am Your love child. I choose to walk in love and I speak well of my enemies. I pay no attention to a suffered wrong, and I believe the best of others. Greater is the Love in me than the hatred that is in the world. Because I walk in love, I will not fail. I will not fail because my Father Who is love never fails. Failure and defeat has no place in my life because I am more than a conqueror in Christ Jesus. [Romans 8: 14-17, 37; 1 Corinthians 13: 4-8, AMP]

I will not judge others; rather I operate in love and I am a blessing. I am a giver, and as I give my Father causes men to give to me good measure, pressed down, shaken together and running over. Because I determine to what extent I enjoy God's blessing, I choose to be a blessing to others. [Luke 6: 37-38, NKJV]

I keep out of debt and I choose not to owe any man anything, except to love him. As I walk in love, I fulfill the Lord's command to love my neighbor as myself. Because I am love I will not do wrong to my neighbor. I will not hurt anybody because God my Father has enabled me to walk in love by His grace. I choose to love the brethren, and this reminds me that I have passed over from death into Life. Because I abide in love I remain in Life. I choose to put the love of God to work in my life daily. Therefore, I am not unforgiving, resentful, or touchy. [Romans 13; 8-10; 1 John 3: 14, 18, 1 Corinthians 13: 4-8, AMP]

I know and believe the love that the Father has for me. God is love, and because I abide in love I abide in God, and God in me. Love has been perfected in me in this: that I may have boldness in the day of judgment; because as You are Lord Jesus, so I am in this world. As You are Love, so I am love. I walk in love and I do not fear because there is no fear in love; but perfect love casts out fear because fear involves torment. I choose to be perfected in Love, therefore, fear has no place in me. I love You Father God because You first loved me. [1 John 4: 16-18, NKJV]

I refuse to return evil for evil or insult for insult (scolding, tongue-lashing, berating), but on the contrary blessing. I have pity and love for those the enemy uses against me and I pray for their welfare. I know that to this I have been called, that I may myself inherit a blessing [from God - that I may obtain a blessing as an heir, bringing welfare and happiness and protection]. I keep my tongue free from evil and my lips from guile (treachery, deceit), therefore I will live long and enjoy many good days. I shun every form of wickedness, and I search for peace (harmony; undisturbedness, from fears, agitating passions, and moral conflicts) and pursue it. Thank You Lord for Your eyes are upon me, and Your ears are attentive to my prayer. I walk in love and will not gratify the desires of the flesh. Since I have chosen to walk in love, the devil and his cohorts cannot hurt me because You oh Lord are my defense. [1 Peter 3: 8-11; Galatians 5: 16, AMP]

Prayers for Presenting Firstfruits and Tithes

A Prayer for Presenting Your Firstfruits to the Lord

Lord Jesus I lift my firstfruits to You to worship the Father with it. I give thanks to You, my Lord and God, this day that I have come into Your Kingdom. Once I was in darkness and I called upon Your Name Lord Jesus, and Father You saved me. You brought me out of the control and dominion of the power of darkness with signs and with wonders which You wrought through Jesus at the cross. You brought me into the Kingdom of the Son of Your love, the Kingdom of Your Blessing. Now, behold, I bring the firstfruits of my income (labor) which You, O Lord, have given me. I worship You oh Lord and I rejoice in all the good which You the Lord my God has given me and my household. Thank You Father for a double portion blessing, blessing me above all others, and prospering me in everything I do. I believe I receive and I thank You for it, in the Name of Jesus. [Deuteronomy 26: 2-11, AMP]

A Prayer for Presenting Your Tithes to the Lord

Lord Jesus I present my tithe to You to worship the Father with it. I have not used it for a wrong purpose nor given it to the dead (dead church or ministry). Father look down from Your holy habitation, from heaven, and bless me and my household as you did Abraham. Thank You Father for opening the windows of heaven and pouring out a blessing (ideas, concepts, innovations, witty inventions) on me, that there shall not be room enough to receive it. Father I thank You for rebuking the devourer for my sake, and he will no longer steal from me and my family. All peoples shall call me happy and blessed, for You have made home a "land" of delight unto you. I believe I receive my tithing blessing (ideas, concepts, inventions, innovations, and strategies to implement the ideas, concepts, inventions, and innovations), and I will see the manifestation in Jesus' Name. Thank You Father for favoring me with Your blessing and making me and my family a land of delight unto You in the Name of Jesus. Thank You Father for pouring Your blessing that is indefinite and limitless upon me and my family. [Deuteronomy 26: 12-14; Malachi 3: 10-12; Genesis 14: 18-20, AMP]

A Sample Prayer Giving (Sowing) Your Offering (Seed)

I thank You Father releasing my harvest of blessing even as I sow my seed of faith right now. By faith, I receive my harvest right now according Mark 11: 24. In the Name of Jesus, devil loose your hold and grip over my 100-fold blessing. Ministering angels go forth and bring my harvest to me. I thank You Father for giving me sensitivity in my spirit man to recognize my harvest. By faith I will reap my harvest, and I will not let my harvest pass me by in the Name of Jesus. Amen. [Mark 11: 24; Genesis 26: 12-14; Luke 6: 38; Mark 10: 29-30]

Harvest Manifestation

Heavenly Father, I have worshipped You with my firstfruits, tithes, and offerings as my seeds of faith. Thank You father for rebuking the devourer for my sake. I thank You because You are growing my seeds and changing them into my harvests. Ministering angels, go forth and bring my harvests to me in the Name of Jesus. Father, thank You for causing my harvests to come to me in a perfect way. Thank You Lord for enabling me to recognize my harvests in the their due seasons and reap them in Jesus Name. [Proverbs 3: 9-10; Malachi 3: 10; Galatians 6: 7-9]

Financial Prosperity

Father I thank You for it is Your will for me to prosper and be in health even as my spirit prospers. I have been redeemed from the curse of poverty; therefore, I enjoy abundance. Jesus came that I may have and enjoy life, and have it in abundance (to the full, till it overflows). The abundance anointing is on me and in me. The blessing of Abraham is in me and on me. Father, Your favor profusely abounds towards me, and You surround me with favor as with a shield. Therefore I declare, "I will never be broke another day in my life." I have surplus of prosperity because I hearken to the Word and voice of God. [1 John 3: 2 (HCSB); John 10: 10; Genesis 12: 3, Deuteronomy 28: 1-2,11, AMP]

Father, I thank You for commanding Your blessing upon me, in my bank accounts, investments, and in all that I undertake. I have been redeemed from the curse of the law, therefore, I am debt free. I am a lender and not a borrower because of the grace of God on my life. I am willing and obedient; therefore, I enjoy the best of the land. Hallelujah! [Psalm 5: 12; Galatians 3: 13; Deuteronomy 28: 8, 11-12, Isaiah 1: 19, AMP]

I am blessed (prospered), and I am a blessing prospering others. Everything I lay my hands to do prospers and succeeds. I am blessed when I come in and I am blessed when I go out. I have favor everywhere I turn. Thank you Father for multiplying and increasing me and my family. I seek first the Your Kingdom Father God and all its righteousness, and You add all other things to me over and above. [Genesis 12: 3, AMP; Psalm 115: 13-15, AMP]

I love to give. I love to sow, and I always have plenty of seed to sow and food to eat. I am a reaper of abundant harvests of the seeds of faith that I have sown. My cup of blessing (prosperity – spiritual, physical, and financial) runs over. Goodness and mercy accompany me all the days of my life. I have more than enough to meet my needs and to be a blessing to others in the Name of Jesus. [Proverbs 11: 17 AMP; *Luke 6: 38; Psalm 23; 2 Corinthians 9: 8*]

Father I thank You for making all grace [every favor and earthly blessing] come to me in abundance, so that I always [under all circumstances, regardless of the need] have complete sufficiency in everything, and have an abundance for every good work and be a blessing to others. Thank You Father for You have made me to be a merciful, kind, and generous man; therefore I benefit myself. The harvests of my generosity return to bless me. I generously scatter abroad by being a blessing to others; therefore, I increase more and more. Because I am a liberal person, I am enriched. I am the righteousness of God in Christ Jesus, therefore I flourish like a green plant. My fruit as the righteous is a tree of life, and I win souls for Christ because God's wisdom is mine. I meditate on Your Word Father, and whatever I do prospers and comes to maturity. Thank You Father for daily prospering me as Ephraim and Manasseh in the Name of Jesus. Prosperity is a reward for me as the righteous. [2 Corinthians 9: 8; Psalm 1: 1-3; Proverbs 11: 17, 24, 25, 30; Deuteronomy 33, AMP]

I trust in You oh Lord my God and I prosper. Good fortune comes to me in everything I do. I am a giver, and I thank You Father for causing men to give to me pressed down, shaken together, running over, to make room for more do they pour into my bosom. A 100-fold (a complete series of) return is mine in Jesus' Name. [2 Chronicles 20: 20; Psalm 1: 1-3; Luke 6: 38, TLB; Mark 10:30]

I am one with God. Because Jesus is "Abundance," I am "abundance." I am not looking for abundance outside; abundance is in me because Jesus is in me. Lord, I receive abundance from You right now. Abundance, I command you to manifest in me now! Wisdom of God manifest in me now! Witty inventions come forth now! Ideas, concepts, and innovations come forth now! "Money comes to me now!" in Jesus' Name! "Money come to me now!" "Money comes to me now in Jesus' Name!" [*Thompson,1996] *Father, I thank You and praise You for the manifestation right now in the Name of*

Jesus. Glory! Hallelujah! [1 John 4: 17; proverbs 8: 12 (KJV); 2 Kings 12: 4 (KJV)]

Because I give liberally for the spreading of the Gospel, Father You liberally supply (fill to the full) my every need (the employment I need, healing, contracts, favor, success in everything I do, my necessity and wants) according to the wealth of Your power, favor, anointing that carries all that You are and do in the Anointed Jesus. In this time and in this economy I enjoy abundance and I am *satisfied with plenty.* [Philippians 4:19, AMP; Psalm 37: 19]

I am a generous man, and I prosper. I water others, and I am watered. Because I am a giver, the harvests of my giving come back to me multiplied. Thank You Father for the great deal more and indefinite blessing of tithing is mine because I am a tither. People call me happy and blessed because I am blessed of You oh Lord. Thank You Father for You have made me to have abundance and no lack. Thank You Father for redeeming me from every curse of the law. You set me free from the curse of poverty; therefore, I walk in abundance. I am debt free. I declare, I am a lender and not a borrower; and I have prosperity demonstration in my life daily. Hallelujah!! [Malachi 3: 10-11; Matthew 6: 33; Galatians 3: 13-14; Deuteronomy 28: 6-13; Luke 6; 38; Mark 10: 30; Proverbs 11: 17; 13: 21; 28: 25 (NIV)]

Because I am a benevolent person, I open my hands wide to be a blessing. I give to the poor and needy; and my deeds of justice and goodness and kindness and benevolence go on and endure forever! Father I thank You for You are the One Who gives me seed to sow, multiplies my resources for sowing, and increases the fruits of my righteousness which manifests itself in active goodness, generosity, and charity. Thus, I am enriched in all things and in every way, so that I can be generous and my gifts as they are administered by those I bless will bring forth thanksgiving to You Father God. Thank You Lord for blessing me, the work of my hands, and all that I undertake. [2 Corinthians 9: 8-9, Deuteronomy 15: 7-8,10, AMP]

* Thompson, L. (1996). *Money Cometh. Ever* Increasing Word Ministries. Darrow, LA, U.S.A.

Revelation Knowledge and Authority

Confess/pray this daily to receive revelation knowledge from the Lord, and walk in the authority He has given you.

I pray to You the God of our Lord Jesus Christ, the Father of glory, that You may grant me the Spirit of wisdom and revelation [of insight into mysteries and secrets] in the [deep and intimate] knowledge of You.

Father, flood the eyes of my heart with Your light, so that I can know and understand the hope to which You have called me, and how rich is Your glorious inheritance in the saints (Your set-apart ones), so that I can know and understand what is the immeasurable and unlimited and surpassing greatness of Your power in and for us who believe. That power You demonstrated in the working of Your mighty strength, which You exerted in Christ when You raised Him from the dead and seated Him at Your [own] right hand in the heavenly [places], far above all rule and authority and power and dominion (principality and power) and every name that is named [above every title that can be conferred], not only in this age and in this world, but also in the age and the world which are to come. [Ephesians 1: 17-21, AMP] You put all things under Jesus' feet, and gave Him to be head over all things to the church, which is His body, the fullness of Him who fills all in all. [Ephesians 1: 22-23, KJV]

I thank You Father that You raised me up together with Christ, and made me sit down together with Him [giving me joint seating with Him] at Your right hand in the heavenly spheres, and all things (devil and his demons included) are under my feet by virtue of me being in Him. Thank you Father, in the Name of Jesus, that I am not only seated at Your right hand in Christ Jesus, I am walking in my authority in Him. [Ephesians 2: 5-6; Luke 10: 19, AMP]

To Be Strong in the Lord

To be strong (empowered in your inner man) in the Lord confess this daily.

Father, seeing the greatness of Your plan by which I am built together with the Body in Christ, I bow my knees before You my Father, the Father of our Lord Jesus Christ, for whom every family in heaven and on earth is named. You are the Father from Whom all fatherhood takes its title and derives its name. I ask You to grant me out of the rich treasury of You glory to be strengthened and reinforced with mighty power in the inner man by the Holy Spirit Himself indwelling my innermost being and personality.

May Christ through my faith in Him dwell (make His permanent home) in my heart. May I be rooted deep in Agape love and founded securely on Agape love, that I may have the power and be strong to apprehend and grasp with all the saints [God's devoted people, the experience of that love] what is the breadth and length and height and depth [of it]. That I may really come to know practically, through experience for myself the love of Christ, which far surpasses mere knowledge [without experience]. That I by being filled through all my being unto all the fullness of You Father may have the richest measure of Your divine Presence, and become wholly filled and flooded with You Father God Yourself.

Now to You Father Who, by the action of His power that is at work within me, is able to carry out Your purpose and do superabundantly, far over and above all that I dare ask or think - infinitely beyond our highest prayers, desires, thoughts, hopes, or dreams - to You be glory in the church and in Christ Jesus throughout all generations forever and ever. Amen. [Ephesians 3: 14-21, AMP]

Prayer of Salvation and Baptism in the Holy Spirit

Jesus I acknowledge and confess that You are Lord, and today I make you the Lord of my life. I believe in my heart that God raised You from the dead, therefore I am saved. With my heart I believe and I am justified, declared righteous, and acceptable to God, and with the mouth I confess (openly declare and speak out freely my faith) and confirm my salvation. Because You are the Lord of my life, I am delivered, prospered, made whole, and set free from every curse (generational and otherwise). I put my trust in You Lord, and I will never be put to shame or be disappointed. I have called upon You and I am saved. Thank You Lord for saving me, and thank You Father God for making me Your child in the Name of Jesus. Amen. I am now a new creation in Christ. My old life is gone, and I now have a new life in Christ Jesus. Hallelujah!

Now Father God I ask You to baptize me with Your Spirit. I believe and I receive the in-filling of the Holy Spirit and I begin to glorify You by speaking in other tongues as You give me utterance in the Name of Jesus. [Romans 10: 8-13; Mark 11: 24; Luke 11: 9-11]

OTHER TITLES BY ENE I. ETTE

The Mechanics of Faith:

If you want to understand faith and how to put it to work to get God's results, this is the book for you. It is written in in a practical, how to, manner, providing you with tools you need to believe and receive from God, and how to appropriate the blessings of God in your life. You will learn how to position yourself for the manifestation of God's goodness in your life, pray the prayer of faith, and how to release your faith to meet the challenges of life.

Power to Transform

You are governed by your words because they set the course for your life. It is time to change and set your life on God's trajectory for you. Your change has to begin with your speech. When you change your speech, you change your thinking, believing, and the course of your life. This book will help you get on course as well as help you cancel negative things you have spoken over your life in the past. You will know how to handle trouble and how to cooperate with God to turn your troubles and crises into triumphs. You will learn how God wants to use your crisis to bring about a material change such as wealth transfer, promotion, healing, etc. in your life. In addition, you will learn the importance of confessing God's Word as a key to manifesting God's goodness in your life.

Dominion Power

This is one of the most important books you will read on your God-given authority as a believer. As a child of God, you are a king and a priest to God. The takes you on journey from understanding the finished work of the cross, the importance of faith and love for walking in victory, what it means to believe in the Lord and how that opens the door for you to work the works of God, through keys to operating in authority, knowing Satan and his strategies, to the understanding of what it means to put on the whole armor of God, and the dynamics of dominion power.

The Power of a New Life

If you want to know how to activate the power of the new life in Christ Jesus that is in you and let Him manifest His glory in your life, this book is for you. In this book, Dr. Ette shares biblically based insights and testimonies to enable you grasp the revelation of the power of a new life in Christ Jesus and how to activate it in your life. Thus, you will learn: what Jesus did for us at Calvary's cross; how to appropriate the power of a new life that stems from salvation in Christ Jesus; how to grow in Christ; how to establish yourself in the righteousness of God and enjoy its benefits; how to overcome fear and oppression; the importance of the blood of Jesus and how to appropriate it; how to renew your mind to the realities of who you are and what are yours in Christ, and walk in them.

Coming Soon; Other Titles by Dr. Ene I. Ette

The Name

Jesus gave us the legal right to use His Name, a name His received by inheritance, by conferment, and by conquest. In that Name is our victory over the adversary and his demons. In The Name we have miracles, provision, protection, and deliverance. This book introduces to The Name and the power you have in it, how to exercise the authority you have in the Name, and walk in victory. You will also learn how to use Name of Jesus for God to bring life into dead situations, and cause what was dead to live again.

How Do You Script Your Life

You words define you and set a course for your life. What you are today is what you said yesterday. Your words shape your future. This book will teach you how to get your words to work for you and not against you. It is a must have because you will learn how to speak the Word and in line with the Word to become who God created you to be.

The Timeless Zone

God lives in the eternal now. When we operate in faith, we operate in the now where God operates. You will learn how to move into the timeless zone – the now zone. You will also learn how to get the cardinal law of seedtime and harvest to work for you in every area of life. You will learn about communing effectively with God in prayer for the right results, and much more. *The Timeless Zone* will teach how to speak, think, and act like God using His faith that He has given you.

They will be available at Amazon.com.

For more information and sample chapters,

visit www.alaythace.org

Additional copies of this book and other book titles from Amazon.com.

For a complete list of our titles visit us at www.alaythace.org

Alaythace Publishing

www. alaythace.org

Publishing the truth of the Gospel of Christ, The Anointed One.

AUTHOR CONTACT INFORMATION

ene.ette@alaythace.org